D1617343

A GEORGE HERBERT COMPANION

GARLAND REFERENCE LIBRARY
OF THE HUMANITIES
VOL. 921

A GEORGE HERBERT COMPANION

Robert H. Ray

GARLAND PUBLISHING, Inc.
New York & London / 1995

Library of Congress Cataloging-in-Publication Data

Ray, Robert H., 1940–
    A George Herbert companion / Robert H. Ray.
        p.   cm. — (Garland reference library of the
    humanities ; vol. 921)
    Includes bibliographical references.
    ISBN 0–8240–4849–0
    1. Herbert, George, 1593–1633—Handbooks,
    manuals, etc.   2. Poets, English—Early modern,
    1500–1700—Biography—Handbooks, manuals, etc.
    I. Title.   II. Series.
    PR3508.R39   1995
    821'.3—dc20   94–30947
                                                        CIP

Printed on acid-free, 250-year-life paper
Manufactured in the United States of America

CONTENTS

v

PREFACE

This book provides for the reader of George Herbert a reference
and resource volume similar to the companions, dictionaries, guides,
and handbooks existing on several other major writers. I especially
have modeled it upon my own *A John Donne Companion*, as well as
F.E. Halliday's *A Shakespeare Companion*, Edward S. LeComte's *A
Milton Dictionary*, and D. Heyward Brock's *A Ben Jonson Companion*.
I am greatly indebted to these works, and, while learning much from
their formats, criteria for sections and entries, and decisions on
inclusions and exclusions, I institute modifications that seem more
appropriate to Herbert's life and work and more pertinent to my
primary audience. Throughout the writing I have kept before me the
kinds of questions I had when first reading, studying, teaching, and
researching Herbert. I attempt, then, a compendium of useful
information for any reader of Herbert to have at hand, especially
information not easily accessible to the nonspecialist. I include key facts
about his life, works, and times, to enhance understanding and
appreciation, without being exhaustive. In fact, my citations,
bibliography, and suggestions for further research direct the reader to
those books, articles, scholars, and critics that can best satisfy curiosity
stimulated herein on any topic or work related to Herbert. Therefore,
the book should be most helpful to the following groups: (1) general
readers or undergraduate students coming to Herbert for the first time
for any extensive reading or study, (2) postgraduate students seeking
both a basic background in Herbert and some initial guidance to
methods and tools for research in primary and secondary materials, and
(3) nonspecialist teachers, particularly those teaching Herbert's works
commonly found in anthologies and covered in survey courses. The
scholar and critic, the Herbert specialist, however, will find in several

of my entries on individual poems many explications of structure, words, phrases, and lines, with suggestions of wordplay and multiple meanings, not previously noted. I am assuming that the user of this *Companion*, especially in consulting entries in the "Dictionary" portion, has before him or her either an anthology with selections of Herbert's works or an edition of Herbert. This *Companion* is designed to be especially helpful to those with an edition or anthology having few or no notes or other aids in reading and understanding. I emphasize Herbert's poetry over his prose, as well as the most frequently anthologized poems and prose over the more specialized pieces and the selections of lesser popularity and fame. Specifically selected for concentration are major poems from *The Temple*, the two sonnets to Herbert's mother (entered in the "Dictionary" portion of this volume as "Sonnets 1 and 2"), and *The Country Parson* (also known as *A Priest to the Temple*).

The preceding aims and primary audiences largely determine the precise sections included, as well as their lengths, divisions, content, format, tone, and language. "Research in Herbert: Tools and Procedures" notes the most important tools for further research, as well as a step-by-step method of beginning with the "Selected Bibliography" at the end of this volume and then widening one's net to even more comprehensive and complex matters of criticism and scholarship. These steps allow the general reader to stop at the level most useful for his or her purposes, while the student or teacher eventually might wish to pursue more research into seventeenth-century originals and commentaries or into the complexities of text and scholarship: this brief section provides a way to begin. "A Herbert Chronology" presents an overview of dated highlights of Herbert's life and works in order to provide a perspective for absorbing the larger picture and further details in the succeeding "Herbert's Life" and "A Herbert Dictionary." The section "Herbert's Works" provides a list of his major works by customary titles and groups, and the critical studies listed in the "Selected Bibliography" are largely classified according to these works. The lightly annotated "Selected Bibliography" is divided into major categories (with subcategories), such as editions of primary works, tools for research and reference, biographical studies, studies of Herbert's reputation and influence, and criticism. The books, essays, and articles selected are those of first importance to anyone wishing to explore further the field represented within any given division or subdivision of Herbert's life and works. The coverage of the bibliography extends to some works published in 1993. Compact annotations in brackets conclude those items of prime significance that need more description than is given in the titles.

The major portion of the volume, both in importance and size, is "A Herbert Dictionary." Its entries are arranged alphabetically: they identify, define, and explain the most important and influential *persons* in Herbert's life and works (mainly theologians, thinkers, family, friends, and aristocrats); *places* either frequented by Herbert or important in his life and works; *characters, allusions, ideas,* and *concepts* in his works and from his time; *words* and *phrases* of most importance and difficulty in his works, as well as those conducive to multiple meanings and puns in their interpretation; the most significant, famous, and frequently anthologized *books, poems,* and *prose works* of Herbert; other important *writers* and *works* that are relevant to understanding portions of Herbert's own life or works or his influence and reputation; and *literary terms* important to or arising from Herbert's writing and influence. Maintaining my focus on the relevance of the content of each entry to Herbert's life and works is uppermost: for example, I resist being led astray into too many details about an individual's life (e.g., King James's or Sir Francis Bacon's), but rather include only those facts that convey the essence to understand him or her and the role played by that individual in the course of Herbert's career and in the content of his writings. Other reference works, biographies, and histories can provide additional matters for anyone interested in the full details of the lives of such individuals.

The format for the entries in "A Herbert Dictionary" is designed to highlight and distinguish elements. The designation of each entry is capitalized and **Bold**: if it is a long work or book, it is also ***Italicized***; but, if it is a short work, it is in **"Quotation Marks."** The same system of italics and quotation marks is employed within the content of an entry, but without the boldface. In addition, for any mention that appears elsewhere as an entry, I use ALL-CAPITALS as a cross-reference.

Other principles foster clarity and ease of reading. With the exception of the "Selected Bibliography," I modernize spelling and punctuation for all titles of books, prose works, and poems, as well as for any quotations from Herbert's or others' Renaissance original editions, manuscripts, and letters. Through the entire volume I spell out fully the names of Herbert's works, of professional journals, and of scholarly and critical books, rather than employ a lengthy list of abbreviations: for the nonspecialist reader, such abbreviations likely would be cryptic and frustrating, causing one continually to turn back to the key in an early part of the volume.

In writing this book, I have drawn from my own reading, teaching, and research of over twenty-five years, and I feel that some new perspectives in close readings of several of Herbert's poems appear in the entries of the "Dictionary." I must acknowledge the study of works of reference, biography, history, philosophy, theology, scholarship, and criticism that enabled me to accomplish this task. Even though it is impossible to separate one's own readings at every point from the cumulative and mutual debts scholars and critics owe, I attempt to cite noteworthy readings that can be specified without burdening such a work as this with scholarly apparatus. I do, however, want my entire "Selected Bibliography" to be a grateful acknowledgment of and a granting of due credit to the authors of those works found to be most helpful as sources of knowledge and insight, both in my years of studying Herbert and in composing this volume. In listing them I encourage readers to seek these items for fuller discussions and information on works and topics. Also, *The Oxford English Dictionary*, the *Dictionary of National Biography*, the *Cyclopedia of Biblical, Theological, and Ecclesiastical Literature*, the *Encyclopedia Britannica*, the *Dictionary of Phrase and Fable*, the *Gazetteer of the British Isles, An Encyclopaedia of London, The London Encyclopedia*, and *The Shell Guide to The History of London*, out of countless resources, have been of primary value and deserve singular mention. If I seem to have slighted or if I have been unaware of some work pertinent to my own readings and provision of information in this *Companion*, I apologize most deeply for the oversight.

I am indebted to many groups and their associated individuals for generous assistance. Garland Publishing has been exceedingly understanding and helpful, especially Phyllis Korper, Senior Editor. For continuing encouragement and generosity in allotting time and research sabbaticals for this work, I thank Baylor University and its administrators, especially James Barcus, John Belew, William Cooper, Herbert Reynolds, and Donald Schmeltekopf. I particularly am grateful to the College of Arts and Sciences Faculty Development Committee for its vital support in granting the summer sabbaticals necessary to complete this project.

I wish to thank my family, especially my wife, Lynette, for unfailing encouragement.

R.H.R.
Baylor University

A George Herbert Companion

RESEARCH IN HERBERT:
TOOLS AND PROCEDURES

Although the "Selected Bibliography" concluding this volume provides key items for further study, researchers might wish to pursue Herbert's life and works more thoroughly. The following discussion guides one in such a task.

Fortunately for students of Herbert, an annotated bibliography of criticism saves labor and time. John R. Roberts's *George Herbert: An Annotated Bibliography of Modern Criticism, Revised Edition, 1905–1984* (1988) covers virtually every book, article, and essay of significance published on Herbert between 1905 and 1984 (Roberts excludes dissertations). He arranges the volume chronologically by year of publication and alphabetically by author within each year. The annotations succinctly describe the content and nature of each item. Roberts also provides indexes to authors, subjects, and Herbert's works. To survey the dissertations written on Herbert, one should consult *Dissertation Abstracts* and *Dissertation Abstracts International* for the years desired. To find listings of books, articles, essays, and dissertations published from 1985 to the present (i.e., from the end of Roberts's coverage), the individual should employ the *MLA International Bibliography*, the *Annual Bibliography of English Language and Literature*, and the *Essay and General Literature Index*.

Robert H. Ray's bibliographical essay titled "Recent Studies in Herbert (1974–1986)" published in the Autumn, 1988, issue of the journal *English Literary Renaissance* (Volume 18, Number 3) extends coverage beyond Roberts's bibliography to the major books, articles, and essays published in 1985 and 1986 and provides a selective review of major works, topics, and trends in Herbert scholarship and criticism from 1974 through 1986. This review essay is a continuation of an earlier one by Jerry Leath Mills titled "Recent Studies in Herbert" published in the Winter, 1976, issue of *English Literary Renaissance* (Volume 6, Number 1).

The preceding references, then, provide ways to research almost everything written about Herbert for the larger part of the twentieth century, and for many topics these will suffice. However, if one wishes or needs to consult books, manuscripts, articles, essays, and comments regarding Herbert and his works in his own century, another reference tool provides the essentials. Robert H. Ray's *The Herbert Allusion Book: Allusions to George Herbert in the Seventeenth Century* (1986 [Texts and Studies, *Studies in Philology*, 83:4]) is a compilation of 849 allusions to Herbert and his works in books and manuscripts from 1615 through 1700.

A highly selective survey (seventy-four excerpts) of references to Herbert from 1615 to 1936 is by C.A. Patrides in *George Herbert: The Critical Heritage* (1983). The user of this work should be careful, however, about accepting many of its assertions and transcriptions. One should always verify them by checking against reliable research tools or the original works themselves. Some examples selected only from the portion concerning the seventeenth century are as follows: (1) the poetic fragment attributed to Codrington (pp. 4 and 63) actually is in the handwriting of a "J.H." in the original manuscript, and the fragment is incorrectly transcribed in Patrides's volume; (2) Archbishop Leighton quotes only once from Herbert, not "frequently" (p. 11); (3) rather than three lines of "Virtue," the entire poem is quoted in Hall's work of 1676 (p. 11); (4) Flatman's allusion first appeared in 1679, not 1686 (p. 13); (5) Walton says that *Edmund Duncon*, not Arthur Woodnoth, was asked by Herbert to deliver the manuscript to Nicholas Ferrar (p. 58); (6) Daniel's 1648 ode on *The Temple* was first published in 1878, not 1959 (p. 70); (7) the quoted passage from Dryden's *MacFlecknoe* does not correspond in either spelling or wording to the 1682 edition cited (p. 137); (8) the uses of Herbert in Thomas White's work are more extensive than indicated (p. 145). For other errors to be noted and warnings to be heeded by the potential user, one should also read the review of this volume by Fram Dinshaw in *The Review of English Studies* (36: 566-68 [November, 1985]).

For even more comprehensive research that calls for the use of early editions and manuscripts, further tools are necessary. The various reference volumes known as the *Short-Title Catalogue of Books Printed in England* and the *National Union Catalog* note libraries and collections possessing copies of early editions. (The researcher unfamiliar with these tools should consult a reference librarian for help.) Actually, if one cannot physically hold and examine the original books because of limited access to them, seeing early publications of Herbert's works (and those of writers who refer to and comment on Herbert) is much easier than the researcher might think. Because of some microfilms made of English books by University Microfilms International, many libraries now possess Herbert's works filmed from original editions. Armed with the number assigned to a particular book in the *Short-Title Catalogue*, the researcher can locate which reel of film that book appears on in a set of microfilms by using the reel guides that accompany the collections. (Again, seeking a reference librarian's help in orienting oneself to this search is quite valuable.) If a person needs information on extant manuscripts of Herbert's works (their contents and locations), the primary reference tool is the *Index of English Literary Manuscripts*, compiled by Peter Beal and others. Many of the modern editions of Herbert cited in my "Selected Bibliography" also discuss the early editions of and the manuscript sources for Herbert's works, a complex matter indeed.

The standard edition of Herbert's works is F.E. Hutchinson's *The Works of George Herbert* (1941; rev. 1945). Other modern editions are listed in my "Selected Bibliography."

The *George Herbert Journal* specializes in articles on Herbert and his age and is published twice a year. The editor is Sidney Gottlieb.

A HERBERT CHRONOLOGY

1593 George Herbert born on April 3 in Montgomery, Wales.

1596 Herbert's father (Richard) dies.

1597 Lives with his mother (Magdalen) in Eyton.

1599 Lives with his mother in Oxford.

1601 Lives with his mother in London: household established at Charing Cross.

1604 Attends Westminster School.

1608 Magdalen Herbert marries Sir John Danvers.

1609 Matriculates at Trinity College, Cambridge.

1610 Sends two sonnets (arguing that the love of God is a proper topic in poetry) to his mother for New Year's Day.

1612 Takes his Bachelor of Arts degree. Publication of his two Latin elegies on the death of Prince Henry.

1614 Elected minor fellow at Trinity College.

1616 Elected major fellow at Trinity College. Takes his Master of Arts degree.

1618 Appointed Praelector in Rhetoric, Cambridge University.

1619   Appointed deputy for Sir Francis Nethersole, University
        Orator.

1620   Named University Orator.

1622   Sir Edward Herbert (brother of George) dedicates his *De
        Veritate* to George Herbert and William Boswell.

1623   Delivers oration during Prince Charles's visit to Cambridge.
        Elected as Member of Parliament from Montgomery.

1624   On leave from Cambridge. Archbishop of Canterbury gives
        dispensation allowing Bishop John Williams to ordain George
        Herbert as deacon. Granted a share in the church living at
        Lladinam, Montgomery, by Bishop Williams. Probably does
        not return to Cambridge after his leave expires.

1625   Death of James I and accession of Charles I. Bacon dedicates
        his *Translation of Certain Psalms* to Herbert. John Donne and
        Herbert stay at the Danvers home in Chelsea in December
        during time of plague in London.

1626   Death of Bacon. Publishes Latin poem on Bacon's death.
        Installed by proxy as canon of Lincoln Cathedral and
        prebendary of Leighton Ecclesia. Installed at Leighton
        Bromswold and probably visits Little Gidding near there.

1627   Herbert's mother, Lady Danvers, dies. John Donne preaches a
        memorial sermon for Lady Danvers at Chelsea. Herbert's
        Memoriae Matris Sacrum published with Donne's sermon.

1628   Sir John Danvers (Herbert's stepfather) marries Elizabeth
        Dauntesey. Herbert resides in the home of his stepfather's
        brother, Henry Danvers, the Earl of Danby, in Wiltshire.

1629   Marries Jane Danvers, his stepfather's cousin. They live at
        Baynton House, his wife's home.

1630   Presented the living of Bemerton St. Andrew and Fuggleston
        St. Peter near Salisbury in Wiltshire. Becomes Rector of
        Bemerton, with induction at St. Andrew's Church in
        Bemerton. Ordained priest at Salisbury Cathedral. Arthur
        Woodnoth visits Herbert at Bemerton.

1631   Death of John Donne. Serves at Bemerton and writes on poems of *The Temple* and on his prose work *The Country Parson* (or *A Priest to the Temple*).

1632   Continues serving at Bemerton and writing. Corresponds with Nicholas Ferrar at Little Gidding.

1632/3   January, 1632 (Old Style calendar)/1633 (New Style): Edmund Duncon delivers Herbert's poems to Nicholas Ferrar. February, 1632/3: Dictates will to Nathanael Bostocke, his curate. March 1, 1632/3: dies of tuberculosis in Bemerton Rectory. March 3, 1632/3: buried beneath or very near the altar in St. Andrew's Church, Bemerton.

1633   *The Temple* published.

1640   *Outlandish Proverbs* published.

1651   *Jacula Prudentum* (enlarged edition of *Outlandish Proverbs*) published.

1652   *Herbert's Remains* (including the first publication of *A Priest to the Temple* [or *The Country Parson*]) published.

1670   Izaak Walton's *The Life of Mr. George Herbert* published.

HERBERT'S LIFE

George Herbert was born in Montgomery, Wales, on April 3, 1593, one of the children of Richard Herbert and Magdalen Newport. There were ten children born to these parents (seven sons—George being the fifth—and three daughters). Richard Herbert died in 1596 when George was only three and one half years old. After the estate was settled, Herbert's mother took the family to her own mother's home in Eyton, Shropshire. After her mother's death Mrs. Herbert moved her family again (1599), this time to Oxford where her oldest son Edward was attending the University. The household remained there until 1601 when the family moved to London, specifically in Charing Cross.

The household at Charing Cross was made up of twenty-six people, including nurses, chambermaids, and servingmen. Mrs. Herbert was known for her hospitality, with many guests frequently in the home for dinner, with musicians, dancers, and card-playing as entertainments. In her role as patroness of artists, Mrs. Herbert included John Donne as one whom she supported and to whom she was a friend: their friendship began in earnest in 1607. Donne sent to her his *La Corona* (a series of sonnets, or, as Donne calls them, "hymns"). Donne also addressed a poem to Edward Herbert. George Herbert attended Westminster School during many of the Charing Cross years, and, at this young age, would be acquainted with Donne personally in his visits to the household and with Donne's writings. George Herbert also was exposed during this time to several musicians who would visit the home. George himself became an accomplished musician, especially on the lute and viol. At Westminster School Herbert was thoroughly polished in Latin, Greek, and music.

In 1608, during the latter part of George Herbert's period at Westminster School, his mother married Sir John Danvers. He was a handsome man and much younger than Magdalen Herbert: Danvers was apparently about the same age as her oldest son (Edward). But George Herbert found his stepfather to be a man whom he could trust and whom he regarded as a friend. In addition to the Charing Cross home, the Danvers household also spent time (especially summers) in Sir John's Chelsea home on the north bank of the Thames, a home with grounds especially famous for the beautiful gardens.

George Herbert was admitted to Trinity College, Cambridge, in May, 1609. Early in his Cambridge years (1610) Herbert wrote a letter to his mother in which he speaks of the vanity of the many love poems daily written and consecrated to Venus, and he tells her that his poetic abilities will always be consecrated to God's glory. He sent her two sonnets exemplifying this vow. Herbert took his Bachelor of Arts degree in 1612, was elected minor fellow in 1614, and then was elected major fellow and took his Master of Arts in 1616. As fellow, Herbert served as a tutor to several students. In 1618 he was named Praelector in Rhetoric at Cambridge and in 1620 became University Orator, after serving in 1619 as deputy to Sir Francis Nethersole, the previous Orator. As Orator, Herbert wrote the University letters and delivered orations to official guests of the University, including royalty and other prominent figures in the state. During his years at Cambridge Herbert wrote much of his Latin poetry, and he wrote early versions of several English poems that would many years later find their final form in *The Temple*.

In late 1623 Herbert stood for a position in Parliament representing his family seat of Montgomery and was selected as a Member. He sat in Parliament in 1624 and was granted a leave from his position of Orator until December, 1624. Herbert did not return to his Cambridge life, although he did not resign officially his Orator's position until a few years later. His deputies performed his duties. By late 1624 Herbert apparently anticipated his pursuit of divinity and prepared to take holy orders. In fact, during his leave he applied to the Archbishop of Canterbury for permission to be ordained at any time by the Bishop of Lincoln, John Williams. The Archbishop granted this permission on November 3, 1624. If this permission were not granted, Herbert would have to wait the customary year following his declared intention for ordination before he could indeed take holy orders. Herbert and Williams had become friends apparently, and Williams undoubtedly recognized Herbert's promise in the church. Probably Williams ordained Herbert soon after receiving permission to do so. On December 6, 1624, the Bishop granted Herbert a portion of the rectory of Llandinam, Montgomery, thus giving him income that he now lacked without his academic post.

In the summer of 1625, following the death of King James I in the spring, an epidemic of plague occurred in London. John Donne stayed at the Danvers home in Chelsea from June to December of that year and writes in a letter that George Herbert was also there in December.

In 1626 George Herbert probably lived in the home of his brother Henry Herbert in Woodford: Henry was Master of the Revels and a Member of Parliament. Francis Bacon died in 1626, and George Herbert published a Latin poem on his death in a commemorative volume. In July of 1626 Herbert was installed (by proxy) as canon of Lincoln Cathedral and prebendary of Leighton Ecclesia. Herbert's duty was to preach an annual sermon in the cathedral on Whitsunday (Pentecost). Herbert probably appeared in person at Leighton Bromswold for his induction, with his friend and fellow deacon Nicholas Ferrar from nearby Little Gidding present and/or Herbert himself visiting Ferrar at Little Gidding. The church at Leighton Bromswold had fallen into such a state of decay that it had not been fit for public worship for many years. Herbert, with the help of Ferrar and benefactors solicited for funds, made plans to restore the church, a task not completed until after Herbert's death. During 1626 Herbert was subject to a severe period of illness, apparently from "consumption" (i.e., tuberculosis).

Herbert stayed at Chelsea in May of 1627: his mother was ill and eventually died in early June. After her death Herbert wrote *Memoriae Matris Sacrum*. John Donne preached a memorial sermon for Lady Danvers on July 1. Herbert's poems in her memory were subsequently published with Donne's sermon.

In 1628 Herbert moved to the Wiltshire home (Dauntesey House) of his stepfather's older brother, Henry Danvers, Earl of Danby. Possibly Herbert became his chaplain. Also, in 1628, Sir John Danvers married Elizabeth Dauntesey. Herbert undoubtedly was able to devote time at Dauntesey to continue writing the English poems that would come to form *The Temple* eventually.

Twenty miles from Dauntesey was Baynton House, the home of Charles Danvers. His daughter Jane was the cousin of John and Henry Danvers, and Herbert probably had met her even before his time spent in the Earl of Danby's household, despite Izaak Walton's contention in his seventeenth-century *Life of Herbert* that Herbert met her only three days before their wedding! At any rate, he renewed or struck up a fruitful acquaintance with her during his time here because he married her on March 5, 1629, in the parish church at Edington. The couple then lived with her mother (a widow), brothers, and sisters in Baynton House for a period of about a year following their marriage.

In April, 1630, Herbert was presented with and inducted into the living of Fugglestone-with-Bemerton, encompassing the parish church of Fugglestone St. Peter and the chapel of Bemerton St. Andrew. George Herbert probably was nominated for this parish by his cousin William Herbert, 3rd Earl of Pembroke, before William's death on April 10, 1630. If not upon his nomination, undoubtedly it was upon that of William's brother Philip, the 4th Earl of Pembroke. King Charles I, who frequently visited Wilton House, the ancestral home of the Earls of Pembroke, approved the presentation. Walton's account of Herbert's induction at Bemerton supposedly comes from Arthur Woodnoth who was with Herbert on that day. Herbert was closed in the church to toll the bell and pray. Woodnoth looked in at a window and saw Herbert lying (in humility and subservience to God) before the altar. In September Herbert was ordained priest, this act giving him the power of speaking words of absolution and administration of the sacrament, rather than simply the power of a deacon to read the daily offices.

During the few remaining years of his life Herbert served as priest at Bemerton, completed his poetic masterpiece *The Temple*, and completed his prose work *A Priest to the Temple* (or *The Country Parson*). Herbert's love of music continued to thrive in his proximity to Salisbury Cathedral, where he would attend Evensong two times a week and play in musical groups after the services.

During Herbert's final illness from tuberculosis, according to Walton, Edmund Duncon was sent to visit Herbert at the request of Nicholas Ferrar. Herbert gave his manuscript of the poems later published as *The Temple* to Duncon to deliver to Ferrar and said, "He shall find in it a picture of the many spiritual conflicts that have passed betwixt God and my Soul, before I could subject mine to the will of Jesus my Master: in whose service I have now found perfect freedom." Herbert also reportedly said that if Ferrar thinks that the book of poems will be to the advantage of "any dejected poor soul," then let it be published, but, if not, Ferrar should burn it. Herbert later made his will. On March 1, 1632 (Old Style calendar)/1633 (New Style), Herbert died in the Bemerton rectory. On March 3 he was buried beneath or near the altar in St. Andrew's, Bemerton, with the stone over his grave not marked. Later in 1633, however, his true memorial in poetry was formed with the first publication of *The Temple*, as seen through the press at Cambridge by Nicholas Ferrar.

(For fuller study of Herbert's life, see the works cited in my "Selected Bibliography," especially Amy M. Charles's *A Life of George Herbert*.)

HERBERT'S WORKS

As customarily classified by titles and/or groups, Herbert's major works are as follows:

A. Poetry

    Latin Poetry
    Sonnets (from Walton's *Lives*)
    The Temple
    To the Queen of Bohemia
    To the Right Hon. the L. Chancellor (Bacon)

B. Prose

    The Country Parson (also known as *A Priest to the Temple*)
    Letters
    Orations (Latin)
    Outlandish Proverbs (also known as *Jacula Prudentum*)

A HERBERT DICTIONARY

A

Abraham. See SARA(H).

Abroach. *Adverb*: in phrase "to set abroach"—to pierce and leave running, especially in speaking of puncturing a barrel or cask of liquor, wine.

Admire. *Verb*: (1) to wonder, marvel, or be surprised; (2) to view with wonder or surprise; (3) to look upon with pleasure or approval or affection.

Admit. *Verb*: (1) to allow to enter, to let in; (2) to permit or allow; (3) to acknowledge; (4) to accept as true, to concede as fact.

Affect. *Verb*: (1) to aspire to or seek to obtain, (2) to like or love, (3) to frequent or inhabit, (4) to influence or act upon.

Affection. *Noun*: (1) emotion or feeling; (2) passion; (3) disposition, inclination, mental tendency; (4) fondness; (5) biased feeling.

Affects the metaphysics. See METAPHYSICAL.

"Affliction (1)." Many scholars and critics feel that this poem is one of Herbert's most autobiographical. The speaker (or Herbert) is attracted to serve God (simply as a creature of God from childhood or as a Christian). In the first stanza he pictures himself as one offered a position as a servant to God, and the "service" is appealing because it is quite attractive in its beauty and elegance ("BRAVE"). God seems a generous employer, seeking to better his servant's welfare with "gracious benefits," not just with physical enjoyments, of course, but with his grace and spiritual provisions. The analogy of the speaker as a servant or laborer in relation to God as a master or landowner recurs in Herbert's poetry. The "furniture" and "household-stuff" of the second stanza continue the analogy of a household servant to a master. These terms may be taken specifically to refer to the furnishings and trappings of God's house, the church—i.e., the pews, altar, chalice, and other beautiful physical elements of the environment in which a Christian worshipper would serve or simply the accouterments in any vocation or calling in which he can serve God. The household-stuff is indeed "glorious," in physical and worldly senses, but possibly also implying that these elements are means to lead to spiritual and heavenly glory. But the comment on counting "such stars" (line 11) suddenly expands the idea of God's earthly house or place of vocational service into one encompassing the whole creation: the speaker is joyful to serve God in the creation itself, with its elements of beauty surrounding him. Continuing the servant and monetary analogy, the speaker receives his "wages," then, in both the pleasures of God's MACROCOSM and of his MICROCOSM on earth.

Stanza three pictures the rather naive and self-concerned speaker as ecstatic in his optimism contemplating his rosy future: he feels that he will never lack (WANT) any pleasures, since he will be able to serve the ultimate King and provider, God himself! But he has ignored the possibility of "grief or fear" in the life of a servant of God. His rash, hasty (see SUDDEN) soul briefly realizes these possible spoilers of the good life and brashly looks to God for some reassurance and encouragement. (One should note Herbert's use of "her" in line 18 to refer to the soul: see SOUL, FEMININE.) Most of stanza four reinforces his naive nature—and indeed his pathetically childlike view of God's first nurturing him like a mother with the very "milk and sweetnesses" he had earlier anticipated. His early life (as a human? as a Christian?) seemed a veritable eternal spring ("May") with all the pleasures and beauties in life that he could wish. But "sorrow" intrudes with his accumulating years and begins to fight on the side of "woe" and against pleasure in life.

Stanza five presents the body ("flesh") complaining to the soul: lines 26, 27, and 28 of the poem should be read as if quoting the body's statements (its three complaints) to the soul. To understand this, one must remember the concept of the TRIPARTITE SOUL: the sensitive (or sensible) soul is responsible for the functioning of the five senses (and thus feeling and pain). "Grief" and "fear" (stanza three) do now have a large part in his life.

Stanza six (the middle one of the poem) enforces the "affliction" of the poem's title quite explicitly: the speaker is now suffering not just periods of fluctuating physical health and well-being (significantly quite typical of the sickly Herbert throughout his life), but periodic losses of emotional well-being and "life" through deaths of friends. Decline in his sense of humor and penetrating wit was "lost," "blunted." At this stage he felt physically weak and wasted ("thin and lean") and emotionally isolated, unprotected, and unsupported ("without a fence or friend"). He was aware of being afflicted with the "storms and winds" of life and mortality.

Stanza seven has obvious reflections of, or at least parallels to, Herbert's own life. His birth into a prominent family and some of his own initial desires might suggest an inclination toward a position in the government and/or court, but he instead became immersed in academic life, with "book" and academic "gown," as a student, fellow, and University Orator at Cambridge. The troubles of the larger world were not excluded from the academic world, however. The "strife" inherent in humanity and the world impinge on him increasingly, as well as conflict felt within himself about his true goals and purposes in life. This imagery of conflict and battle carries into stanza eight with his wish to end the "siege" of God's force pressuring him either (1) to serve God in his academic calling or (2) to serve God as a clergyman. God's praises and the sweetnesses of Christian service keep him serving God. But the speaker discovers (stanza nine) that this new life of Christian service also has afflictions: he is not immune to earthly afflictions that all mortals are subject to, and God promises him no such immunity and no poetic justice for the good in this life. God turns (see "CROSS-BIAS") his direct, apparently simple path in life to an oblique, indirect one to reach his ultimate goal.

The last stanza pictures him settled into his service for God, but with uncertainty for its future course, with no simple assurances and predictions and no help from academic and theological scholarship ("None of my books will show"). His own uncertainty in being subject to flux and suffering, of course, is not unique in this world: in fact, it is the typical lot of mortal humanity in a fallen world, and this is what the speaker must learn. The speaker's sense of frustration is conveyed well by line 57 of the poem ("I read, and sigh, and wish I were a tree"): the regular iambic meter with alternating short and long words corresponding to the short and long stresses give a sense of his life seeming to be one of weary impatience, of being suspended uselessly. To gain a sense of simple purpose and certainty, he makes his slightly sarcastic wish to be a tree that at least provides fruit, shade, and a nesting place and is not subject to the consciousness of misery as humans are.

He attempts to calm himself early in the final stanza by trying to convince himself that he must meekly and stoically bear any afflictions he is subject to and, paradoxically, also be "strong" in times of spiritual weakness that might cause him to stray from God's service. Suddenly, as any inconstant mortal tends to do, he changes his mind and wants to go find another "service" for another "master," throwing away his present way of life for something on the horizon that always seems better: the servant/master analogy begun in stanza one is thus brought full circle at the end of the poem. Suddenly in the last two lines the speaker seems shocked at himself to realize how fickle and disloyal and self-serving he has just been: he asks for the capacity to fully love and serve God and implies that if he cannot still love God even in the midst of affliction, then he does not really deserve to serve God (i.e., to serve because of his love). Herbert has made the last two lines capable of two interpretations, in fact, but both are relevant to the larger meaning of the poem. The ambiguity is in "I am clean forgot": he can mean that he has completely forgotten God (and his debt and love to God) and/or he can mean that temporarily or at intervals (of affliction) that the speaker feels that God has forgotten him. In either case, his love and service to God should continue, and he should ideally be capable of transcending the changes and trials of this earthly life. His experience reflects in miniature, then, that of Job.

Afford. *Verb*: (1) to perform or accomplish, (2) to grant or bestow or give of what one has, (3) to be capable of yielding, (4) to supply from resources or to yield naturally.

"The Agony." The title refers to the biblical event of Christ's praying in agony by himself in the Garden of Gethsemane on the Mount of Olives (see MOUNT OLIVET). The account in Luke says that his sweat was like great drops of blood falling. Immediately after praying, he was betrayed by Judas and arrested. These events led to his crucifixion.

The first stanza gives an expansive view of the accomplishments of "philosophers," only to then satirically deride them because of the relative unimportance of their discoveries, compared to some in the spiritual realm. "Philosophers" here primarily designates natural philosophers, i.e., scientists, including astronomers, geographers, mathematicians, and others who have "measured" the physical world and universe from the top of the earth ("mountains") to the bottom ("depths of seas") and have even "walked with a staff to heaven." This last statement plays on two meanings of "STAFF": one is a measuring rod (thus, an astronomer's means of measuring), and the other is a staff used as an aid in walking. By implying both, Herbert effectively conveys not only the scientists' attempts to measure everything in the physical universe (distances of planets, etc.), but their extreme pride and presumption in doing so (or in *thinking* that they have done so). Walking to heaven conveys the scientists' egotistical feeling of doing something apparently with ease and nonchalance that most mere mortals cannot conceive of doing. Geographers have measured mountains, seas, and traced "fountains" (springs and/or the sources of streams and rivers). Herbert does include, along with these scientists, "philosophers" in the sense of lovers of wisdom, applied to politics and statecraft ("states, and kings"), implying their pride also in this mastery of worldly and physical matters. (See PHILOSOPHY and NEW PHILOSOPHY.) Herbert must be playing on meanings of both "MEASURE" and "FATHOM" in these first three lines of the poem, and his wordplay creates further his satirical and critical tone. He implies that scientists feel that they have "measured," in the sense of determined the size of mountains, but also feel that they have "measured" in the sense of correctly judged the value of these physical heights. Also, the scientists feel that they have "fathomed," in the sense of measured the depth (i.e., sounded with a fathom-line) of seas, but also feel that they have "fathomed" in the sense of having understood the seas thoroughly. Of course, they only understand the land and sea of earth *physically*, not in any larger senses, and there are other matters much more important *spiritually* to be examined. And "fathomed the depths of," applied to "states" and "kings" is clearly playing on "fathom" as *understanding* political systems, implying the shallowness of this knowledge when compared to matters of more importance. Thus, Herbert drives home common human limitations and ignorance in lines 4–6 by noting that Sin and Love remain unexamined: his satirical, critical tone depends largely on the continuing wordplay on "measure" in line 5: clearly here the emphasis is on the greater importance of *judging the value of* sin and love, in contrast to merely determining the physical size of mountains. Similarly, the wordplay on "fathom" is completed in line 6: to "sound" or "fathom" sin and love in the sense of *understanding thoroughly* their natures is in contrast to merely probing the physical depth of seas. One also notes Herbert's careful variation of metrical stresses at a key point in line 4: "two," "vast," and the first syllable of "spacious" all are heavily stressed, violating the normal iambic pattern and slowing down the reading. The sense of stretching the syllables out conveys the impressive dominance in importance of the two elements he is about to name (Sin and Love), in comparison to the several lesser things that he has catalogued very rapidly in the first three lines. So, by the end of the first stanza, Herbert has punctured and deflated the ego of seemingly

all-knowing "philosophers": they *think* that they can range over the
earth and universe and even walk to heaven very familiarly, but they
only know "heaven" physically. To truly walk to heaven spiritually,
one must understand sin and love, things that cannot be simply sized and
quantified physically.

Herbert's use of CLASSICAL form becomes evident in the
careful structure of the poem, as he names "Sin" and "Love" at the end
of stanza one and then devotes the succeeding two stanzas to first the one
("Sin") and then the other ("Love") in that order. One also sees the
development of METAPHYSICAL content and conceits, combined with
this classical form. With the second stanza, the reader also begins to see
the application of the title to the poem more clearly. Christ's "agony"
in the Garden of Gethsemane best exemplifies the effect and pain of
human sin, for which Christ will suffer and die. Significantly, one
envisions "a man" (line 9) suffering this pain because God took on
man's nature in Christ to suffer for man in the flesh. Herbert pictures
the pain as so great that Christ is sweating blood (cf. Luke 22:44).
Christ is being "wrung" or squeezed by mankind's Sin, as if Sin were a
"press" (implying conceits of both a *wine-press* that squeezes juice out
of the grapes in order to make wine and an *apparatus for torture* with
which a person is subjected to heavy weights placed on the body).
Herbert also calls Sin a "vice," playing on its meaning as both (1) evil
conduct and (2) a screw-press, "vise," instrument for squeezing. Christ
as in a wine-press alludes to the Old Testament cluster of grapes (in
Numbers 13:23) as a TYPE of Christ (also see Herbert's "THE BUNCH
OF GRAPES"). Christ's agony, then, presses him and results in his
flowing blood just as a wine-press squeezes grapes and causes the juice
to flow out. The juice of grapes turned into wine implies a parallel to
Christ's blood as the wine of Holy Communion.

The wine-press conceit carries into the third stanza, as Christ's
crucifixion and blood flowing from him there complete the process.
Christ's crucifixion does not only exemplify Love, but also it defines
Love. The "juice" that the soldier's spear ("pike") caused to flow from
Christ's side (see John 19:34) is Christ's blood, like wine made from
grape juice flowing out of a punctured (see ABROACH) cask. Herbert's
use of "taste that juice" forces the reader to perceive the love evinced by
Christ to be embodied for the worshipper in Holy Communion, the
point made even more explicit in the last two lines of the poem.
Drinking the wine of the Eucharist, then, is a tangible tasting of Christ's
love expressed through his sacrifice. Significantly, here Christ is
referred to as "my God," not just as "a man" as in stanza two. Sin is
human, and Love is divine. Paradoxically, mankind's Sin conveyed to
Christ is repaid to mankind in the form of Christ's Love. And, further,

the Love that is pressed out by the Sin becomes the very thing that overcomes Sin.

Ague. *Noun*: a fever accompanied by chills and shaking.

Air. *Noun*: (1) one of the four ELEMENTS, (2) the atmosphere or space just above the earth, (3) breath or sigh.

Alarms. *Noun*: calls to arms or battle (with trumpets or drums).

Alchemist. See ALCHEMY.

Alchemy. The "science" or "chemistry" of the Middle Ages and Renaissance that attempted to turn base metals into gold by the use of a "philosopher's stone." Also, these practitioners of alchemy, the alchemists (or "chemics"), wanted to concoct or extract an "elixir" (or "elixir vitae"), a miraculous medicine that supposedly would cure all disease and prolong life. This elixir was also referred to as the "quintessence" (or "fifth essence"), an absolutely pure substance that could purge impurities. It was believed by some to be latent in all matter, and it was thought to be what makes up the heavenly bodies. *One must note that Herbert and other writers commonly do not distinguish between the "philosopher's stone" and the "elixir" and the "quintessence," but use these terms interchangeably.* See, for example, Herbert's "The Sinner" and "THE ELIXIR."

Allow. *Verb*: (1) to praise or commend, (2) to approve of, (3) to accept as reasonable or valid, (4) to permit.

Allure. *Verb*: (1) to tempt, entice, charm; (2) to draw to oneself, to draw forth, to elicit.

"Altar, The." This poem is an example of Herbert's PATTERN POEMS (or "shaped verses"). Here the poem is in the shape of an altar. Another example of a pattern poem in Herbert is "EASTER WINGS."
      This poem is the first one in the section *The Church* of *THE TEMPLE*. Herbert thus dedicates his heart (the real altar) to God: line 1 echoes Psalm 51:17 ("The sacrifices of God are a broken spirit: a broken and contrite heart, O God, thou wilt not despise"). The parts of his heart are those that God himself did "FRAME," in the sense of "create" or "form" (line 3). This broken, sinful, repentant (note "tears") heart is the altar presented to God. Line 4 specifically alludes to God's words to Moses in Exodus 20:25 ("And if thou wilt make me an altar of stone, thou shalt not build it of hewn stone: for if thou lift up

thy tool upon it, thou hast polluted it"). From this Old Testament image in line 4 Herbert proceeds to apply a New Testament image in lines 5–6 ("A heart alone / Is such a stone"): he alludes here to St. Paul's assertion in 2 Corinthians 3:3 ("Forasmuch as ye are manifestly declared to be the epistle of Christ ministered by us, written not with ink, but with the Spirit of the living God; not in tables of stone, but in fleshy tables of the heart"). The Old Testament literal stone, then, becomes a TYPE of the New Testament human heart that only God (through Christ) can affect. So, the sinner's or speaker's (or Herbert's?) "hard heart" (line 9), in all of its broken pieces, come together in this "FRAME" (line 10): here "frame" is a noun designating a structure put together of parts, thus applying both to the heart as an altar and to this very poem put together of pieces and embodying the symbol of the heart as altar.

Lines 12–13 ("That if I chance to hold my peace, / These stones to praise Thee may not cease") refer to Christ's answer to the Pharisees who wanted him to rebuke his disciples who were praising him—see Luke 19:40 ("And he answered and said unto them, I tell you that, if these should hold their peace, the stones would immediately cry out"). It is important to note that this biblical allusion is to Christ's entry into Jerusalem before his crucifixion, since lines 14–15 of the poem end it with the request that Christ let his "sacrifice," his crucifixion and death, apply its redemptive power to this sinner's heart. The end of the poem acknowledges that only Christ's crucifixion can sanctify this "altar," his heart and his Christian poetry, with Christ's death as the offering upon the sinner-poet's altar. Significantly, the next poem in *The Church* is Herbert's long poem "The Sacrifice" that portrays Christ's crucifixion and death.

Amalgamating disparate experience. See DISSOCIATION OF SENSIBILITY.

Amber-greese. *Noun*: ambergris—waxy, oily substance secreted from a whale, used in cooking and in perfumes.

Amerce. *Verb*: to fine.

Amiens. City in France taken by Louis XI ("the Fox") in 1471. His enemy was Charles the Bold ("the Lion").

Anatomy. *Noun*: (1) dissection, (2) a body or corpse for dissection, (3) a skeleton.

Andrewes, Lancelot (1555–1626). Preacher, theologian, chaplain to Queen ELIZABETH I; one of the translators of the Authorized Version of the Bible under King JAMES I; and ultimately Bishop of Winchester. One of the most popular preachers of the time.

Andrewes became Dean at Westminster Abbey in 1601 and possibly sponsored Herbert when he entered Westminster School. While Herbert was at Cambridge, he wrote a Latin letter (in the autumn of 1619) to Andrewes. He obviously was a person whom Herbert greatly respected and one whom Herbert regarded as a friend until Andrewes's death.

Angel. *Noun*: (1) spiritual being, above man and below God in the hierarchy of creation, who attends God and serves as a ministering spirit and a divine messenger (see also HIERARCHY, THE HEAVENLY); (2) an English coin stamped with the image of the Archangel Michael piercing the Dragon (of Revelation). Writers of the sixteenth and seventeenth centuries, including Herbert, frequently pun on the word: e.g., see "THE PILGRIMAGE."

Anneal. *Verb*: to make permanent the colors painted on glass by heating the glass.

Anon. *Adverb*: (1) at once, immediately; (2) soon, in a little while.

Anthony. Christian hermit in Egypt in the 4th century A.D.

Apothecary. *Noun*: a pharmacist, one who mixes and prepares drugs or medicines.

Approve. *Verb*: (1) to try, (2) to experience, (3) to corroborate or confirm.

Aquinas, Saint Thomas (1225–1274). The most famous and influential of the scholastic philosophers or SCHOOLMEN. Born of a noble family in Italy. Studied the philosophy of ARISTOTLE at the university in Naples and later became a Dominican friar. He taught at Cologne and Paris. Was made a Doctor of Theology at Paris. Later taught in several Italian universities, eventually remaining in Naples. His most famous and influential work is *Summa Theologica*, although it was unfinished at his death: his works reconcile Christianity with the philosophy of Aristotle (about whom he also wrote commentaries). This massive work analyzes parts of creation (including angels, men, the soul, and the body) and discusses righteousness, free will, original sin, the Seven Virtues (faith, hope, and love are added to the four Cardinal Virtues of justice, prudence, fortitude, and temperance), the Incarnation, seven sacraments, the Word made flesh, and numerous other topics spanning theology, morals, and metaphysics. He argues that reason and revelation do not contradict each other, since God is the author of both reason and revelation. Ideas of Aquinas appear in Herbert, as well as references to the Schoolmen.

Archangels. See HIERARCHY, THE HEAVENLY.

Aristotle (384–322 B.C.). Greek philosopher. Studied under PLATO for twenty years. Was tutor to Alexander the Great. Established a school (the Lyceum) in Athens and taught there for twelve years. His thought survives largely in his and/or his students' lecture notes, and his study covers all realms of knowledge in his time. His influence dominated thought for 2,000 years after him, reaching its height in the Middle Ages when he was idolized as the final word on all knowledge: he was particularly central to the SCHOOLMEN. In logic, his development of deductive reasoning held sway until the scientific advances following BACON and the rise of science and induction in the 17th century. Ultimately disagreed with and challenged Plato and PLATONIC thought, arguing rather for the reality of the physical and material world, and for the duality of body and spirit. In contrast to an idealistic mode of thought, Aristotle tends toward the pragmatic, the practical: *Nicomachean Ethics*, *Politics*, and *Poetics* treat conduct, government, and literature in this light.

Many of the assumptions underlying both NATURAL ORDER and the view of the universe ascribed to PTOLEMY have their sources in Aristotle, especially in his *Metaphysics*. He envisions a ranked, hierarchical nature that leads to the pure Unmoved Mover at the top that is the source of all energy in the universe. His philosophy was ultimately brought into agreement with major Christian conceptions and was embraced by the church.

The ideas of intelligences directing the SPHERES, of the human TRIPARTITE SOUL, and of the four ELEMENTS owe much to Aristotle, and they frequently appear in Herbert and other writers of his time. Herbert also uses Aristotle's conception of man as a MICROCOSM.

Ark. *Noun*: (1) the ark God had Noah build to save himself and his family from the flood: see Genesis 6–9; (2) the Ark of the Covenant, a holy chest eventually containing the Ten Commandments and carried from place to place by the Hebrews in their wanderings and battles, finally being placed in Solomon's Temple, where it is believed to have been destroyed in the Babylonian destruction of the Temple. Herbert, in *THE CHURCH MILITANT* (lines 19–20), pictures Abraham (see

SARA) taking it on his journeys to and from Canaan (see Genesis 12:5, 21:34, and 22:2). In general, this ark symbolizes the religion of Israel.

"Artillery." The speaker portrays himself sitting before his small dwelling (see CELL) and seeing a shooting star fall into his lap. As he shakes it off his clothes, the speaker hears "one" (obviously God) tell him rather sarcastically to go on and do as he usually does (see USE), that is, to disobey and/or ignore suggestions or motives of a God-ordained, divine nature. Thus, to "expel good motions from thy breast" is the symbolic import of the speaker's shaking off the heavenly bit of fire that has been directed (by God) to fall into his lap. Herbert seems to be suggesting a double meaning in line 8 ("Which have the face of fire, but end in rest"). It is deliberately ambiguous in that in one sense it presents God suggesting that these "good motions" from heaven that are fiery might seem to be dangerous but actually lead to "rest," spiritual peace. However, a second reading suggests that the speaker is being accused by God of ignoring his own spiritual, fiery thoughts that are left to cool and die away without action.

   In the second stanza the speaker suggests his surprise at hearing this voice from the stars, although he has heard of music in the spheres (see SPHERE). He attempts to answer God's message, acknowledging that the stars and all things are God's ministers: these lines echo Psalm 104:4 ("Who maketh his angels spirits; his ministers a flaming fire"). The speaker grants that he might be guilty of often refusing to pursue good motives and notions but that he now vows not to refuse to cleanse himself of his stubbornness: he says that he will now act ("do") on these divine suggestions or suffer the consequences. The use of "blood" to "wash" his nature suggests the importance of Christ's blood to a redeemed sinner and Christian. In other words, he should acknowledge that Christ's blood has cleansed him and that he should be willing to risk his own suffering to enact his own Christlike nature. He acknowledges that he indeed should be known by his own fruits and that his faith is as dead as the sparks that he allows to die without action in works, in deeds. God's "artillery" has caused a partial capitulation of the speaker to God in this battle of wills, in this conceptual war between God and the speaker.

   The METAPHYSICAL CONCEIT of the title becomes even clearer in the third stanza. At the poem's mid-point the speaker begins to threaten to return military volleys. His own "stars" and "shooters" (i.e., shooting stars) are his "tears" and "prayers" (line 19) that he fires up at God from earth: these are his bullets fired to God. But he accuses God of not responding to them ("yet thou dost refuse"). He feels that God is not granting his own wishes expressed by tears and prayers. In the rest of the third stanza (lines 21–24 of the poem), the speaker, in a rather convoluted and syntactically awkward statement (thus effectively conveying his own hesitant stumbling in challenging God here), admits that he is much more obligated to do God's will than is God to grant the speaker's will. However, in a final volley, he throws up to God the fact that "Thy promise now hath even set thee thy laws." This statement seems to have multiple meanings that express the speaker's challenge to God. If God's "promise" is taken to be generally the promise of redemption and salvation in New Testament terms of Christ's love, mercy, and sacrifice on man's behalf, then God's Old Testament "laws" are "set" aside and have "set" like the sun: even to God himself, love and grace now rule over law. But one must note also that "promise" can be taken much more specifically (especially in light of the speaker's implorings of God through tears and prayers) to refer to Christ's promise in Matthew 7:7–8, "Ask, and it shall be given you; seek, and ye shall find; knock, and it shall be opened unto you: For every one that asketh receiveth; and he that seeketh findeth; and to him that knocketh it shall be opened." So, these New Testament "laws" pronounced by God obligate God to abide by them, the speaker insists, and he feels that his own askings, seekings, and knockings through tears and prayers have been ignored.

In the fourth stanza the speaker concludes that both he and God are like soldiers who fire artillery ("shooters"). His attitude also becomes more humble and grateful. He recognizes that God "deigns" to enter combat with humans, thus condescending to a level on which he dignifies man by communicating with him and being concerned about him. Paradoxically, God is even willing to "contest" with his "own clay": man is the clay, and this part of the poem and much of the poem itself echoes Psalm 40:1–3 ("I waited patiently for the Lord; and he inclined unto me, and heard my cry. He brought me up also out of an horrible pit, out of the miry clay, and set my feet upon a rock, and established my goings. And he hath put a new song in my mouth, even praise unto our God: many shall see it, and fear, and shall trust in the Lord"). Suggested also at this point is Romans 9:20–21 ("Nay but, O man, who art thou that repliest against God? Shall the thing formed say to him that formed it, 'Why hast thou made me thus?' Hath not the potter power over the clay . . .?"). The speaker would gladly (see FAIN) "parley"—i.e., he wishes to make peace, to negotiate and discuss with this enemy. Yet, regardless of the outcome of his attempts to shoot at and negotiate with God, he still capitulates: he is truly God's and can only have his true identity through God's. He confesses that ultimately there is no "articling," no arranging of matters by articles in a treaty, with God. What does he have to offer God? All he is and all he possesses is already God's, in his own source, being, and end. He is only finite man facing an infinite God, but, paradoxically, complete capitulation to God grants to man infinity, eternal life.

"Art of love." See lines 45–47 of "The Thanksgiving" and OVID.

As. Frequently means "that" and "since" (or "because").

Assay. *Verb*: to test or try.

Assume. *Verb*: (1) to adopt or take, (2) to take food or drink into the body, (3) to take upon or put on, (4) to lay claim or usurp.

Attend. *Verb*: (1) to pay attention to or consider or listen to; (2) to apply oneself to; (3) to wait upon or serve or accompany; (4) to wait for or expect; (5) to wait or stay.

Augustine, Saint (354–430). Bishop of Hippo in Africa from 396 to 430. Recognized as one of the greatest thinkers, writers, and theologians in Christianity. His mother (Monica) was a devout Christian and continually wished Augustine to become one. He lived a rather dissolute early life, with a mistress and an illegitimate son. At the age of 28 he went to Milan as a teacher of rhetoric where he heard Ambrose preach and was impressed by his use of Neoplatonic philosophy (see PLATONIC). He experienced a mystical conversion in Milan that was confirmed by a reading of St. Paul. He turned more ascetic and philosophical. He was baptized by Ambrose in 387. On his return to Africa his mother died, just after a conversation between mother and son on the ascent to heaven and its glories. After returning to Africa, he became assistant priest to the bishop at Hippo, and, after the bishop's death, Augustine was made Bishop in 395 and remained so until his death during the siege of the city by the Vandals.

Augustine wrote sermons, commentaries, essays, and letters. Two of his works, however, are his most famous and influential. His *Confessions* detail his early life and conversion, expressing extreme guilt for the sexual and other sins of his youth. *The City of God* proposes that there are two cities in existence vying for man's adherence, Jerusalem and Babylon or the heavenly city and the earthly city or the city of God and the city of man. Although heavily influenced by PLATONIC philosophy and its ability to be reconciled with some facets of Christianity, Augustine increasingly saw the differences. He could agree that looking into himself at his own soul can reveal God and felt that he could find in God the author of all and the illuminator of truth. He is one of the four traditional Doctors of the western church.

Augustine's formulation of the concept of the BOOK OF
CREATURES also influenced Herbert and other writers, thinkers, and
clergymen of his time. In Herbert's will he left "St. Augustine's works"
to NATHANAEL BOSTOCKE.

B

Babel, Tower of. The tower of brick erected by men who wanted its top to reach to heaven. God, seeing their pride, confounded their language so that they could no longer understand each other. They then ceased their building and scattered to various parts of the earth. See Genesis 11:1–9.

Bacon, Francis (1561–1626). Studied and practiced law, served in Parliament, and held the position of Lord Keeper of the Great Seal under Queen ELIZABETH. His advancement was even more rapid under King JAMES, serving as Solicitor General, Attorney General, Lord Keeper, and Lord Chancellor. Knighted in 1603, created first Baron Verulam in 1618, and made Viscount St. Albans in 1621, Bacon accumulated many political enemies, and he was tried and convicted by the House of Lords in 1621 on the charge of accepting bribes as a judge. He was barred from holding public office: thus in public disgrace, Bacon retired to his estate to concentrate more on philosophical and scientific speculations and proposals and on writing. His *Essays* had first appeared in 1597, but subsequent editions through 1625 expanded their number. His most influential works are *The Advancement of Learning* (1605) and *Novum Organum* (1620), containing key proposals in his visionary plan to refute Aristotelian and medieval authority and means of reasoning. Bacon proposes the inductive (or scientific) method of arriving at truth, wishing to eliminate the human tendency to be misled by subjectivity. Bacon's works placed him in the vanguard of the rise of science, endorsing both an attitude of objective observation of physical matter outside of the individual and an increase of practicality and utility in outlook in the seventeenth century. His *New Atlantis*, proposing a type of scientific Utopia, appeared a year after his death.

Bacon dedicated his *The Translation of Certain Psalms into English Verse*, published in 1625, to George Herbert, whom he calls his "very good friend." He thanks Herbert for the "pains" that Herbert took about some of Bacon's "writings." Hutchinson (see "Selected Bibliography: Works") notes that this refers to Herbert's share in translating *The Advancement of Learning* into Latin for incorporation in *De Augmentis Scientiae* (1623). Bacon also says in the dedication that he could not make a better choice of a person than Herbert in whom he sees "Divinity and Poesy" met. Herbert wrote some Latin poems and an English poem to Bacon.

Balm. *Noun*: (1) aromatic substance exuding from some trees and valued for fragrance and medicinal qualities, (2) a soothing and healing substance, (3) according to PARACELSUS, the life-preserving fluid existing in every living being, the absence of which means death. Most frequent in Herbert is sense 2, especially used metaphorically to suggest Christ's blood and its spiritually healing power.

Balsam, balsome. See BALM.

Bandy. Herbert's one use of this verb in "Humility" ("bandying") means to band together (i.e., "bandying" is banding together).

Banquet. *Noun*: (1) a sumptuous feast of food and drink; (2) sweets, fruit, and wine; (3) dessert; (4) Eucharist or Lord's Supper ("heavenly banquet").

Baynton House. Home (in WILTSHIRE) of JANE DANVERS, cousin of JOHN DANVERS, Herbert's stepfather. Herbert married Jane in 1629, and the couple lived in the house with Jane's mother, brothers, and sisters for about a year after the marriage.

Bays. *Noun*: leaves of the laurel, traditionally depicted as woven into a garland or celebratory wreath, and commonly used to reward poets and poetic achievement.

Bear the bell. Take first place. See line 187 of *THE CHURCH-PORCH*.

Becomes. *Verb*: (1) comes to be, (2) befits or suits.

Behind. *Adverb*: (1) [spatially] in the back of or toward the rear of; (2) [temporally] following in time, later.

Bell(s). For specific bells associated with death, see DEATH BELL, FUNERAL BELL, and PASSING BELL.

Bemerton. Village where Herbert lived upon becoming rector of the chapel of Bemerton St. Andrew and the parish church of Fugglestone St. Peter.   Herbert probably was granted this living upon the recommendation of his kinsman WILLIAM HERBERT, 3rd Earl of Pembroke, to CHARLES I. George Herbert was installed and inducted (on April 26, 1630) here shortly after the death of William, however, when PHILIP HERBERT, 4th Earl of Pembroke, had succeeded to the title and to WILTON HOUSE. George Herbert and his family lived in the Bemerton rectory, just across the road from St. Andrew's. Today Bemerton is essentially a suburb of SALISBURY and is called Lower Bemerton.

WALTON says that at Herbert's induction ARTHUR WOODNOTH waited outside the door of St. Andrew's while Herbert was shut inside the church to toll the bell and pray. After some time Woodnoth looked in and saw Herbert lying prostrate before the altar.

Betimes. *Adverb*: (1) at an early time; (2) early in life; (3) early in the morning; (4) in due time, before it is too late; (5) soon, speedily.

Betray. *Verb*: (1) to reveal or to disclose something or someone, (2) to place into the hands of an enemy by treachery, (3) to expose to punishment, (4) to be false or disloyal.

Blast. *Verb*: (1) to blow violently, (2) to wither.

Board. *Noun*: (1) a thin piece or slab of wood, (2) a table, (3) food served at the table. *Verb*: to approach.

Bohemia, Queen of. See STUART, ELIZABETH.

Book of Creatures. See BOOKS OF GOD.

Book of Life. See BOOKS OF GOD.

Book of Nature. See BOOKS OF GOD.

Book of Scriptures. See BOOKS OF GOD.

Books of God. The concept held by many writers, clergymen, and philosophers that God "wrote" two "books" which mankind can "read" and thus learn of God and truth. One is the "Book of Scriptures" (i.e., the Bible or Divine Revelation). The other is the "Book of Creatures" or the "Book of Nature" (i.e., everything God created in the universe). There is also a third, the "Book of Life," that essentially is the roll or register of the Elect, the individual saved souls known only by God [see, for example, "H. Baptism (1)"].

Bostocke, Nathanael. George Herbert's curate at BEMERTON. Herbert's will was dictated to Bostocke: it is written in Bostocke's hand, and he also is a witness to it. Herbert left him his copy of ST. AUGUSTINE's works.

Brahe, Tycho (1546–1601). Danish astronomer. In 1572 he discovered a "new star" in the constellation Cassiopeia. After a change of Danish rulers and withdrawal of state funds to support his work, Brahe went to Prague in 1599 after the emperor Rudolph II offered support. He died there in 1601. Brahe argued for a view of the universe that was a compromise between those of PTOLEMY and COPERNICUS: Brahe argued that the earth does not move but that the other planets revolve around the sun and that the planets and the sun revolve around the earth yearly. Although many of his views remained relatively conservative, several of his discoveries and accurate observations contributed to the full development of the "NEW PHILOSOPHY" under KEPLER and GALILEO.

Brave. *Adjective*: (1) courageous, daring; (2) splendid, showy, beautiful, handsome, grand; (3) finely-dressed; (4) worthy, excellent; (5) boastful.

Break. *Verb*: (1) to separate forcefully into parts; (2) to divide or part; (3) to wreck [a ship]; (4) to burst the surface; (5) "break the heart": to overwhelm with sorrow; (6) to demolish or ruin; (7) to dash against an obstacle [especially water or waves against a bank or wall, etc.]; (8) to cease or end; (9) to discipline, train, tame [especially animals, such as horses]; (10) to violate; (11) to penetrate; (12) to disclose, reveal, utter; (13) to escape confines, to emerge.

"Brief Notes." See VALDÉS, JUAN.

Bright. *Adjective*: (1) shining, (2) beautiful, (3) of vivid or brilliant color, (4) glorious or splendid.

"British Church, The." The title significantly does not limit the subject to the English church, but apparently encompasses that of the whole of Britain, including Wales and Scotland. In his edition of Herbert and Vaughan Louis L. Martz (see my "Selected Bibliography" under "Works: Poetry and Prose") argues convincingly (pp. 458–59) that Herbert might have in mind the legend that British Christianity came directly from JOSEPH of Arimathea who supposedly came to Britain after Christ's death and established a center of worship at Glastonbury. Thus, this implication carries the note of independence from Rome and Roman Catholicism that Herbert wishes. In addition, Martz also notes that the Welsh most certainly were regarded as Britons and that Herbert came from a Welsh family.

Herbert regards the British Church as his "Mother," one that has nurtured him spiritually from his infancy. Her physical features are "perfect." Calling her hue "bright" (line 3) suggests the clarity and brilliance of truth: the British Church embodies truth in faith and worship, to Herbert. In line 4 he sees beauty itself residing in the British Church, implying that this Church is the epitome of the principle of beauty. Beauty is seen as dating "her letters from thy [the British Church's] face." Here Herbert refers to the fact that under the Julian (or "Old Style") calendar the year began on March 25, regarded as the vernal equinox. This day, however, in England also was Lady Day (the Feast of the Annunciation), honoring the Virgin Mary. So, Herbert implies that one of the holy days observed by the British Church determined the year's beginning—and thus the date of beauty's "letters."

The METAPHYSICAL CONCEIT of various churches as types of women develops more explicitly beginning with the images of dressing and clothing in the third stanza. The clothing worn by the British Church is "fit," appropriate. It is not too MEAN (shabby and sorry in appearance), and it is not too "gay" (not extreme in its bright, rich, luxurious colors and material). Metaphorically, Herbert is thinking of the physical trappings and ornaments in church worship: the British Church strikes a happy medium between the bare, plain appearance of the churches adhering to CALVINISM (or extreme Protestant and Puritan churches in general) and that of Roman Catholicism (with its sumptuous, excessive display of ceremonial trappings, priestly dress, statuary, art, etc.). "Outlandish" (i.e., any "foreign") churches (Roman Catholic or Calvinistic) cannot compare in looks, in beauty, to the British Church (line 10). Those churches (as if they were women) are either "painted" or "undressed": the "painted" ones are like women overdoing things with cosmetics (Roman Catholic churches with excessive emphasis on colors, art, ornamentation), and the "undressed" ones are like women with no clothes at all (the Calvinistic churches that frown on any physical beauty or ornamentation in worship). Thus, these are the two extremes that the British Church avoids.

After this general condemnation of the two excessive churches in the fourth stanza, Herbert then more specifically delineates the excessive natures of each of these churches, describing them still in terms of his conceit of the churches as women. Stanzas 5 and 6 discuss the Roman Catholic Church, and stanzas 7 and 8 concern the Calvinistic Church. "She on the hills" is the Roman Catholic Church, associated with the seven hills of Rome. She is like a woman who acts "wantonly" and who "allureth": she tempts men to succumb to her painted beauty. Those so tempted hope to be "By her preferred." Herbert here is playing on the word "PREFER": in one sense it is simply to be liked better by "her" (the woman as the Roman Catholic Church), but in another sense it is to be advanced in status or promoted by her. In this latter sense Herbert slyly criticizes the many who literally would use the Roman Catholic Church to further their worldly status in both wealth and power. But also the idea is present that people are attracted to Roman Catholicism "in hope" ultimately to be advanced in status into heaven itself. This latter implication is not without its satirical slant by Herbert either, since it seems paradoxical and incongruous for such a worldly temptress as this Church is portrayed to be able to elevate individuals spiritually into heaven! In stanza 6 "painted" emphasizes the ornamentation and artificiality in the surface beauty, rather than the substance, of the Roman Catholic worship. Stanzas 7 and 8 turn to the other extreme, Genevan Calvinism. Again, this church is presented as a woman ("she"): in contrast to the one on the hills, this one dwells "in the valley," since Geneva, the center of Calvinism, is in a valley. The very plain form of worship here is implied in the picture of her being "shy of dressing" and even so extreme that she "nothing wears": all ornamentation, vestments, ceremony, art, liturgy, etc., are stripped away from worship in this extreme Protestantism. She deliberately does not beautify herself. She does not have her "neighbor's pride": her neighbor is the Roman Catholic Church, playing on the fact that Switzerland and Italy are neighboring countries, with Geneva and Rome, then, quite close together geographically. The churches they symbolize, however, are great distances apart ecclesiastically!

Stanzas 9 and 10 bring the poem full circle with the final focus on the best and dearest church, again addressed as "Mother," just as in the first line of the poem. The British Church, then, metaphorically is presented now as the best kind of woman, a fact perceived now in contrast to both the artificially painted temptress and the plain and ugly sloven presented above. Now "Mother" implies the naturally beautiful, loving, nurturing woman as an image of the British Church. The "MEAN" (here used as a noun denoting the happy medium, the quality of being equally removed from two extremes) is her "praise and glory." This church is appropriately the true bride of Christ, the true wife to God, then, and her true children are those adherents of this church. God's love for his bride is apparent in the "love" he has shown to her in using his grace to "double-moat" her, and only her. The precise meaning of this phrase ("double-moat") has been interpreted differently among editors and critics. Joseph H. Summers's edition (see my "Selected Bibliography" under "Works: Poetry") explains it by saying (p. 162), "Only the British Church has God defended not only by his general grace promised to all churches but also by the beautiful mean." In contrast, Barbara K. Lewalski and Andrew J. Sabol, editors of *Major Poets of the Earlier Seventeenth Century* (1973), gloss the phrase (p. 292) as "the British Church is protected [moated] against both ostentatious pride and nudity." Still different is the explanation by Tobin (see my "Selected Bibliography" under "Works: Poetry and Prose") as follows (p. 380): "Britain is already surrounded by a moat of water; God has added a second protective moat of grace." Thus, although the general idea of God's protective favor granted the British Church is clear, the specific references in this seemingly simple phrase are by no means clear and settled in the minds of scholars, critics, editors, and readers. Some ambiguity remains to tease and stimulate us, as in much of Herbert's work, in fact.

Buckingham, 1st Duke of. See VILLIERS, GEORGE.

"Bunch of Grapes, The." The title specifically refers to the cluster of grapes taken by the spies sent from Moses into Canaan, the Promised Land. They cut a branch with a cluster of grapes near the brook of Eshcol and brought it back to show Moses and the Israelites in the wilderness (see Numbers 13). The story of the Israelites wandering in the wilderness is a symbol of the spiritual state of the speaker, but also, by implication, for all Christians. The speaker's "joy" has been lost, and, just as the Israelites, he is wandering in a circle, back to the same dearth of spiritual joy that he had previously. He felt that he had progressed from the Red Sea to the promised Canaan in his own life, but now he is back to the Red Sea, the "sea of shame" (line 7). This parallels the progress of the Israelites. They had reached an area near Canaan, but, because of the "evil report" (see Numbers 13:32) given about the Promised Land by the spies and the subsequent disbelief of God's promise and rebellion against God by the Israelites, they were kept wandering in the wilderness toward the Red Sea again. So, then, do weakness and sin overcome joy in this life, for the speaker and for any Christian at times.

The second stanza makes this parallel, this analogy, much more explicit with "For as the Jews . . . / So now each Christian. . . ." Each Christian's "journeys" are "spanned" (limited)—i.e., the Israelites' physical journey over earthly space is a symbol of each Christian's emotional and spiritual journey over earthly time. "Their story [i.e., the Israelites'] pens [writes] and sets us down [i.e., writes ours down on paper]" (line 11). In addition, however, Herbert seems to be using "sets us down" with another meaning that suggests that we are being warned and that our own tendency to rebel is being quelled by seeing how the Israelites were brought low by their own foolish rebellion. This sense is enforced by Herbert's echo here of St. Paul in I Corinthians 10:11 ("Now all these things happened unto them [Israelites in the wilderness] for ensamples: and they are written for our own admonition. . . ."). I also feel that Herbert is using "pens" with a double sense: it not only means "writes" but also "confines" or "encloses." So, we are penned up, restricted from our own foolish straying and from our own perceived deservings that are independent of God's will and guidance. This additional meaning is supported by its consistency with "spanned" (limited) in the previous line. God's restrictions and admonitions (as shown in the story of the Israelites) reveal his greatness and power, his "ancient justice." Also, his many "wide works" are contrasted to the smallness and insignificance of any individual's one deed. Just so does God's Bible extend significance beyond any human individual's deed or life, but into all humanity through all time. At the end of this stanza, Herbert indeed does provide the transition from the Old Testament example of God's power and justice to his New Testament love and mercy by emphasizing how God's works "let in future times." In other words, these Old Testament events, people, and things are TYPEs that foreshadow New Testament events, people, and things important to the Christian, and all are brought to fruition in Christ, redemption, and the true Canaan provided for the Christian. The second half of the poem (stanzas three and four) elaborate on how these types of the Israelites' story are to be interpreted.

Line 15 alludes to Exodus 13:21 ("And the Lord went before them by day in a pillar of a cloud, to lead them the way; and by night in a pillar of fire, to give them light; to go by day and night"): so, we have "guardian fires and clouds" in our Christian life (in instruction? liturgy? clerical guidance?) to help us. We also have "Scripture-dew" (line 16), alluding to Numbers 11:9 ("And when the dew fell upon the camp in the night, the manna fell upon it"): so, we have the Bible that nourishes us and continually teaches us. We have our afflictions, hardships, and disappointments ("sands and serpents, tents and shrowds [temporary shelters]") in our Christian life as the Israelites had in their Old Testament wanderings. We also give out "murmurings" of dissatisfaction, complaining, and rebellion as they did. Recognizing our parallels to their unhappiness and sorrow, however, causes the speaker to long for the taste, the foreshadowing also of the joy that the Israelites had in the bunch of grapes brought to them from the Promised Land. The speaker says to God that if I must borrow the Israelites' "sorrow" in my own life, then let me also have a sample of the "joy" that they had. The final stanza has the speaker providing the answers to his own questions asked in this third stanza.

Line 22 implies that he cannot "want" (i.e., lack) the "grape" (i.e., the bunch of grapes) since he has the "wine" from the grapes. Line 23 is the speaker telling himself that he has the "fruit" that the Israelites had and even "more": the bunch of grapes to the Christian is Christ himself who was "pressed" (line 28) as in a wine press, but also he was "pressed" as in an instrument of torture (see PRESS and also similar double meaning used in "THE AGONY"). These two pressings of Christ occurred at the Crucifixion, which caused the flowing of Christ's blood, just as the juice of grapes flows from crushed grapes in a wine press. Christ's blood, then, is the "wine," and this recognition is enacted in Holy Communion, with the wine as Christ's blood. The "joy" sought by the speaker, then, is recognized as already available to him through Christ's sacrifice for him and for all humanity. The "sour juice" of Old Testament Law was transformed into the "sweet wine" of New Testament Love with the Crucifixion. The bunch of grapes is, then, a type of Christ. The same is true of "Noah's vine": in the Old Testament story (Genesis 9:20) Noah's fruitful vineyard was blessed by God and produced grapes and wine, but this is a type of the New Testament "vine" which is Christ (see John 15:1, where Christ says, "I am the true vine, and my Father is the husbandman").

Buttery. *Noun*: a storeroom for provisions of food and drink.

C

Cabinet. *Noun*: (1) a small chamber or room; (2) a case in which to keep jewelry, letters, documents, or other valuable items.

Calvin, John (1509–1564). Jean Cauvin, French theologian and Protestant reformer. Studied law, logic, Latin, Greek, and Hebrew. After accepting many of LUTHER's beliefs, he was forced to flee Paris during a royal proscription of Lutherans. In 1536 he published *Institutes of the Christian Religion* in which he criticizes many facets of Roman Catholicism and promotes reformed Protestantism. Soon after its publication he took up residence in Geneva, Switzerland. The beliefs of Calvinism emphasize human depravity resulting from original sin, salvation only through God's grace (Calvin agreeing with Luther concerning the inability of good works to gain salvation, but emphasizing God's grace more than the individual's faith emphasized by Luther), and the doctrine of the Elect (those predestined by God for salvation). Calvin argues that Christ "imputes" righteousness to the believer (see Herbert's use of this word and idea in lines 33–36 of "Faith"). Calvin argues that the two sacraments are Baptism and the Lord's Supper. These beliefs of Calvin, along with his insistence upon the church being governed largely by individual congregations (rather than by an episcopal hierarchy) and upon the Bible as the true and authoritative one of the BOOKS OF GOD, became most important in the thinking and practices of the English PURITANs of the 16th and 17th centuries.

Calvinism. The doctrines and practices of the Calvinists, following John Calvin. See CALVIN.

Calvinist. A proponent of Calvinism, the doctrines and practices subscribed to by John Calvin and his followers. See CALVIN.

Cambridge University. See TRINITY COLLEGE.

Cardan, Jerome (1501–1576). Italian physician, mathematician, and astrologer. Gave the first clinical description of typhus fever, published the first book on computation of probabilities based on games of chance, and published a book important in the history of algebra. Argued against the existence of a layer of the element of fire in the universe: see NEW PHILOSOPHY.

Cardinal Virtues. See VIRTUES.

Castiglione. See *THE COURTIER.*

Celebrate. *Verb*: (1) to perform publicly [a marriage or funeral or other ceremony]; (2) to proclaim publicly; (3) to praise, to extol.

Cell. *Noun*: a small dwelling or cottage.

Chair. *Noun*: (1) piece of household furniture consisting of a seat with four legs and a rest for the back, designed to accommodate one person; (2) a seat of authority, state, or dignity, such as of a king or judge or high cleric; (3) a portable seat carried on poles held by men; (4) see CHAIR OF GRACE.

Chair of grace. The throne of the king or queen (symbolic of his or her attribute of godlike grace). When the court moved to various residences or subjects' homes, the "chair" would accompany the sovereign.

Charing Cross. A part of London named after a large cross originally erected in this area by King Edward I. The cross existed in Herbert's time, but it was removed in 1647. The area retains its name to this day. It is in this area that MAGDALEN HERBERT established a household when she moved from Oxford in 1601: George Herbert was eight years old at the time. Her household was made up of twenty-six people, including nurses, chambermaids, and servants. Her steward was JOHN GORSE. During his years here George Herbert was exposed to JOHN DONNE through Donne's visits to the household, as well as to many musicians who also would frequent the home.

Charles I (1600–1649). King of England, 1625–1649. Son of JAMES I. Presented George Herbert to the church living of BEMERTON in 1630, apparently upon the nomination of WILLIAM HERBERT, Earl of Pembroke. Increasing conflicts between King and Parliament, as well as among factions in the Church, developed into the Great Rebellion (English Civil War) with Parliamentary and PURITAN forces pitted against those of the King and Court. Charles surrendered and eventually was beheaded.

Chaw(e), chawes (chaws). Chew, chews.

Cheer. *Noun*: (1) joy, (2) comfort, (3) food.

Chelsea. Area on the banks of the Thames River a few miles southwest of central London. MAGDALEN HERBERT (Lady Danvers) lived here in the home (with its impressive grounds and garden) of her husband Sir John Danvers.

Chemic. See ALCHEMY and PARACELSUS.

Chemique. See ALCHEMY and PARACELSUS.

Chemist. See ALCHEMY and PARACELSUS.

Cherbury, Lord Herbert of. See HERBERT, EDWARD.

Chest. *Noun*: (1) a box or coffer; (2) a coffin; (3) metaphorically, a chamber or room or study; (4) the portion of the human body enclosed by the ribs and breastbone.

Choler, choleric. See HUMOR.

Christ-Cross. The sign of the cross placed before the alphabet in some students' horn-books of Herbert's time. By extension, it refers to the alphabet. In lines 53–54 of *THE CHURCH MILITANT* Herbert implies that Plato and Aristotle (i.e., their philosophical inheritors) had to study a new, unfamiliar alphabet of Christian philosophy.

Christ's three offices. Prophet, priest, and king.

Chrysostom, Saint John (about 345–407). Born in Antioch, Syria, where, after some time as a monk and in solitude, he later was ordained and gained the reputation of a great preacher. Noted for his ability to apply the scriptures to everyday life, his humor, his compassion, and his eloquence (he was called "golden-mouthed"). In 398 he became Archbishop of Constantinople. Here he alienated some of the wealthy and powerful by his criticism of the misuse of wealth, and charges were trumped up against him, leading ultimately to his banishment and exile in Cucusus. Since he still wrote powerfully and communicated with Constantinople, he was ordered to be moved to an area farther away, but he died on the journey. His remains were returned to Constantinople about thirty years later. His influential writings survive in his sermons, famous for their commentaries on the Bible and for their practical advice. He also wrote essays, treatises, and letters. St. Chrysostom is one of the four traditional "DOCTORS" of the eastern church. Herbert refers to him in Chapter 34 of THE COUNTRY PARSON.

Church, The. See *THE TEMPLE*.

Church Militant; Militant Church. The band of Christians battling sin on earth. See *THE CHURCH MILITANT*.

Church Militant, The. Poem of 279 lines (in couplets) constituting the last major division of Herbert's *THE TEMPLE*. It is thought that this poem represents a fairly early work by Herbert, one, in fact, written before the other poems of *The Temple*. In general, the poem traces the progress of Religion, and thus of the Christian Church, westward. From the East, it went to Egypt, Greece, Rome, Germany, and Britain. Anticipation of its spread to America is voiced in the poem, and then it is envisioned continuing around the earth until it reaches the East again, where it will be judged. As the Church proceeds around the world, sin always follows and attempts its downfall and destruction. "Church Militant" or "Militant Church" refers specifically to the Christians on earth who are fighting sin. (Contrast "CHURCH TRIUMPHANT.") At the Judgment sin at last will be conquered.
    Many readers and critics of the poem have wrestled with the problem of whether or not *The Church Militant* really is integral in *The Temple* and thus whether or not *The Temple* itself is a unified work. This poem does not seem to fit an architectural unity implied by *THE CHURCH-PORCH* followed by *The Church*. Many critics simply ignore the poem and/or regard it as a disruption of the unity of *The Temple*. However, Gene Edward Veith, Jr., in *Reformation Spirituality: The Religion of George Herbert* sees both *The Church-Porch* and *The Church Militant* as Herbert's depiction of the external, visible church, as opposed to the largely internal, invisible church portrayed in *The Church* (see p. 229 of his book). Veith also argues that Herbert in the final section of his work "presents the institution of the visible Church as it exists corporately and historically, in the context of other institutions" (p. 235). In an essay Kenneth Alan Hovey attempts a close reading of the poem on its own terms, emphasizing the satirical and critical bent of the work, with an insistence on the many guises that Sin (false religion) takes on through the history of the church: see Hovey's article cited under *The Church Militant* in my "Selected Bibliography."

"Church Monuments." This poem, of course, fits well into the structural principle of the physical "Church" (see *THE TEMPLE*). Monuments, statues, busts, reclining effigies, etc., of people buried in graves and tombs under them are encountered inside of, and many times in the entrance to, an English church. One should be aware of the facts that Herbert's original manuscript of this poem does not divide it into stanzas, and neither is it so divided in the later copied manuscript that served as printer's copy for the first printed edition of 1633. The printer divided it into four stanzas of six lines each, thus obliterating some of the effect that Herbert embodied in the structure and style. In addition, Herbert only used six marks of punctuation at the ends of his lines: three commas, one colon, one question mark, and one period. The printed edition of 1633 and most later editions and anthologies add many more marks of punctuation and divide the poem into stanzas. More perceptive and accurate modern editors restore Herbert's original structure and punctuation, thus restoring the sense of the inexorable, unstoppable progress down to dust, earth, and death itself that Herbert conveys through lack of neat stanza stops and through minimal punctuation and pauses at the ends of lines.

The opening of the poem pictures the speaker entering a church and encountering some monuments to people buried there. Here he buries ("entomb[s]") his own body, his own flesh, since he leaves the sense of the physical here in favor of his emphasis on the spiritual as his "soul repairs to her devotion" within the church. (Typical of the time, Herbert refers to the soul as feminine ["her"]: see SOUL, FEMININE.) Also, this separation of body and soul is a foreshadowing of death itself. The word "repairs" has two senses here: commonly at the time it meant simply "to go," but also relevant is the sense of restoring to a sound condition. As the flesh is left with the monuments, it also will learn valuable lessons. With a touch of humor, Herbert says that his flesh will "take acquaintance of this heap of dust": this pictures the encounter of his body with the other bodies (dead ones) there as almost a social occasion, a meeting at a party! But, of course, the situation turns out to be a much more serious and grim one. The "heap of dust" deliberately has more than one meaning. It refers to the bodies buried there as now only dust, but it also suggests that the monuments themselves are only dust, the latter implication supported by "dusty heraldry and lines" in line 9 and the entire development of the poem. The word "betimes" also carries multiple meaning here: it primarily means in due time, before it is too late, but it also can mean early in life, as well as speedily. Lines 3–6 note that the "blast," the storm wind, of "Death's incessant motion" drives *all* (all bodies and all physical things) at last into a "heap of dust." This is the important fact that the speaker wishes his own body to "take acquaintance of." This powerful, driving, incessant "motion" of Death is what Herbert's original structure and punctuation for the poem embody and what is partially lost by the 1633 printing and later reprintings that use stanzas and added punctuation.

Death's motion is nourished, energized ("Fed" in line 5) by the "exhalation of our crimes"—i.e., our original crime, original sin by Adam, became the crime(s) of all humanity thereafter, and Adam's fall introduced death for humanity. We all repeat and participate in Adam's sin and its consequent death. Our very breathing, our very life, itself is sin and death, and every breath ("exhalation") leads us inexorably closer to death. God breathed life into Adam, but Adam's (and thus "our") crime is breathed forth from us as death instead.

Lines 6–9 use a METAPHYSICAL CONCEIT of the speaker's body attending a "school," in which it learns to "spell" and to read. Herbert employs multiple meanings of both "spell" and "elements" here: "elements" was used to refer to the letters of the alphabet, and thus the body is learning to "spell" in the sense of learning the rudiments of the alphabet, the composition, of the body itself and thus of physical mortality. The "school" is the sight of the monuments. But "elements" also refers to the four elements out of which everything physical was believed to be composed: the four elements are earth, water, air, and fire, and any physical entity made of these is subject to decay and death. "Spell" not only means to read letter by letter, but also to decipher and to discover. In fact, the body literally has to study carefully the letters engraved on the monuments in order to decipher them, because they are "dusty"—i.e., the letters themselves are crumbling into dust, and the "lines" of letters and words on the monuments giving the names and family ancestry are steadily being obliterated by their deterioration and are literally difficult to read. However, this fact in itself is part of what the body discovers ("spells") in this "school": the decay of the letters and the crumbling of them and the monuments into dust point directly to the origin ("birth") of the monuments, of the dead bodies under them, and of the living body of the speaker contemplating them (and another meaning of "spell" is to contemplate) as only dust. And to dust indeed they *all* are returning! Very much in the background of this whole poem is a part of Genesis 3:19 ("for out of it [the ground] wast thou taken: for dust thou art, and unto dust shalt thou return"). This surely is the lesson that the speaker has sent his body to this "school" to learn. Herbert plays on "lines" here as the engraved lines of letters, but also as the genealogical lines, family lines, of the people buried there: both are "dusty" in being hard to read and understand. Ultimately the only genealogy that matters is the origin of all from dust itself! One might note the use of "his" in line 8 to refer to the body in possessive form. This is a common use in Herbert's time for what in modern English would be "its." However, the use of "its" was already beginning in Herbert's time, and Herbert himself writes it several times in both his poetry and prose. So, it is interesting that he refers to the body as "it" in line 7, but then uses "his" twice in line 8. I feel that Herbert probably is wanting to raise the ambiguity here that the reference can also be to "Death" in the possessive in line 8, in addition to referring to the body. The traditional personification of Death lends credence. So, it is valid to see the body here learning its own elements and Death's elements, and it is also valid to see the body learning its own "birth," but, most paradoxically, it is also true that physical Death's "birth" is evidenced in dust!

Lines 10–11 support the preceding implications. "Dissolution" of both the buried bodies and their monuments, with all crumbling into dust, best shows that the speaker's body has both its origin and destination in "dust" and "earth," that the body's "elements" are only "dust" and "earth," and that the only genealogy that matters is that traced back to "dust" and "earth." Herbert here seems again to create functional ambiguity, irony, and multiple meaning, as he does throughout the poem. For example, to "discern" implies to perceive the *difference* between things, but in this case what is revealed, ironically, is the *similarity*, the lack of distinction among bodies and monuments! They are indistinguishable dust and earth, in fact. When one compares "dust with dust" and "earth with earth" (or bodies with monuments that have dissolved into dust and earth), there is no difference, certainly. Herbert's humor comes through clearly here. Also, his phrasing of "dissolution sure" suggests that "sure" is comparable to the adverb form "surely"—i.e., that dissolution surely does best discern. . . . But also one feels that just as valid is its suggested use as an adjective—i.e., "dissolution sure" has the sense of "sure dissolution," and this is indeed the insistence of the whole poem as to the certainty of mortality and decay for all earthly matter.

Lines 12–16 continue Herbert's humorous (and even satirical) picture to make a most serious point. Most editors and other commentators gloss "These" in line 12 as referring to "dust" and "earth" in line 11, and this does seem to be the primary reference. However, this ambiguous pronoun probably also has a secondary, but relevant, echoing of "dusty heraldry and lines" in line 9: not only the dust and earth of the crumbling monuments, but also even the crumbling inscriptions on the monuments "laugh" at the monuments themselves. The monuments are made of "jet" (black marble) and other kinds of marble and thus are seemingly permanent, according to the usual human way of regarding them. But Herbert insists that they are quite impermanent and that the dusty inscriptions and their own dust and earth and earth falling from them ridicule the monuments themselves as feeble attempts at immortality. The monuments were placed there as permanent signs to memorialize the persons buried there. They were meant to "sever the good fellowship of dust" in two senses: (1) they were to separate each individual body from other bodies, and (2) they were to separate the monument above from the person beneath it. But the joke is that as surely as each person buried there is crumbling into dust and mingling with the dust of other individuals, just so are all the individual monuments crumbling into dust and joining the dust of the bodies they were placed there to memorialize! Their efforts to "spoil the meeting" of bodies with bodies and monuments with bodies are futile. Herbert's most sarcastic comment on this utterly futile attempt at earthly immortality is the question in lines 14–16: when these monuments themselves have all crumbled and joined the dust of the bodies they now are entrusted to memorialize, what will memorialize these "dead" monuments? Will a monument be erected to memorialize the monument that once stood there memorializing a body? The sarcasm is heightened, of course, by the personification of the monuments as bowing, kneeling, falling down flat, and kissing the bodies under them, as if they worshipped them. This, in essence, reflects on the proud people buried there who wished such monuments erected for their own physical preservation and worship of themselves and of their supposed physical, earthly immortality. The word "heaps" of line 16 also effectively demolishes any semblance of dignity and pride in the bodies: they now are only "heaps," and thus this explicitly echoes the "heap of dust" of line 3. The satirical sarcasm of the speaker is directed to those people who have not learned to face the fact of mortality. His own body is learning that fact, however, from this "school."

The remainder of the poem addresses his body ("flesh"). Continuing the "school" conceit, the speaker tells his body some specific facts to "learn" (line 17). The flesh should learn its "stem"—i.e., its origin, its birth, which specifically is from Adam, earth, and dust. The "true descent" (line 18) that the body should learn, then, is the true genealogy of every human, one that traces back to Adam, earth, and dust. This genealogy is contrasted to what, by implication, is the lesser genealogy of family lines that are in the inscribed "dusty heraldry and lines." The body then will be resistant to succumbing to deceptive worldly, physical pleasures and values. Herbert at this point employs another metaphysical conceit (lines 20–22) that expresses in a concise analogy some of the major thought of the poem. The "flesh," the body, is like an hourglass: both contain only dust. This additionally implies an analogy to the monuments that also contain the dust of the people buried within. So, the body, the monuments, and an hourglass are all containers of dust, but the *containers themselves* (body, monument, and hourglass) "also shall / Be crumbled into dust." This is the important fact of all-pervasive mortality that the speaker says that his body can learn from the monuments. The monuments represent a kind of pride in humans who are only dust but who live as if they were otherwise.

With ironic understatement in lines 22–24 the speaker tells his body to notice how "tame these ashes are" of the dead bodies "here below" the monuments. They are "free from lust" now. This should allow the body of the speaker to "fit thyself against thy fall." "Fall" has multiple meaning. It is a fall through pride (repeating Adam's sin) that can now be avoided by the body, since it sees its most humble, lowly outcome as only dust. And "fall" also means the final fall into death itself: the body now should be prepared for it.

One notes that Herbert repeats the word "dust" through the poem, and this repetition itself drives home his major point about all earthly elements, including the flesh. I also feel that Herbert's construction of the poem with 24 lines may suggest the inexorable progression through 24 hours of the day, especially with the importance of the hourglass conceit and the insistence in line 21 on "measures all our time." One might also note that "which" in line 21 ambiguously may refer to "time" itself crumbling into dust (in addition to referring to body, monument, and hourglass doing so). The sifting down of all dust on earth every hour of the day measures our limited time. Thus the day becomes an implied metaphor for a lifetime with death at the end, just as the poem ends with the word "fall."

My own detailed reading of this poem has been stimulated by the excellent comments on it in *George Herbert: His Religion and Art* by Joseph H. Summers. For further suggestions about the meter, syntax, rhyme, and other techniques it is recommended that one read Summers's discussion.

"Church Music." This poem relates to the structural principle of the physical "Church" (see *THE TEMPLE*) in that it comments on the beauty of music played in the church. The relationship between the speaker and church music is pictured metaphorically as that between a male lover and his lady, his sweetheart. In this analogy or METAPHYSICAL CONCEIT, Herbert plays with and against secular love poetry of the Renaissance. The mistress, church music, is addressed as "sweetest of sweets": she is the sweetest of all sweethearts, as well as the sweetest of all delights or pleasures. She has given him a supremely delightful ("dainty") lodging within her "house of pleasure": this image that suggests a love nest of sorts actually refers, of course, to the church itself as a "house of pleasure" but also to the state of spiritual ecstasy in which he finds himself as he responds to the music. So, Herbert establishes in the first stanza an image suggesting a physical, sexual relationship that expresses, paradoxically, one that actually is spiritual.

This suggested conceit is further supported and developed in the second stanza. His almost-mystical ecstasy (a separation of soul and body) is described as if his soul's union with his music-mistress were sexual ("Now I in you without a body move, / Rising and falling with your wings"). The suggested *sexual* intercourse here conveys his ecstatic *spiritual* union felt in the rise and fall of the music, paradoxically. The love relation is further suggested with "We both together sweetly live and love," a phrase that echoes that of Christopher Marlowe's lyric "The Passionate Shepherd to His Love" in which the shepherd says, "Come live with me and be my love, / And we will all the pleasures prove." This was a quite famous pastoral love lyric in the late 16th century and was parodied by both Sir Walter Raleigh and JOHN DONNE. Herbert's version here, then, has church music as the love and *spiritual* pleasures as the ones proved (i.e., experienced). The speaker imagines their living together in blissful isolation and in a superior status to even the greatest of worldly rulers: "God help poor kings" expresses pity for such lesser beings with lesser pleasures than those that the speaker and church music enjoy with one another. In fact, I believe that Herbert here might be alluding to a major theme recurring in DONNE's secular poetry: in such lyrics as "The Good-Morrow," "The Canonization," "The Anniversary," and "The Sun Rising" Donne portrays two lovers in their own self-sufficient, superior world or universe, looking down with contempt and/or pity on mere "princes" (as in "The Sun Rising") and on the mundane world and human existence outside of them.

In the last stanza the speaker says "Comfort" (i.e., take comfort) to the mistress, church music. He says, "I'll die": here he uses two of the common meanings of "DIE" in the Renaissance. To part or to be apart from the lady was to "die," and to experience sexual consummation was to "die," since the belief was that each sexual consummation subtracted time from one's life. So, if church music leaves him ("post" is to ride away with haste), he will die in the former sense. But if he remains the companion of church music (last two lines of the poem), he experiences death in the latter sense (continuing the analogy of spiritual ecstasy as sexual intercourse). Being with church music, then, makes this existence a heaven-on-earth (as many secular lovers and poets always said of their fleshly mistresses). But, in addition, church music leads to the door of heaven itself: it is part of worship on earth that helps direct one's spiritual path toward heaven and salvation. It is interesting to note that Herbert's presentation of the beauty, power, and value of music in the church, with its directing one, in fact, to "heaven's door" differs extremely from the PURITAN attitude that denigrated church music and other forms of art and beauty in the church. Indeed, this poem is an effective criticism of such an attitude. Herbert's own love of music, specifically church music, is evident in the fact that he would attend Salisbury Cathedral services and participate in musical groups himself (see my "Herbert's Life" section, WALTON's *The Life of Mr. George Herbert*, and Amy M. Charles's *A Life of George Herbert*).

Church Triumphant; Triumphant Church. The souls of Christians who have reached salvation in heaven.

Church-Porch, The. Poem of seventy-seven stanzas (462 lines) constituting the first major division of Herbert's *THE TEMPLE*. This didactic poem advises and instructs in matters such as temperance, lying, dress, gambling, conduct, friendship, and cleanliness. The poem is subtitled "*Perirrhanterium*," Greek for an instrument to sprinkle holy water: the implication is that this poem is a cleansing instrument for one before entrance into *The Church* portion of *The Temple*. The topics focus on physical, social, ethical, and moral means of cleansing, with worship a topic at its end. Thus, these cleansings prepare for the larger Christian, spiritual concerns in *The Church* that one makes a transition into from this "porch." Stephenie Yearwood, in fact, contends that *The Church-Porch* presents a classical, not a Christian, value system and that its limited perspective must be corrected and expanded in *The Church*, with its more clearly Christian and sacramental views: see Yearwood's essay cited in my "Selected Bibliography" under "*The Temple*: In General and Its Unity."

The speaker of the poem gives proverbial, pithy advice to one addressed in the first stanza as "Thou," one who is young and has worldly hopes of achievement. The speaker clearly states that his poetry is a pleasurable "bait" within which is the "good" he wishes to inculcate in his listener-reader and that "verse" can be more effective than a "sermon" in grabbing the attention of the audience.

Stanzas 2–4 argue against lust; 5–9, against excessive drinking, drunkenness (noting that one should "stay at the third glass" and picturing the drunkard as exemplifying man's bestial nature); stanzas 10–12, against swearing; stanza 13, against lying; stanzas 14–19, against "idleness," "sloth," and improper education; stanzas 20–21, against inconstancy and lack of integrity; stanzas 22–25 argue for self-restraint, self-discipline, and self-analysis; stanzas 26–30, for thrift, generosity, economy, and avoidance of greed; stanzas 31–32, for discretion in clothing; stanzas 33–34, against gambling; stanzas 35–42, for substantive, civil, pleasant, and moderate conduct; stanzas 43–45, for proper respect to eminent and authoritative people; stanzas 46–48 concern friendship, family relations, and the single life; stanzas 49–55, social relations and communication; stanzas 56–59, ambition and character; stanzas 60–61, foreign influence; stanza 62, cleanliness; stanzas 63–65, charity and giving to the poor; stanzas 66–75, proper behavior and attitude in worship; and stanzas 76–77 emphasize the general goal of virtuous, respectable behavior.

This poem was Herbert's most popular work in his own century: more allusions to it and quotations from it exist in 17th-century books and manuscripts than to and from any other single poem or prose work by him.

Chymick. See ALCHEMY and PARACELSUS.

Cicero, Marcus Tullius (106–43 B.C.). Roman orator, statesman, and prose writer. Studied philosophy, literature, rhetoric, and law. Practiced law. Elected Consul in 63 B.C. He discovered Catiline's conspiracy to overthrow the government and suppressed it. After the assassination of Julius Caesar, Cicero made speeches attacking Antony. After the Second Triumvirate of Antony, Octavian, and Lepidus assumed power, Cicero was killed by Antony's army. Speeches, treatises, and letters by Cicero survive. He is influential in the rhetoric, politics, and philosophy of his prose works, as well as the primary model for the polished, lengthy clause or sentence known as Ciceronian prose style. He is commonly called "Tully" or "Tullie": see, for example, Chapter 34 of *THE COUNTRY PARSON*.

Circe. In Greek mythology, the sun god's daughter who was exiled to the island of Aeaea after murdering her husband. She was an evil enchantress. The companions of Odysseus were changed into swine when they visited her island. Odysseus himself was not changed, having been given an herb by Hermes to resist Circe's power. After seeing Odysseus unchanged, Circe transformed the men back to their normal state, entertained them and Odysseus lavishly as her guests for a year, and bore Odysseus a son. See SIRENS.

Circle. Frequently used in the Renaissance as the symbol of perfection, infinity, immortality, and God.

Classical. As used in this "Dictionary," "classical" refers to the particular style and content of poetry stemming from "classicism," especially as viewed and practiced by BEN JONSON and his followers in the late 16th and early 17th centuries. The assumptions of such classical verse arise from similar assumptions in works of ancient Greece and Rome that provide the major models for Renaissance classicism. The term "classical" is extremely complex and is applied in numerous ways, but the following working definition, albeit a greatly simplified one, may serve to illustrate the major characteristics of it, especially those that differ in important respects from those of much METAPHYSICAL poetry.

As far as content, many classical poems are complimentary in nature, praising certain individuals. Praises for the country life and for good food and drink also are common. The *carpe diem* theme (literally, "seize the day": urging one to live and love fully and actively now, for time is passing rapidly and death is approaching) is a recurring one. Epitaphs (compact poems memorializing individuals who have died) appear frequently in classical verse. In many (especially in JONSON) the poet is in a public role as a social, moral, and ethical critic. Generally the speaking voice is rather formal and polite in word choice and tone, with emotion kept restrained.

In style and structure a classical poem is overtly well-organized, displaying strict divisions, logical progressions, and stages clearly defined from beginning to end. The structure and style of the poem, stanzas, and lines employ careful balance, parallelism, and symmetry. The metrics generally are regular, avoiding excessive variations. Frequently the classical poet writes in couplets, many of which have carefully placed and clear caesuras. All in all, clarity is valued in syntax, word choice, and thought. Some relevant examples of classical poetry in which one can see these characterisitics are the following by Ben Jonson: (1) the song beginning "Still to be neat," (2) the song beginning "Come, my Celia, let us prove," (3) No. 4 of "A Celebration of Charis," (4) "To William Camden," (5) "To Penshurst," (6) "On My First Son," and (7) "Inviting a Friend to Supper."

Although Herbert traditionally is classified as a metaphysical poet, one should be alert to the great extent to which he actually fuses the classical with the metaphysical.

Clifford, Lady Anne (1590–1676). After the death of her husband Richard Sackville, 3rd Earl of Dorset, this intelligent and learned lady married PHILIP HERBERT, 4th Earl of Pembroke, on June 1, 1630. She then became Countess of Pembroke and resided at WILTON HOUSE during the time that George Herbert lived in and served his parish at BEMERTON, only a short distance away. He visited her at Wilton House: ARTHUR WOODNOTH refers to her (in a letter written to NICHOLAS FERRAR) and to an occasion upon which he spent an hour to himself at Wilton while Herbert was with the Countess. One of Herbert's own letters is addressed to her (dated December 10, 1631). He thanks her for the cask of metheglin (spiced mead) that she has sent to his household. She wrote of herself that she made good books and virtuous thoughts her companions. Her library contained DONNE's and Herbert's poems and some of Donne's sermons, a fact evidenced by a large portrait of her with those volumes prominently displayed in the background. She also erected the monument to EDMUND SPENSER in Westminster Abbey.

Clod. *Noun*: (1) a lump of dirt, earth; (2) a stupid or unthinking person, a blockhead, a clodhopper or common farm laborer.

Cloister. *Verb*: (1) to enclose; (2) to place in a monastic house or cloister. *Noun*: (1) an enclosure; (2) a place of religious seclusion, such as a nunnery, convent, monastery.

Close. *Noun*: a specialized use in Herbert refers to the conclusion of a musical phrase (see "VIRTUE," line 11).

Cock. *Noun*: (1) rooster, (2) victor.

Cockatrice. *Noun*: basilisk, a serpent reputedly able to kill by a glance and supposedly hatched from a cock's egg.

"Collar, The." The speaker of this poem is rebellious against the restrictions imposed upon him by the Christian life, with all of its spiritual, ethical, and moral demands. Herbert conveys the speaker's emotion and anger and internal disorder partially through the irregular line lengths, through irregular stress pattern, and by ending sentences, questions, and exclamations within, rather than at the end of, lines. The structure, style, and syntax are very like those elements in many poems by DONNE, and thus are quite METAPHYSICAL in nature. In fact, the emotional and irregular beginning of this poem is quite similar to the beginnings of such Donne poems as "The Canonization" and "The Sun Rising." Although the larger import of the poem applies to any Christian, perhaps it may reflect something of Herbert's own life. IZAAK WALTON relates that Herbert said the following to EDMUND DUNCON as he gave him the manuscript of his poems to deliver to NICHOLAS FERRAR: "Sir, I pray deliver this little Book to my dear brother Farrer, and tell him, he shall find in it a picture of the many spiritual Conflicts that have past betwixt God and my Soul, before I could subject mine to the will of Jesus my Master: in whose service I have now found perfect freedom. . . ."

    The title of the poem is another of Herbert's in which he suggests multiple meanings that relate to various themes and motifs in the poem. "Collar" suggests a restraining collar on an animal and/or slave. Generally, it is a symbol of restriction that the speaker wishes to be liberated from. It also suggests the "yoke" that Christ urges on one in Matthew 11:28–30. Critics and editors argue about whether or not it could also suggest a clergyman's collar, the clerical collar. Some argue

that such a distinct collar was not worn by clergymen in Herbert's time
and thus would not have our own modern assumptions. However,
others (for example, Mary Ellen Rickey in *Utmost Art*, pp.
99–100) feel that this meaning is possible because of an order early in the reign
of JAMES I that those holding "any ecclesiastical living, shall usually
wear gowns with standing collars and sleeves strait at the hands" (quoted
from Rickey, p. 100). If this meaning also is present, then the poem is
even more clearly autobiographical in applying the restrictions felt by
the speaker to Herbert, the Christian priest. Another implication in the
title clearly suggests a pun on "choler," one of the four HUMORs (noted
by Dan S. Norton in 1944–45 in *The Explicator*: see my "Selected
Bibliography"). This meaning relates to the anger of the speaker
throughout the poem, even to the point that he "raved, and grew more
fierce and wild" (line 33). Still another important pun in the title
suggests "caller" (see the note of 1951–52 by Jack M. Bickham cited in
my "Selected Bibliography"). The "caller" is God at the end of the
poem who is "calling" the speaker back into submission to accept again
his Christian calling.

The emphatic beginning expresses the speaker's anger and
frustration as he strikes the "board," the table. He is determined to
leave ("will abroad") this life of severe restraint and discipline, as he
now sees it. In lines 3–6 he does not want to "sigh and pine," as if he
were a frustrated PETRARCHAN lover who never achieves his desire.
He no longer wishes to be "in suit," as if he were a lover suing for favor
or a servant suing for a better reward for his labors from his "lord" (or
from the Lord God, in his case). He argues with himself that he is free:
in fact, his freedom is as plentiful as abundance ("store") itself! When
he asks if he shall be "still" in suit, primarily he uses "STILL" in its
adverbial sense of *always*; however, John Tobin notes in his edition (see
"Selected Bibliography" under "Works: Poetry and Prose") that "still"
could well suggest *silent* here, a condition that the speaker no longer is
submissively honoring. I feel that another adjective use is relevant here:
"still" can mean *motionless*, which he also no longer wishes to be, since
he has said that he "will abroad" and that he is free to move on to other
things in his life.

In lines 7–13 the speaker more explicitly pictures himself as an
unsuccessful tenant farmer to the lord he serves. He seems to be the
only one who has not had an abundant harvest, or, at least, one who has
had his harvest destroyed by wind and rain ("sighs" and "tears"). So,
through this METAPHYSICAL CONCEIT the speaker implies that the
secular life is full of fertility and abundance that he cannot experience
or retain as a Christian who serves the Lord God. His own harvest is
painful and sterile ("thorn," "blood," "dry," "drown"). He sees no
sensuous, worldly pleasures for himself in his restricted life. The

"thorn" and "blood" suggest Christ's crown of thorns and crucifixion, the pain and sacrifice of Christ that all Christians take on themselves to follow Christ: at this point he sees no fertility, even spiritual fertility, in this Christian life. The "wine" and "CORN" may suggest also the wine and bread of communion, the blood and body of Christ, and thus also suggest that the "board" of line 1 may allude to the communion table.

Lines 14–18 develop further the tenant-lord-harvest conceit. He has no "bays," no crown of laurel (traditionally the reward for poets, but generally suggesting secular, worldly accomplishment). He has no "flowers" or "garlands gay" that typify a secular merrymaking, such as at a harvest festival concluding the taking in of the last of the year's crop. He asks if all of these are withered (see BLAST) and wasted away for him. He sees the lack of these elements of worldly, physical beauty and pleasure in his currently restricted Christian life; therefore, he tells himself (lines 17–18) that "there is fruit" waiting to be plucked by his hands. In other words, the "fruit" exists out in the secular life that he sees and is tempted by for its apparently satisfying pleasures and worldly successes. So, he sees the secular life as one of freedom and fertility, as opposed to his present life of subservience in the Christian life that he sees as restricting and sterile. At this point he seems ready to repeat the original rebellion of Adam and Eve, to pluck the "fruit" against God's wishes. Ironically, with the background of Christ's crown of thorns and blood in the previous lines, we become aware that Christ's crucifixion was necessary for human salvation after Adam's fall. Christ's atonement was the actual means to "restore" (line 8) with "CORDIAL" fruit what Adam "lost" (line 9) through "fruit" (lines 9 and 17). Christ's provision of spiritual fertility and abundance as of prime importance is not yet recognized by the speaker, but it will be by the end of the poem. And the temporal, earthly, secular "year" (line 13) is of no consequence in the face of eternal life that can only be granted through Christ's spiritual restoration and abundance. But the speaker must discover for himself that the harvest he now experiences is really the most fruitful for him, that it is provided by Christ, and that it is the answer to his own rebellion.

Lines 19–26 continue the speaker's forceful urging of himself to break away from his present life. He will make up for lost time (his "sigh-blown age") by living a life of "double pleasures." He wants to stop ("leave" off) debating what is spiritually, ethically, and morally right ("fit"). One notes that he sees such a debate as "cold," appropriate to other images of sterility and of lacking warmth and life, as he sees it. He wants to break out of his self-imposed "cage" of the Christian life of moral restrictions, regarding true freedom at this point as an untrammeled experience of the secular life. Another metaphor for his self-imposed Christian life is a "rope of sands": this is a medium of restraint that will hold no one who wishes to free himself of it, and "sands" further enforces the sterility he sees in his present life. It is only self-deception, he tells himself, that has made the Christian life seem to be a strong restraint ("good cable"), while it actually is not. He has only closed his eyes (see WINK) and refused to see that nothing actually binds or imprisons him to submit to his self-imposed, restricted life.

Lines 27–32 embody the climactic point in his rebellion. He urges himself emphatically to walk away from his present life. He tells himself to "call in thy death's head there" and "tie up thy fears" (line 29): he wants to dispense with his MEMENTO MORI, a skull that many Christians would have to remind them of human mortality. He does not want to be reminded of or have to fear death, since he wishes to free himself of concern for his sure physical fate, without any hope of the spiritual immortality that he now is casting aside. His ultimate accusation of himself (lines 30–32) is that anyone (i.e., such as he) who does not have the courage to go and take what he wants from life deserves the burden, the hard life that he has.

Lines 33–36 note the anger (choler) that builds in the speaker through the poem. But, ironically, his anger and rebellion collapse in the face of the one word "Child" that is spoken by "one," obviously God. And God is pictured as "calling," which suggests God as the "Caller" and implies that the Christian resubmits himself to his own Christian "calling" and to the "Collar" in order to serve God. The powerful submissiveness in the speaker's "My Lord" completes the servant-tenant-lord conceit through the poem. Some critics suggest also that the ending of the poem recalls I Samuel 3, in which Eli tells the child Samuel to say, if the Lord calls, "Speak, Lord; for thy servant heareth." Also relevant is the injunction by Christ in Matthew 18:3 ("Verily I say unto you, Except ye be converted, and become as little children, ye shall not enter into the kingdom of heaven"). One notes also in the last four lines a regular *abab* rhyme, in contrast to the irregular occurrences of rhyme prior to this. As the disorder is quelled in the speaker, so is it in the rhyme of the poem. (For more on the rhyme and line lengths of the poem, see Joseph H. Summers, *George Herbert: His Religion and Art*.)

Collett, Anna. See FERRAR, NICHOLAS.

Collett, Mary. See FERRAR, NICHOLAS.

Combination of dissimilar images. See METAPHYSICAL CONCEIT.

Come. *Verb*: (1) to move towards or to approach, (2) to be derived [from], (3) to arrive [in course of time], (4) to happen, (5) to approach for sexual contact, (6) to experience sexual orgasm.

Common. A special sense of the term refers to "common land," to be used by everyone. Opposed to this is "enclosed land," fenced off for private use. For example, see stanza 4 of *THE CHURCH-PORCH*.

Complexion. *Noun*: the type of physical appearance, personality, disposition, and temperament resulting from the dominance of a particular HUMOR in the body: choleric, sanguine, phlegmatic, or melancholic. Also see ELEMENT and GALEN.

Conceit. See METAPHYSICAL CONCEIT.

Conjurer. *Noun*: magician.

Conserve. *Noun*: a medicine or confection made from some part of a plant and preserved with sugar.

Considerations. See VALDÉS, JUAN.

Constantine (280?–337). Roman emperor, 306–337. First Christian emperor. His father died at York in 306, where soldiers then proclaimed Constantine to be the new emperor. His mother was believed to be of British birth. In essence, Constantine instituted state protection of the Church.

Consumption. *Noun*: (1) action of consuming or destroying; (2) evaporation of moisture; (3) decay or wasting away; (4) pulmonary consumption, tuberculosis: the apparent cause of Herbert's recurring illnesses, weakness, and eventual death.

Conversation. In some contexts, the word in Herbert's time refers to general conduct in public.

Copernican. Referring to Copernicus and/or his concept of the universe. See COPERNICUS.

Copernicus, Nicolaus (1473–1543). Polish astronomer. Studied in Poland and Italy. Well-versed in astronomy, mathematics, law, medicine, and theology. Increasingly disagreed with the theories of PTOLEMY, and he formulated a heliocentric theory for the structure of the universe (i.e., one with the sun as the center, rather than the earth). Argued that the earth and other planets move around the sun in orbits. His work profoundly influenced later astronomers such as KEPLER and GALILEO and others of the "NEW PHILOSOPHY."

Cordial. *Noun*: a medicine, food, or drink that invigorates the heart.

Corn. *Noun*: (1) grain, (2) seed. [Does not designate Indian corn, as in later American usage.]

Country Parson, The. See *HERBERT'S REMAINS* and BARNABAS OLEY. Apparently Oley gave this prose work its title *A Priest to the Temple*, with *The Country Parson* as its alternate title. Undoubtedly Herbert's own title for it, however, is *The Country Parson*. The work reflects the ideal set for himself or for any ideal pastor: he says (in the prefatory "The Author to the Reader"), "I have resolved to set down the Form and Character of a True Pastor, that I may have a Mark to aim at." In addition, the full title is *The Country Parson: His Character, and Rule of Holy Life*. Paradoxically, critics increasingly are noting Herbert's indebtedness to secular courtesy books for his picture of the ideal parson. See *THE COURTIER*.

The work is divided into 37 chapters as follows: (1) "Of a Pastor," (2) "Their Diversities," (3) "The Parson's Life," (4) "The Parson's Knowledge," (5) "The Parson's Accessory Knowledges," (6) "The Parson Praying," (7) "The Parson Preaching," (8) "The Parson on Sundays," (9) "The Parson's State of Life," (10) "The Parson in his House," (11) "The Parson's Courtesy," (12) "The Parson's Charity," (13) "The Parson's Church," (14) "The Parson in Circuit," (15) "The Parson Comforting," (16) "The Parson a Father," (17) "The Parson in Journey," (18) "The Parson in Sentinel," (19) "The Parson in Reference," (20) "The Parson in God's Stead," (21) "The Parson Catechizing," (22) "The Parson in Sacraments," (23) "The Parson's Completeness," (24) "The Parson Arguing," (25) "The Parson Punishing," (26) "The Parson's Eye," (27) "The Parson in Mirth," (28) "The Parson in Contempt," (29) "The Parson with his Churchwardens," (30) "The Parson's Consideration of Providence," (31) "The Parson in Liberty," (32) "The Parson's Surveys," (33) "The Parson's Library," (34) "The Parson's Dexterity in Applying of Remedies," (35) "The Parson's Condescending," (36) "The Parson Blessing," and (37) "Concerning Detraction."

Interesting to modern readers and critics of Herbert is the way in which the work suggests that a true pastor must be a living example of Christ in the daily life of his parishioners: an interesting poetic counterpart to this fully developed idea in the prose may be seen in "THE WINDOWS." In addition, one sees that teaching pervades the life of Herbert's parson: he teaches by example, by catechetical instruction, and by sermon.

Also of great interest to modern readers of Herbert's poetry are the many parallels in ideas, phrases, and words between *The Country Parson* and the poems of *THE TEMPLE*. For example, in addition to the parallel idea cited above of the Christlike preacher found in "The Windows," one also notes that the end of the first chapter ("Of a Pastor") is as follows: ". . . a priest is to do that which Christ did, and after his manner, both for doctrine and life." One should compare line 11 of "The Windows": "Doctrine and life, colors and light, in one." Only one other example of many such similarities in phrases is one noted by Hutchinson (p. 559) in his edition (see my "Selected Bibliography"): in Chapter 14 Herbert refers to those who labor profanely "like brute beasts," a phrase and idea parallel to line 5 of "THE ELIXIR" ("Not rudely, as a beast").

Interesting parallels and contrasts and/or echoes between Herbert and earlier or contemporary writers are also found in the work. For example, in Chapter 9 Herbert says, "If he [the parson] be married, the choice of his wife was made rather by his ear, than by his eye; his judgement, not his affection found out a fit wife for him, whose humble, and liberal disposition he preferred before beauty, riches, or honor." I feel that this plays seriously a bit with a comment by Sir FRANCIS BACON in his essay "Of Love" in which he says, "For whosoever esteemeth too much of amorous affection, quitteth both riches and wisdom." Bacon suggests the foolishness of one who chooses passion ("amorous affection") over "riches" and "wisdom": riches and wisdom are held up by Bacon as high values. In his variation, however, Herbert holds passion, beauty, riches, and honor all to be of inferior value to the virtues of humility and generosity that the parson should esteem in a wife.

Finally, scholars and critics have examined how influential this work was to writers of Herbert's century who created the idea of Herbert as a model priest for the Church of England. Especially important in this view of Herbert are both OLEY and WALTON.

Couplet. See SONNET.

Courage. *Noun*: (1) spirit, vigor, energy; (2) boldness or bravery; (3) sexual desire or lust.

Courtier, The. Book written originally in Italian (entitled *Il Libro del Cortegiano*) by Baldassare Castiglione (1478–1529). Castiglione was himself a courtier and diplomat and received a humanist education. The book essentially was written during 1513–16, but Castiglione continued revising it until it was published in 1528. It is the epitome of a "courtesy book," one that delineates the ideal qualities of a gentleman (and thus forms the basis for the ideal, well-rounded Renaissance man). It is structured as a dialogue in four books (representing four discussions on four evenings), with Pietro Bembo (a man Castiglione knew) as the primary speaker. Other real individuals are also made participants in the discussions with Bembo. The work immediately became popular and influential and was translated into several languages in the 16th century. The first English translation (by Sir Thomas Hoby) was published in 1561 and influenced the English court and major writers such as Sidney, Spenser, Shakespeare, and Donne.

The ideal courtier is presented as one who is graceful, modest, learned, skilled in many areas, ethical, and cultivated. The most important part of the work is the fourth book, in which Bembo specifies such central matters of Renaissance philosophy (especially from the perspectives of Christian humanism and Christian Platonism) as the natures of the universe, the soul, beauty, and love. Beauty is described as a circle with goodness at its center. The individual as a MICROCOSM and as a partaker of both angelic and animal characteristics and potentiality is an important consideration. The conflicts of reason and passion, the spiritual and the physical are discussed. For some of the other fundamental concepts embodied in this book, see PLATONIC.

For examples of criticism probing further the subtleties of the courtly tradition and background from Castiglione adapted in Herbert's works, see Marion White Singleton's *God's Courtier: Configuring a Different Grace in George Herbert's "Temple"* (1987), Kristina Wolberg's "All Possible Art: *The Country Parson* and Courtesy" in the *John Donne Journal*, 8 (1989), 167–89, and Michael C. Schoenfeldt's *Prayer and Power: George Herbert and Renaissance Courtship* (1991).

Couzin. See COZEN.

Cozen. *Verb*: to cheat, deceive, defraud.

Crazy, crazie. *Adjective*: (1) cracked, flawed; (2) damaged, unsound, liable to break or fall to pieces.

Creature. *Noun*: (1) a created being, animate or inanimate; (2) an animal; (3) a human being; (4) anything created; (5) a person who owes his or her position, wealth, or power to another person [including a patron] and who is willing to carry out the will of the benefactor.

Cross. *Noun*: (1) the instrument of crucifixion, Christ's cross; (2) a burden or suffering. *Adjective*: contrary or perverse. *Verb*: to prevent.

Cross(e)-bias. *Verb*: to cause to incline away from or cross the intended path or direction. The metaphor is taken from bowling on the grass, in which the bias may refer to a lead weight or shape added to or created in the ball that causes it to take an oblique, rather than a straight, path, or the word may also refer to the oblique path so taken. Herbert's use of the term in "AFFLICTION (1)" also seriously plays on Christ's CROSS.

Curious. *Adjective*: (1) carefully or skillfully made, (2) ingenious, (3) inquisitive, (4) fastidious.

D

Dalton, Michael. Writer of *The Country Justice*, first published in 1618. Referred to by Herbert in Chapter 23 of *THE COUNTRY PARSON*.

Damp. *Noun*: (1) visible vapor, such as fog or mist; (2) moisture, dampness, humidity; (3) stupor or loss of consciousness; (4) a state of dejection; (5) a discouragement.

Danby, Earl of. See HENRY DANVERS.

Danvers, Charles. Father of JANE DANVERS, Herbert's wife.

Danvers, Henry (1573–1644). Earl of Danby. Older brother of Sir JOHN DANVERS, Herbert's stepfather. Herbert lived in his home (DAUNTESEY HOUSE) during 1628 and 1629. Member of Privy Council under CHARLES I.

Danvers, Jane. Married George Herbert on March 5, 1629. Cousin of JOHN DANVERS and HENRY DANVERS. Despite the argument by WALTON that Herbert had only known her three days before the wedding, it is most likely that Herbert had met her long before: she was the cousin of Herbert's stepfather (John Danvers) and the cousin of the man whose house Herbert had been living in over a year (Henry Danvers). She lived in BAYNTON HOUSE and continued to live there with Herbert until they moved to BEMERTON. After Herbert's death, she returned to Baynton House to live.

Danvers, John (1588?–1655). Married MAGDALEN HERBERT in 1609, thus becoming George Herbert's stepfather. Sir John was much younger than the widow he married and had a beautiful home with gardens in CHELSEA, which JOHN DONNE, FRANCIS BACON, and others of importance visited. Danvers was almost universally respected as a wise, generous, and kind man. He and George Herbert developed a mutually trusting friendship that lasted for the rest of Herbert's life. Herbert named him as the overseer of his will. Married Elizabeth Dauntesey in 1628, a little over a year after his first wife's death.

Danvers, Lady. See HERBERT, MAGDALEN.

Dauntesey, Elizabeth. Married Sir JOHN DANVERS in July, 1628, a little over a year after the death of MAGDALEN HERBERT, Sir John's first wife.

Dauntesey House. Residence of HENRY DANVERS, Earl of Danby, in WILTSHIRE. Herbert lived in this house owned by this brother of his stepfather (Sir JOHN DANVERS) in 1628 and 1629. It is likely that many of the poems of *THE TEMPLE* were written here.

Deal. *Verb*: (1) to share or distribute, (2) to do business or to trade, (3) to associate with or to have to do with a person or thing, (4) to take action.

Dearth. *Noun*: (1) famine, (2) a condition in which food is scarce, (3) scarcity or lack of anything.

Death. See DIE.

"Death." This poem comes near the end of *The Church* (see *THE TEMPLE*). In logical progression following it are "Dooms-day," "Judgement," "Heaven," and "LOVE (3)."
　　The first half of the poem (lines 1–12) presents a twofold perspective: it simultaneously represents individual humans of any time perceiving only the horrible image of physical death with no life beyond that death before they discover the Christian promise of spiritual life and a perspective of all humanity before Christ's crucifixion regarding death as the end of life with no hope beyond it. So, personified Death was "once" (both before the individual awakened to a Christian concept of life and death and before Old Testament humanity experienced Christ's crucifixion and its offered spiritual salvation) "an uncouth hideous thing." Death was "uncouth" in the senses of both *unknown* and *crude*: it was a "thing" that could hardly be defined and seemed so unpleasant that it was not even pondered deeply. Death was only physical bones, the result of sad pain and groaning before death, and looked grimly ludicrous in its appearance with the mouth of a head open but no sound emanating. No ability to "sing" (line 4) enforces the sense of sadness present when one only sees life in physical terms and when one assumes that physical death terminates all life.
　　The second stanza seems conducive to two possible readings, and both indeed seem relevant. The first seems to point to the non-Christian perspective of one's own death. The human who concentrates on life as only physical tries to avoid contemplating and anticipating death: it is something one does not want to think of, and he or she tries to resist

acknowledging its presence by always seeing it at some future point ("at some six or ten years hence"). However, a second possible reading here is that after someone's death, then we see that six to ten years of decay later all the body's "flesh" has turned to "dust" and its "bones" to "sticks." The reduction of living matter to the most insignificant and trivial "dust" and "sticks" drives home vividly our perception of Death as "uncouth" and "hideous" (as mentioned in line 1).

Either way that the second stanza is read, it becomes clear in the third one that "we" were only perceiving this physical, worldly side of death, rather than seeing the longer view of spiritual, eternal life beyond our physical vision of death. All we saw were corpses ("shells") of souls that escaped the body at death: Herbert here makes explicit a METAPHYSICAL CONCEIT in which the soul is like a bird that is truly born into life with physical death. The body is like the shell that a bird emerges from in "FLEDGE(d)" form: it has feathers and is able now to fly, which the soul does to reach heaven and is now beyond our physical sight. It is possible that Herbert has prepared for this conceit subtly with the earlier image of the open mouth that could not sing (line 4), since now the flown bird is singing in the spiritual realm. But our limited physical perspective has us seeing only the open mouth of the carcass, the shell of the soul, and the dry dust of that shell which no longer has life to "sing" or even to "shed tears" itself, but it does "extort" tears from mourners. This sense of sadness, then, pervades the limited human perspective of life as only physical.

At the middle of the poem (line 13) occurs the important turning point with the entrance of Christ into the picture. "Our Savior's death" paradoxically put new life into Death! This is a new awareness for fallen humanity before Christ's death, and it is true for any human since Christ who has not yet seen or accepted the view of death as the birth of the spirit which Christ has enabled. Paradoxically, Christ's death "put some blood" into the face of death: Herbert humorously and seriously plays with the image of Christ's literal blood shed on the cross at his death becoming the invigorating and beautifying rosy blush on the face of Death, as we now can see it as full of spiritual life. Christ's physical blood to us becomes the spiritual blood of life. Herbert wittily notes that now we can see Death as not "hideous" but as "fair" (i.e., beautiful) and now full of "grace" (jokingly, the opposite of "uncouth," as well as significantly full of God's free grace to save our spiritual lives through Christ's death and resurrection). The humor injected into this fourth stanza appropriately begins to change the mood of sadness in the limited perception of the first half of the poem into the triumphant joy of the last half, representing the longer Christian view of death as true life. This is why Death is now much requested and sought [by Christians] as a "good." This new view wipes away the extorted tears and gives one victory over them.

The fifth stanza asserts that we now experience the "glad" (rather than sad) view of death as it appears on "dooms-day," the end of the world (i.e., of everything physical and mortal) that will usher in the last judgement: significantly, of course, this poem titled "Death" is followed immediately by "Dooms-day" and "Judgement." Like birds with their new, brilliant feathers, the souls will then wear their new "array." This beauty of the soul will cover the mere bones after physical resurrection on "dooms-day."

The peaceful joy and even anticipation of death brought by the Christian perspective on life is emphasized in the last stanza. With calm and lack of fear toward death now, we can approach death just as we do sleep: we can look forward to reinvigoration and greater vitality upon our awaking into eternal life beyond physical death. We can peacefully "trust half that we have" [i.e., our physical body: the soul is our other half] to "an honest faithfull grave," since we can be assured of our physical resurrection and rejoining of our soul and body at "dooms-day." Significantly, the structure of the poem embodies the two halves of our self: the first half of the poem focuses on the body, and the last half on the soul. The ultimate emphasis is on their being reanimated and rejoined. The grave is "HONEST," not only in its Christian, truthful nature of assuring the holding of the body until dooms-day, but also in its *chaste*, *pure* nature, since the bones and dust now are not seen as dirty, "uncouth," and "hideous" at all. I think that it is important that Herbert spells "faithful" in this particular poem as "faithfull": he did so in the existing earlier manuscript version in his own hand, and it also exists with this spelling in the copied manuscript used for the first printed edition. He apparently wants to emphasize that this Christian grave indeed is *full of faith* in the resurrection and new life beyond this grave. Herbert, in fact, implies that sleep and death indeed are approached identically now: we can sleep with joy, even if we unexpectedly die in that sleep, and we can deliberately prepare for our death as if going to sleep. There are no differences in the feelings, assurances, acts of lying down in a bed or grave, or in the visions of new life beyond sleep or death. So, there is no difference in lying on an everyday pillow of "down" in a bed or on a pillow of "dust" in the grave. The use of "down" interestingly and subtly echoes the analogy of the soft new feathers of the fledged bird/soul from earlier in the poem.

Death bell. Bell rung in a "death knell" (mournful tolling) after someone has died. Compare FUNERAL BELL and PASSING BELL.

Death's head. See MEMENTO MORI.

Deign. *Verb*: (1) to condescend to bestow or grant; (2) to condescend to accept, to take or accept graciously; (3) to treat someone as worthy, to dignify someone.

Demean. *Noun*: (1) demeanor, (2) demesne—i.e., estate or land possessed.

"Denial." This poem suggests that both humanity as a whole before Christ's birth and the individual at any time may experience "denial," or what he or she perceives as God's denial, at least. It is significant that this poem occurs in *The Church* (see *THE TEMPLE*) just shortly after "Anagram" and "To all Angels and Saints," which celebrate Mary as the tent for the Lord of Hosts and the mine from which Christ as the gold was taken. This poem immediately precedes "Christmas," in which any sense of God's "denial" to mankind is completely dispelled with the birth of Christ. Rather than denial, God's giving is exemplified in full with the gift of Christ to complete spiritual harmony for the universe and for the individual.

The note of spiritual harmony and music is a central one, in fact, in "Denial." This music is carried into "Christmas," as well, with images in it of singing and of music that shines. The METAPHYSICAL CONCEIT of a musical instrument, such as a lute, permeates "Denial." The speaker's heart is like a "broken" lute (stanza 1), and his "bent thoughts" are like a "brittle bow" (stanza 2). His soul is "untuned, unstrung" (stanza 5). His request in stanza 6 is for God to "tune" his "heartless breast." The condition of the speaker at the beginning of the poem, then, is that he is out of harmony and order spiritually: he feels that God is not listening to his "devotions" and responding to his spiritual disappointments, and he expresses his resentment of God's lack of response with the paradoxical attribution of "silent ears" to God. God, then, is denying him a hearing, just as one refusing to harmonize or participate in a musical performance: the speaker is playing, but God refuses to. God denies him harmony, from the point of view of the speaker. Disharmony and disorder in his "verse" clearly symbolize that disorder he feels in his own spirit and disorder in his relationship with God and the universe. The idea of his "broken" heart symbolized by "broken" verse is reflected by the fact that the fifth (last) lines of each of the first five stanzas are unrhymed and isolated in each stanza. Only with the sixth (last) stanza does the last line rhyme with another line, and the rhyme is with the immediately preceding line, bringing an effective harmony and closure: the mended "rhyme" depicts the mended heart, soul, order between man and God. And one notes that the regular iambics of the last stanza stand out in contrast to the frequent variations and "broken" nature of them that reflect the "disorder" through the first five stanzas. Any "denial" (of order, harmony, responsiveness, rhyme, etc.) between the soul and God is swept away. The mending is done immediately after the speaker finally asks God to "cheer and tune my heartless breast" (implying that the speaker now accepts responsibility himself, rather than blaming God for his own spiritual disharmony). And God indeed "defer[s] no time," but at once grants his "request."

This ending humble "request" is significantly in a different spirit from his earlier bitter, sarcastic, and accusatory tone and statements to God. For example, in the third stanza he resentfully says that it does no good to make one's heart and knees numb by kneeling before and imploring a God who gives "no hearing." Particularly sarcastic is stanza 4, which notes that God gave "dust" (i.e., man) a tongue to cry to him, but that God refuses to listen.

Descry. *Verb*: (1) to declare, make known, reveal; (2) to reveal something hidden or secret; (3) to cry out against or denounce; (4) to see or perceive; (5) to explore or investigate.

Destiny. *Noun*: (1) whatever is fated to happen, (2) the power or agent that determines events, (3) supernatural or divine preordination, (4) God's divine providence, (5) mythological goddess of destiny.

Devest. *Verb*: (1) abandon, (2) forego a claim to, (3) undress, unclothe.

Die. *Verb* used in various senses in Herbert's time, but particularly in the following: (1) to cease living; (2) to experience rejection by a lady (in the PETRARCHAN love convention); (3) to part from a loved one; and (4) to experience sexual intercourse, orgasm (since each sexual consummation was believed to subtract some moments from a person's life).

"Discipline." The long and slender physical shape of this poem suggests a "rod" with which to discipline a child. The speaker, God's child, is asking God to dispense with his Old Testament anger, "wrath." Instead, God should take the "gentle path" (line 4) of New Testament "grace" (line 16) and "love" (lines 18, 19, 21, 22). The speaker claims that all of his wishes and words are in harmony with God's "book," the Bible (lines 9–12). It is there that God's love and grace are manifested in Christ and that God is as merciful as he is just. The phrase "stony hearts" of line 20 echoes the heart of stone in "THE ALTAR," the heart sanctified by Christ's sacrifice. Personified "Love" will win souls effectively.

Lines 21–24 picture Love as a warrior who can move rapidly and shoot accurately. Herbert here is playing on the image of God as presented in Exodus 15:3 ("The Lord is a man of war"). Very likely also is the image of an armed sailing vessel of a country's navy, a use of the phrase quite common prior to and during Herbert's life. But Herbert emphasizes the God of Love, exemplified in Christ, rather than the frightening God of wrath implied in Exodus and in a violent naval assault. Herbert also plays here with the traditional image of Cupid, the God of Love, with his "bow" (line 25) that no one escapes. Paradoxically, he says that even God the Father was struck with Love's arrow (in his love for mankind), since love even "Brought Thee low" (line 27): God was brought low by humbling himself in the form of Christ as God taking on human nature and even dying for humanity. The speaker says that since God himself was struck by love, certainly a mere human such as the speaker will be struck by God's love and will respond to that, with no need for wrathful discipline from the "rod." The last stanza echoes the first one, emphatically urging that God completely reject wrath in favor of love. The speaker even implies that God should have no "frailties," in contrast to man, and thus God should not show "wrath" (a frailty) but instead should show love.

Discover. *Verb*: (1) to uncover, (2) to disclose or reveal, (3) to show, (4) to manifest or display, (5) to find out, (6) to see.

Discovery. *Noun*: (1) the action of uncovering or fact of becoming uncovered, (2) the action of disclosing or revealing, (3) manifestation, (4) finding out, (5) exploring or investigating, (6) viewing.

Discovery of occult resemblances in things apparently unlike. See METAPHYSICAL CONCEIT.

Discry. See DESCRY.

Disgest. Digest.

Disparate experience. See DISSOCIATION OF SENSIBILITY.

Dispark, disimpark. *Verb*: literally, to turn out of a park—by extension, to evict or cast out of anything.

Dissociation of Sensibility. A famous phrase used by the poet and critic T.S. Eliot in a 1921 *London Times Literary Supplement* review of H.J.C. Grierson's 1921 volume entitled *Metaphysical Lyrics and Poems of the Seventeenth Century*. Eliot says that later in the 17th century (after DONNE and the other major METAPHYSICAL poets) a "dissociation of sensibility set in." He apparently means a separation of thought and feeling or thought and experience in verse, since he praises Donne by saying that "a thought to Donne was an experience." He also asserts, "When a poet's mind is perfectly equipped for its work, it is constantly amalgamating disparate experience." He also calls sensibility "the feeling" in verse.

As far as Herbert is concerned, Eliot's respect for and elevation of his poetry rose through the century. In his *George Herbert* (1962) Eliot says that one cannot appreciate fully Herbert's "genius" and "art" without studying *THE TEMPLE* as a whole. Eliot calls Herbert a major poet.

Dissolution. *Noun*: (1) reduction of any body or mass to its constituent elements; (2) disintegration or decomposition; (3) death.

Divest. See DEVEST.

"Divinity." This poem is one of Herbert's most satirical and sarcastic in criticizing the foolish and wayward nature of humanity. The first stanza ridicules the elaborate cosmological schemes concocted by astronomers' and philosophers' intellects: they seem foolish in trying to undergird the stars by postulating the existence of SPHERES (also see PTOLEMY) in the Ptolemaic cosmology, spheres which supposedly contain each heavenly body. Men seem quite foolish and egotistical in deluding themselves by thinking that their own intellectual fabrications actually support elements of the physical heaven above them, while, in fact, the stars have done quite well in maintaining their own positions ever since the creation, without the help of pompous men. The speaker's attributing to men an attitude of superiority over stars that seem (to these men) even more stupid than a "CLOD" makes his satire even more caustic, especially when he underlines the fact that the star really has no need of a "guide" such as man.

Stanzas 2 and 3 then argue that humanity has taken the same attitude toward the "other heaven," the *spiritual* heaven of God, that it has toward the *physical* heaven of the cosmos. "Divinity's transcendent sky" has been subjected to human intellect ("wit"), as if that wit were a carving knife with a sharp "edge": "cut" and "carve" imply destruction and fragmentation of something previously whole and unified. "Divinity" suggests both theology and the concept of the godhead, upon which Christian theology depends. Divinity's "transcendent sky" transcends the physical realm of the senses, and it is thus contrasted to the physical cosmos of the stars that are accessible to the senses; however, Herbert's point is that men wield their intellect like a weapon that serves to separate and distinguish *both* the physical and spiritual "skies," as a consequence of human pride and misplaced values, with resulting disunity and superfluousness added to what previously was unified, clear, and concise. In man's application of himself to "Divinity," human "reason" is victorious over "faith" that is ignored (line 8), and this is a most unfortunate, deplorable situation, the speaker is implying. Stanza 3 asks if human reason, "wisdom" (used with much sarcasm) has not obscured, rather than clarified, the "wine" of Christian divinity with definitions and other disputed theological distinctions. More than one meaning resides in Herbert's use here, however, of the phrase "broached the wine." First, this alludes to mankind, in the form of the soldier at Christ's crucifixion, piercing Christ's side with a spear and making the blood flow: this suggests the recurring image (see "THE AGONY," for example) of Christ as a cask of wine that is "broached" (pierced to open it—see ABROACH) for the wine to flow. But also suggested is "broached" in the sense of introducing a matter or topic for discussion: here, the "wine" (Christ's nature, divinity, Christian theology) is broached by man continually for debate, definition, distinction, etc. The effect is that human "reason" has added obscuring layers to what originally was clear and easily seen by means of simple faith. The nature of the "wine" (Christ's blood, Christ, etc.) also implies its use in the Last Supper and in Holy Communion (about which humanity and churches and factions of churches were endlessly debating in Herbert's time and in centuries before). Also related to the crucifixion is the use of "his [Christ's] seamless coat": in John 19:23–24 Christ's coat is described as being "without seam," and the soldiers decided not to tear it but to cast lots for it. It remained whole. This represents the unity of the simple Christian faith (beginning with Christ's crucifixion) that humanity since has insisted on making "jagged," divided and torn into disunified pieces by extraneous, inessential, busily inquisitive human "questions and divisions" concerning theology. Thus, proud human "reason" has served only to obscure and divide "divinity," the essential Christian "faith."

   Stanzas 4 and 5 serve to drive home this point of utter clarity and simplicity that foolish humans have only taken pains to obfuscate. The clear "beams of truth" from Christ are the only precepts which can "save," grant eternal salvation. In other words, all the added assertions and speculations from human "reason" are of no use in granting God's salvation for humanity through clear faith. The first two lines of stanza 5 give examples of Christ's "doctrine." "*Love God, and love your neighbor*" is found in Matthew 22:37–40 and Luke 10:27. "*Watch and pray*" occurs in Matthew 26:41, Mark 13:33 and 14:38, and Luke 21:36.

"*Do as ye would be done unto*" is in Matthew 7:12 and Luke 6:31. Herbert ironically calls them "dark" (i.e., obscure or complex), since they are anything but "dark," a point made obvious through the sarcasm of "dark as day." He also, with seething irony, calls them "GORDIAN knots": they really require no undoing at all! The irony and sarcasm highlight the stupidity and/or pompousness of people who feel that they must elaborate on and pretentiously explain the clear and obvious precepts of Christ.

    Stanza 6 pursues further the implications about Christ's blood introduced in stanza 3 and ridicules human disagreements about the precise nature of the elements of Holy Communion. Herbert refers to Christ's words at the Last Supper regarding the wine (Matthew 26:28— "For this is my blood of the new testament, which is shed for many for the remission of sins") as being clear and "not obscure." The importance to salvation is to "take and taste" the wine and experience it as Christ's blood of salvation. What is not important is to try to obscure the act by attempting to define and speculate on its nature. Thus, Herbert dismisses any controversy over TRANSUBSTANTIATION (a controversy, in fact, which occupied many Protestants and factions of Protestants in their examining, disagreeing with, and postulating new views of this Roman Catholic doctrine) as one of the INDIFFERENT THINGS.

    Herbert's speaker's contempt for the futile and frivolous nature of human speculation on divinity is directly expressed in the last stanza with the address to "foolish man." "EPICYCLES" and "spheres" are examples from Ptolemaic astronomy of foolish human speculation, and reference to them concludes the poem effectively by taking the reader back to the speaker's original statements in stanza 1 about the spheres. Destruction of man's foolish rational, philosophical constructs may cause him, then, to look clearly and simply into the matter of saving himself eternally. Humorously, Herbert also says to "save thy head"— i.e., by no longer concerning himself with such rational postulations, man will not be taxing his brain to the point of exhaustion. This is achieved only by faith, and faith "needs no STAFF of flesh." Herbert here plays on two meanings of "staff": a measuring rod and a stick to aid in walking or climbing. "Flesh" is humanity, with its reason. Neither a measuring instrument (such as human reason pretends to be in computing "epicycles," for example) nor an aid in one's mobility toward heaven (such as human reason claims to be in its theological speculations) is needed at all for the faithful soul to find heaven: faith goes to heaven strongly on its own (i.e., with no help from reason), and it leads the soul to heaven (i.e., the soul needs no guidance from reason, but only from faith). Faith, in fact, is like the "star" of the first stanza:

each "knows his way without a guide," without any guidance needed in either case from "foolish man."

Do. *Verb*: (1) to put forth action or effort; (2) to perform or carry out; (3) to accomplish or finish; (4) to copulate, have sexual intercourse.

Doctors. (1) Teachers; (2) learned men; (3) eminently learned early Church FATHERs who were given the special title of "Doctor": e.g., AUGUSTINE, Ambrose, Jerome, CHRYSOSTOM, and Nazienzen; (4) eminent SCHOOLMEN; (5) physicians or medical practitioners.

Donne, John (1572–1631). Poet, prose writer, clergyman. Attended Lincoln's Inn and then served as a soldier briefly. Became a secretary to Sir Thomas Egerton, Lord Keeper of the Great Seal, but lost this position after secretly marrying Egerton's niece, Ann More. By 1608 he enjoyed financial support and respect from two patronesses, the Countess of Bedford and MAGDALEN HERBERT, the mother of George Herbert. Donne sent his *La Corona* series of sonnets to Mrs. Herbert. Donne also was acquainted with EDWARD HERBERT, BEN JONSON, and other respected writers and titled people of his time.

Donne's wishes for secular employment eluded him, ultimately because King JAMES wanted Donne to serve in the English church. In 1615 Donne was ordained. Subsequently he became Reader in Divinity at Lincoln's Inn, a chaplain serving King James, and Dean of St. Paul's Cathedral. In 1624 was published Donne's prose work *Devotions Upon Emergent Occasions*, following a serious illness at the end of 1623. In the summer of 1625 Donne visited the home of Magdalen Herbert, now Lady Danvers, at CHELSEA. He was forced to stay there much longer than originally planned because of an outbreak of plague in London. Donne refers in one of his letters to the fact that George Herbert was also here at the time. Donne preached a memorial sermon after Lady Danvers's death in 1627: according to WALTON, Donne did "weep and preach" the sermon. This sermon was later printed with George Herbert's *Memoriae Matris Sacrum*. After a serious illness in late 1630 and early 1631, Donne died on March 31, 1631.

Many of Donne's sermons were published some years after his death, and these sermons and his *Devotions* have assured his reputation as a great preacher and prose writer. However, his reputation as a great poet rests primarily on his secular *Songs and Sonnets*, although his *Holy Sonnets* and other *Divine Poems* are not to be ignored by any means. Herbert must have grown up reading Donne and knowing him personally, since his mother was a close friend and patroness. Donne also gave Herbert one of his seals with Christ crucified on an anchor and a poem that accompanied it. Herbert wrote verses in response.

Donne is now regarded as the first METAPHYSICAL poet, and Herbert generally is seen as his greatest follower in this group. He does use many of the characteristics regarded as typical of Donne and the metaphysicals (e.g., colloquial language, irregular metrics, and metaphysical conceits) in certain poems and in parts of poems; however, debts to Ben Jonson and the CLASSICAL strain appear strongly in Herbert's work, as well. Fusion of the influences from Donne and Jonson is integral to understanding and appreciating the work of Herbert and others after Donne.

Dorset, Countess of. See CLIFFORD, LADY ANNE.

Doubt. *Verb*: (1) to be undecided, (2) to mistrust, (3) to fear, (4) to suspect.

Drummond, William, of Hawthornden (1585–1649). Born near Edinburgh, Scotland, at the family estate of Hawthornden. Studied law before inheriting his father's estate and title as laird of Hawthornden. He then spent much time reading and collecting many volumes of books for his library before he began writing poems himself. After a poem in 1617 celebrating a visit to Scotland by King JAMES, Drummond became better known among English poets and readers, including Michael Drayton. In 1618 BEN JONSON walked from London to Edinburgh, met Drummond, and stayed with him for two weeks. Drummond invented several military and other mechanical devices, including different types of pistols, pikes, telescopes, and measuring instruments. He supported the Royalists and CHARLES I and wrote some political prose and poetry in their support.

Drummond's own poems and prose pieces are minor, and his renown rests mainly on his recording of Jonson's comments during the latter's visit to Scotland. This prose account usually is referred to as Jonson's *Conversations with Drummond* (or simply as *Conversations*). Some of the most famous and influential comments about DONNE and METAPHYSICAL poetry (as well as other writers) are those attributed to Jonson by Drummond in this work. For example, Drummond records Jonson saying the following (among other remarks on Donne): "that Donne, for not keeping of accent, deserved hanging," "that Donne said to him he wrote that epitaph on Prince Henry . . . to match Sir EDWARD HERBERT in obscureness," "he esteemeth John Donne the first poet in the world in some things," "affirmeth Donne to have written all his best pieces ere he was 25 years old," and "that Donne himself for not being understood would perish."

Dull. *Adjective*: (1) slow of understanding; (2) lacking keenness in senses and feelings, unresponsive; (3) sluggish or stagnant; (4) depressed, gloomy, melancholy; (5) tedious or uninteresting; (6) lacking sharpness.

Dryden, John. See METAPHYSICAL.

Duncon, Edmund. Rector of Fryarn-Barnet who delivered the manuscript of Herbert's poems (the collection eventually published as *THE TEMPLE*) to NICHOLAS FERRAR, the man who eventually saw it through the press. Similarly, he provided Herbert's manuscript of *THE COUNTRY PARSON* to BARNABAS OLEY, who eventually published it. Duncon is one of the first-hand sources WALTON had for his account of Herbert's life. According to Walton, Duncon was sent at the request of Ferrar to visit Herbert during his final illness. Shortly before Duncon left Herbert (about three weeks before Herbert's death) Herbert gave his manuscript of poems to Duncon to take to Ferrar and said, "He shall find in it a picture of the many spiritual conflicts that have passed betwixt God and my Soul, before I could subject mine to the will of Jesus my Master: in whose service I have now found perfect freedom." Walton, still following Duncon's own account of the scene given to Walton personally many years later, also relates that Herbert requests that Ferrar "if he can think it may turn to the advantage of any dejected poor soul, let it be made public: if not, let him burn it."

E

Earth. *Noun*: (1) one of the four ELEMENTS; (2) the world on which humanity dwells, envisioned in the PTOLEMAIC concept as the center of the universe; (3) the land on this world, as opposed to the seas; (4) the ground and soil; (5) place for burial; (6) the body; (7) anything mortal; (8) personified "Mother Earth," fertile and bringing forth life.

"Easter Wings." This poem is an example of Herbert's PATTERN POEMS (or "shaped verses"). It is in the shape of two wings. Another example of a pattern poem in Herbert is "THE ALTAR."
    The first stanza addresses God ("Lord") as both the Creator (God the Father) and as Christ (God the Son). God created Adam ("man"), giving him an abundance of all things of value to him ("wealth and store") in the Garden of Eden, but through foolish pride Adam fell and forfeited his paradise. Adam's sin introduced mortality and death; therefore, man was "Decaying more and more" (line 3). One notices how the shape of the poem here functions beyond the image of the wing in that the length of line and "store" of syllables representing man's abundance is steadily shrinking, reducing, "decaying" with the progression toward the middle of the stanza. At the mid-point (line 5) "most poor" reflects man's reduced physical and spiritual state, and the idea is embodied in the mere two syllables to the line. Then line 6 begins to reverse the decline and suggests expansion (as do the succeeding lines of increasing length) and elevation with the power of "Thee" (Christ). Christ enables man to "rise" again spiritually. Just as Christ rose out of death, so can "man." The "victories" of Christ on "this day" (Easter) are celebrated with harmony and song, and humanity can be as "larks," birds that rise in flight and in song in the early morning. Humans can celebrate the new "day" of the spirit arising from the night of death. The important Christian paradox of the fortunate fall is employed in the final line of the first stanza: Christian writers over many centuries before Herbert had pointed out that Adam's "fall" was paradoxical in that, even though it was a terrible sin, it did lead to even greater things for mankind than had been possessed before. Of particular importance is the fact that humanity was given Christ as Savior and was granted redemption because of Adam's fall. Man now had heavenly paradise to enter, not just the earthly one given Adam. So, with the wings of Christ's redemption, of God's grace, the speaker has a greater "flight" (into heaven) possible: paradoxically, because of the "fall," he actually rises into eternity.

The second stanza applies the first in a personal way (from "man" to "My" and "I," etc.), an action anticipated by the "me" ending the first stanza. He, as all humanity, begins in "sorrow," with the inheritance of original sin. Sickness is evidence of man's fallen nature and mortality, and he asserts that God punished his sin with "sicknesses and shame": this might be taken on an autobiographical level, since Herbert was subject to continual sickness and indeed was "Most thin" (line 5) in body. But the physical wasting symbolizes spiritual wasting, and what occurs in the life of himself is parallel to the history of mankind portrayed as "decaying" in the first five lines of the first stanza. And the decreasing syllables of each stanza are parallel in order to suggest becoming "poor" and "thin" in the respective stanzas. Then, as in the first stanza, it is "With Thee" (line 6 in each stanza) that provides strength and rising—i.e., for the individual, as well as for humanity. Lines 19–20 emphasize the poem's wing pattern by the speaker seeing himself as a bird that will "IMP" his wing with feathers from Christ's wing (Christ's resurrection and rising to heaven after crucifixion and death). The speaker's own "Affliction" as miniature suffering and crucifixion is overcome by his own ability through Christ's power to rise and make the "flight" to heaven. So, just as the "fall" of mankind leads ultimately to humanity's heavenly salvation, so does personal affliction (or the "fall" exemplified in little) paradoxically lead to eternal salvation through the intervention of Christ's grace and power.

Eclipse. *Noun*: (1) darkening or obliterating of the light of the sun or moon by an intervening body; (2) absence or cessation of light; (3) darkness or shadow; (4) dimness, loss of brilliance. *Verb*: (1) to cause darkening or obliterating of the light of the sun or moon; (2) to cause absence or cessation of light; (3) to cast a shadow upon, to darken, to obscure; (4) to cause loss of brilliance; (5) to hide or screen from; (6) to extinguish life.

Ecliptic line. The route of the sun in its revolving sphere, as envisioned in the PTOLEMAIC concept.

Elected. In its special theological sense, chosen by God to receive salvation.

Elector. See FREDERICK.

Element. *Noun*: (1) in Ancient, Medieval, and Renaissance thought, one of the four simple substances [from lightest to heaviest: fire, air, water, and earth] out of which all material bodies are made: anything composed of any one or more of the four elements is mortal and therefore subject to decay and death [see also HUMOR, COMPLEXION, GALEN, and NEW PHILOSOPHY]; (2) more generally, any constituent substance out of which a more complex substance is made; (3) the bread or wine of the Eucharist; (4) [in plural] the letters of the alphabet. *Verb*: (1) to compose or make up something out of a combination of some or all of the four elements [fire, air, water, and earth]; (2) to constitute or compose.

Eliot, T.S. See DISSOCIATION OF SENSIBILITY.

Elixir. See ALCHEMY.

"Elixir, The." For needed background to understand this poem and its METAPHYSICAL CONCEIT, one should first note the entries in this "Dictionary" for ALCHEMY, TINCTURE, and TOUCH.

The first three stanzas (first half) of the poem argue for both *seeing* God in everything and *doing* everything for the sake of God. Man should not act unthinkingly, without reason ("rudely"). Always God should be "prepossessed" in human action: God has first claim on any action by the individual. In line 8 "his" is the equivalent for modern "its"—i.e., the action's perfection should always be the goal of the individual carrying out that action, and "perfection" is only attainable with God's presence inherent in the action. The third stanza expresses the argument in an analogy that illustrates the two options open to the individual when he or she sees (or does) anything. A person may be limited in perspective, such as one who looks at a "glass" (a window) and only sees or examines the glass itself and not what is beyond it: this individual only sees the worldly, physical, and material in creation. However, one might also look through the window to see not it but the heaven, the sky beyond it. This symbolizes the individual who sees God, God's heaven, in everything he or she sees and does: the thing seen or act taken is not important in itself, but only as it exemplifies and leads to God.

The last three stanzas (last half) of the poem develop the metaphysical conceit from alchemy and apply the title more clearly to the development of the poem. The fourth stanza, in its simplest terms, argues that any task, no matter how lowly ("mean"), can be pure and excellent if done for God's sake. In *THE COUNTRY PARSON*, Chapter 14, Herbert says, "Nothing is little in God's service: If it once have the honour of that Name, it grows great instantly." Metaphorically, using elements of alchemy, Herbert designates the phrase "for thy sake" as a "TINCTURE." This suggests both (1) a spiritual principle, the quality of which can be infused into material things and (2) the essence of a substance that supposedly can be

extracted and used to change other substances. So, doing something for
God's sake, with a sense of dedication to God, changes the lowliest task
to one of spiritual value and excellence. One should note, however (in
light of the rest of the poem), that Herbert also seems here to equate
"tincture" with the philosopher's stone, the quintessence, and the elixir
(see ALCHEMY). Many writers use these latter three phrases
interchangeably, and Herbert seems to add "tincture" as well. Stanza
five simply gives a concrete example of how any action that usually is
regarded as "drudgery," such as sweeping, can be transformed like base
metal into gold, into something divine, by the use of the elixir (or
tincture or philosopher's stone or the quintessence): this elixir is the
phrase "for thy sake." Stanza six makes explicit the equation of all of
these terms, since the "famous stone" is the philosopher's stone. Thus,
the "elixir" of the title is apparent in and equated with all of the other
alchemical phrases used and implied in the poem that point to the same
thing, the phrase "for thy sake." And pursuing the motif of
transformation into gold, Herbert ends the poem by referring to
"TOUCH" in its specialized sense of using a touchstone, a black stone
used to test the quality of gold by the color left when rubbed on the
touchstone. So, if the golden action made so by "for thy sake" is valued
as gold by God, then no one else can value it as being any less than that.
("Told" here is used in the sense of "counted" and "valued.") And
certainly the important fact to a Christian is that God does recognize the
individual's dedication of every action, of every work, to God.
    Inherent in this poem is the Protestant doctrine of the "calling,"
the belief that one can be quite holy in any vocation, in any work, that
he or she is called by God to perform or live by. An ordinary
occupation becomes divine and infused with grace when one is called to
it by God.

Elizabeth I (1533–1603). Queen of England, 1558–1603. Daughter
of Henry VIII and Anne Boleyn, she was the last of the Tudor rulers.
She was learned, witty, politically shrewd, and a supporter of the arts.
Upon her accession she attempted to reconcile the deep conflicts
between Protestants and Roman Catholics by forging a compromise, a
settlement dictating a middle-of-the-road Church of England. Some
Roman Catholic threats continued through her reign, however, in the
form of assassination plots against her and the Spanish Armada sent
against England. Roman Catholics in England were severely penalized
for not attending Anglican services and were not eligible for university
degrees and offices of state and church.
    Herbert, in Chapter 32 of *THE COUNTRY PARSON*, supports
his own recommendation that younger brothers should study civil law

by referring to the fact that Queen Elizabeth employed many of those versed in it.

Ell. *Noun*: unit of measure, specifically 45 inches.

"Enchanting voice." See SIRENS.

Endear(e). See INDEAR.

Engine. *Noun*: (1) a plot or snare, (2) a mechanical apparatus or tool, (3) an instrument of warfare, (4) an instrument of torture, such as the rack, (5) an instrument or means.

Epicure. *Noun*: one who follows the philosophy of Epicurus—a philosophy loosely interpreted to argue that no divine force governs the world, that there is no future life beyond the earthly one, and that no religious concerns should govern conduct.

Epicycle. *Noun*: a small circle made by the movement of one of the seven heavenly bodies (in the PTOLEMAIC view of the universe, these seven being the moon, the sun, Mercury, Venus, Mars, Jupiter, and Saturn) within the circumference of the greater circle of its spherical movement around the earth. An epicycle is a movement postulated by followers of PTOLEMY and the Ptolemaic astronomy in order to account for anomalous motions and discrepancies that otherwise could not be explained by Ptolemaic ideas.

Escurial (Escorial). Grand palace and center of Roman Catholicism in Spain that was built in the 1580's by King Philip II.

Except. *Conjunction*: (1) Unless [a frequent meaning in Herbert's works]; (2) other than; (3) if it were not for the fact that. *Preposition*: with the exclusion of. *Verb*: to leave out, to exclude.

Exhalation. *Noun*: (1) action of breathing forth; (2) evaporation; (3) that which is exhaled, breath, vapor; (4) vapor from damp ground; (5) meteor or comet.

Eyton. Eyton-upon-Severn in Shropshire. Magdalen Newport (see MAGDALEN HERBERT) married RICHARD HERBERT here at her family home in 1581. After Richard's death, Mrs. Herbert took her family to live at Eyton in her mother's home. Upon the death of Lady Newport, Mrs. Herbert left Eyton, taking her family to live in Oxford for the remaining time that her son EDWARD HERBERT was there.

F

Faculty. *Noun*: (1) power of or ability for an action, (2) a capability of the body or of a part of the body for a particular function.

Fain, faine. *Verb*: (1) to be glad, (2) to make glad, (3) to rejoice in, (4) to pretend (feign). *Adjective*: (1) glad or content, (2) obliged or necessitated, (3) willing or eager. *Adverb*: (1) gladly, (2) willingly.

Fair. *Adjective*: (1) beautiful; (2) having light complexion or having light or blonde hair; (3) free from blemish, clean; (4) impartial, equitable.

Fame. *Noun*: (1) public talk, report, rumor; (2) reputation or character; (3) celebrity, renown.

Fancy. *Noun*: (1) imagination, (2) things imagined or unreal or illusory, (3) a whim or mood, (4) individual taste or liking, (5) amorous inclination.

Fashion. *Noun*: (1) form or shape; (2) a particular shape or pattern; (3) a certain (and usually current) style of clothing, attire; (4) a prevailing custom or mode; (5) showy outward form.

Fast. *Adjective*: (1) firm, secure; (2) strong; (3) rapid.

Fat. *Adjective*: (1) well-fed, plump; (2) corpulent, obese; (3) affluent, wealthy; (4) self-satisfied, complacent.

Fatal. *Adjective*: (1) destined, decreed by fate; (2) doomed; (3) prophetic; (4) ominous; (5) deadly.

Father. *Noun*: (1) male parent; (2) ancestor, forefather; (3) one of the "Fathers of the Church": early Christian writers, usually those of the first five centuries; (4) title by which God is addressed or referred.

Fathom. *Verb*: (1) to measure with a fathom-line, to determine the depth of water, to sound; (2) to understand thoroughly.

Favour, favor. *Noun*: (1) friendly regard, (2) exceptional kindness, (3) something given out of kindness or regard, (4) aid, (5) beauty, (6) charm.

Fernelius. Jean Fernel, French court physician of the sixteenth century who wrote *Universa Medicina* and other medical treatises. Referred to by Herbert in Chapter 23 of *THE COUNTRY PARSON*.

Ferrar, John (died 1657). Brother of NICHOLAS FERRAR and a member of the community at Little Gidding. Instrumental in the repair of the church at LEIGHTON BROMSWOLD that George Herbert was prebendary of and that Herbert earnestly wanted restored. John Ferrar oversaw the actual day-to-day repairs.

Ferrar, Nicholas (1592–1637). Born in London on February 22, 1592. Took the B.A. and M.A. at Cambridge University. A member of the Virginia Company and a Member of Parliament for some years prior to 1624. He and his family decided on a life of dedication to God and retirement from the world and, to these ends, purchased the remote manor of Little Gidding in 1625. The small church there had been used as a hay barn and pigsty. The Ferrars immediately repaired it. In 1626 Ferrar was ordained deacon by WILLIAM LAUD at Westminster Abbey. That same evening he recited a vow to his family that the rest of his life would be spent in mortification, devotion, charity, and preparation for death. About thirty people made up the Little Gidding household. They included Nicholas's mother, his brother JOHN FERRAR and his family, and his sister Susanna and her family (the Colletts). Psalms and other parts of the Bible, hymns, and prayers made up a significant portion of daily activity and devotions. Schooling, study, regular worship, charity, and the techniques of bookbinding, gilding, and lettering were important at Little Gidding. Volunteers always maintained a night watch or vigil, with prayers and psalms, in anticipation of Christ's second coming. They staunchly followed the traditions, ceremonies, and Book of Common Prayer of the Church of England.

    Herbert corresponded with Nicholas Ferrar, and Ferrar sought Herbert's opinion on his translation of Valdesso's *Considerations* (see VALDÉS, JUAN), resulting in Herbert's "Brief Notes" on this work. Ferrar's cousin was ARTHUR WOODNOTH, one who visited Herbert at Bemerton, sought Herbert's advice on matters, and served as executor of Herbert's will. Ferrar sent EDMUND DUNCON to inquire of Herbert's health and to comfort him in his last illness: Duncon delivered the manuscript of the poems eventually published as *THE TEMPLE* from Herbert to Ferrar at this time. Ferrar had this original copied by some of the Little Gidding community (his two nieces, Anna and Mary Collett) to make it ready for publication. Ferrar saw it through the press, wrote the anonymous preface to it ("The Printers to the Reader"), and apparently gave the work its title.

Figure. *Verb*: (1) to form or shape, (2) to represent or symbolize, (3) to express in metaphor, (4) to imagine, (5) to prefigure or foreshadow.

Fire. *Noun*: (1) one of the four ELEMENTS; (2) the operative principle in combustion; (3) a flame; (4) in some contexts, a reference to hell; (5) in some contexts, a reference to the fire believed to end the world; (6) the means of lighting a fire, such as a live coal; (7) glowing appearance resembling fire; (8) in some contexts, ardor or enthusiasm; (9) creative imagination or poetic inspiration; (10) in some contexts, passion or emotion.

First Mover. According to the PTOLEMAIC view of the universe, the outermost SPHERE is the one called the "First Mover" or "Prime Mover" or "Primum Mobile." Its function is to give the initial motion to all of the spheres and to keep all of them revolving in perfect harmony. As they thus revolve, they create a perfect music called the music of the spheres (see discussion under SPHERE).

Fledge. *Adjective*: fledged, possessing feathers and ready to fly, as new birds out of the shell.

"Flower, The." The title points to the major METAPHYSICAL CONCEIT of the poem: the speaker (and ultimately every human) is analogous to a flower. God's grace and spiritual joy returning to him rejuvenate him, just as flowers in spring come to life after a period of winter. The speaker apparently has been in a period of sin and despair. His "grief" (line 5) melts like "snow in May" when he feels God returning to him. The period of "cold" when he felt his own guilt and God's displeasure is now over. "DEMEAN" in line 3 has two relevant senses here, *demeanor* and *demesne* (estate or land possessed). He is saying that flowers have both beauty in appearance (demeanor) and worth (demesne) and that both the beauty and worth are increased by and are appreciated more because of the contrast with the frosts preceding them. In fact, frosts pay "tributes of pleasure" to the succeeding flowers, just as a tenant on an estate pays tributes to its owner. So, the import of this analogy is that grief (like frost) increases the beauty and worth of the spiritual joy that succeeds it.

Stanza 2 furthers the conceit. His heart was "shriveled," withered down to the root of the plant in his own winter period of sin, despair. But, as the flower in spring, his heart recovers "greenness" (life, vitality) with the return of God's warmth.

In stanza 3 he attributes these changes in his spiritual and emotional states to the "Lord of power" who can both "kill" and "QUICKEN" (restore to life): God's killing displeasure sends one into a "hell" of sin, guilt, and spiritual despair, but God's grace brings one up to a "heaven" of spiritual joy and renewal. This is like turning a "PASSING BELL" (one tolling a single note while an individual is dying) into a "chiming" bell (i.e., a bell playing harmoniously with other bells in a blending of several joyous notes). In lines 19–21 the speaker acknowledges the absolute power of God to determine everything through God's will (God's "word"). We are incorrect in saying that anything exists ("is") in and of itself, because God's "word" determines the existence and nature of everything, and we would realize this if only we could correctly "SPELL" (in the senses of both *contemplate* and *comprehend*). So, God's will (along with man's obedience or disobedience of it) determines flux in one's earthly spiritual state. This is like the coldness and warmth of seasonal change determining the state of the flower.

Stanza 4 then expresses the speaker's wish that he could transcend this "changing" that one is subject to on earth. If he were in God's "paradise," heaven, he would be in an infinite, unchanging realm. He would be like a flower eternally beautiful and not subject to withering. He, like the flower, grows upward toward heaven, "offering" (i.e., *aiming*) at heaven. His desire to reach it is symbolized by the flower's shooting up and growing toward the sky. He even furthers the conceit of the flower by saying that he also does not *lack* ("WANT") a "spring shower": his spring shower is made up of his tears of repentance for sin. They nurture him for salvation.

Stanza 5 points out the truth and irony of the human condition, for in the very act of longing for heaven the speaker becomes smug ("as if heaven were my own"), and he, like Adam, feels God's "anger" at this pride. His "decline," his withering, again reminds him of being only a flower. God's anger is analogous to the "frost" that withers and kills the flower, but it is so much more powerful than the literal frost! In fact, God's "frown" is so cold that, in comparison to it, even the North Pole (Arctic) or South Pole (Antarctic) [i.e., the coldest areas on earth] seem like the torrid "ZONE," the area around the equator between the Tropics of Capricorn and Cancer [i.e., the hottest areas on earth].

In stanza 6 he again experiences the inevitable flux in this world as he feels again like a flower in spring: he "buds" again, rejuvenated by

the "dew" and "rain" of God's grace. He is given life by the "Light,"
the invigorating sun (and Christ the Son). He now feels so emotionally,
spiritually, and intellectually alive that it is hard to believe that he has
even been subject to those storms ("tempests") of the past sent by the
"Lord of power." Certainly the poem in this stanza suggests possible
autobiographical importance in the fact that the speaker's spiritual
regeneration also involves his creative regeneration as a Christian poet
dedicated to God: he now can "write" again and once more can "relish
versing."

Stanza 7, especially in its first line, is set up in parallel/contrast to
stanza 3, in its first line. In this last stanza he can now recognize and
emphasize the "Lord of love," rather than the "Lord of power." The
climax to the flower conceit is in his statement that, through love, God
makes "us" (all humans) see that "we are but (i.e., *only*) flowers" that
"GLIDE" (pass away gently and imperceptibly, ultimately through death
into eternity). To learn this fact ("find") and to experience it
("PROVE") leads to humility on the part of the individual and will lead
to the ultimate "garden" (heaven, paradise) for the "flower" (the
human). There the flower will "bide" eternally. But one who would be
"more" than only a flower and who would swell with "STORE" in this
earthly life will forfeit paradise by "pride," as did Adam, and as the
speaker has to be reminded not to do periodically (e.g., line 30, "as if
heaven were mine own"). The recurring periods of frost, cold, winter,
etc., from God, then, are reminders to humans that they indeed are only
flowers, reminders given to humanity in this life from God's love—a
love to direct them to heaven.

I feel that Herbert has carefully structured this poem of seven
stanzas with seven lines in each stanza to suggest numerological
symbolism. The number "7" symbolizes perfect order, a complete
period or cycle (see Cirlot, p. 261 [see "Selected Bibliography: General
Background"]). The image of the flower in relation to winter and
spring seasons suggests the continuing cycles through which the
"flower" (the human) proceeds in this life. Ultimately the cycle is from
this life to heaven, a fact emphasized in stanza 7. In large terms the
poem also embodies the cycle from Adam to redeemed man and from
the Garden of Eden to the "garden" in heaven where we will "bide"
(stanza 7). A cycle from pride to humility is also emphasized.
Certainly other cycles appear in the poem: Lord of power to Lord of
love, killing to quickening, hell to heaven, passing bell to chiming bell,
etc. The idea of perfect order symbolized by "7" is clearly assumed by
the speaker as he considers God's universe and "word": it is primary
that the human must recognize this order and his own place in it (i.e., he
must "SPELL" it), a lesson that the speaker has learned by the end of
the poem, in a sense suggesting the completion of life's cycle.

Fly. *Noun*: any winged insect, such as a moth.

Fond. *Adjective*: foolish.

Forbear. *Verb*: (1) to endure, submit to; (2) to dispense with, spare; (3) to give up, part with; (4) to avoid, shun: (5) to abstain or refrain from.

Forward. *Adjective*: (1) early or well-advanced, (2) ready or prompt or eager, (3) presumptuous, (4) extreme.

Fountain. *Noun*: (1) a spring or source of water flowing out of the earth, (2) the source of a stream or river.

Fox, the. See AMIENS.

Frame. *Verb*: (1) to shape, form, create; (2) to direct something to a certain purpose; (3) to attempt; (4) to adapt oneself or conform; (5) to form in the mind, to conceive, to imagine; (6) to cause or produce. *Noun*: (1) a structure consisting of parts put together, (2) heaven or earth regarded as a structure, (3) a structure that provides support.

Frederick, Elector Palatine (1596–1632). Count, Elector Palatine, and eventually King Frederick V of Bohemia. Succeeded his father in 1610. Married ELIZABETH STUART, daughter of King JAMES, in England on February 14, 1613. As Rhineland Elector, he was one of the rulers in Germany and vicinity who could vote for the Holy Roman Emperor. His rule was assertive of Protestantism. Accepted the election as King of Bohemia in 1619. He was crowned in November, 1619, but he ruled only until November, 1620, when his army was defeated by the Catholic League. He was nicknamed "the Winter King." He and his family fled. Eventually the League and the Spanish occupied the Palatinate. Frederick and his family became financially dependent upon the Dutch States General and Gustavus Adolphus of Sweden and died in exile in November, 1632.

Fugglestone St. Peter. See BEMERTON and WILTON HOUSE.

Funeral bell. Bell tolled at a person's funeral. Compare DEATH BELL and PASSING BELL.

G

Galen (about 130–200). Greek physician and writer who eventually lived, lectured, and wrote in Rome. His experience in anatomy contributed significantly to knowledge of the circulatory and nervous systems. In the Middle Ages and Renaissance his writings were most influential in proposing a theory of HUMORS and COMPLEXIONS, all related to the four ELEMENTS. His work was particularly popularized and made available in English by Sir Thomas Elyot in the early 16th century, most notably in *The Castle of Health*, which undoubtedly influenced Shakespeare, DONNE, JONSON, Herbert, and others. See also GALENIST and contrast to PARACELSUS.

Galenist. *Noun*: one subscribing to the teachings, theories, or medicine proposed by GALEN, particularly the idea that to combat an imbalance in HUMOR and COMPLEXION, one ingests food and substances of opposite qualities. See also GALEN and ELEMENT. Contrast to PARACELSUS.

Galileo [Galileo Galilei] (1564–1642). Italian mathematician, astronomer, and physicist. Studied and made fundamental discoveries about gravitation and laws of motion. One of the major proponents of the basic truths of the theory of COPERNICUS and thus (with KEPLER, BRAHE, CARDAN, and others) one of the developers of the NEW PHILOSOPHY, as opposed to the older cosmology of PTOLEMY.

Galileo developed the first telescope that could be used for astronomical observation. In 1609 and 1610 he announced some discoveries and published *Sidereus Nuncius* (1610). He noted that the surface of the moon is irregular, that the Milky Way is a galaxy of distant stars, that the planet Jupiter has satellites, that there are spots on the sun, and that the planet Venus has certain phases. In 1613 Galileo asserted that Copernicus was right and Ptolemy wrong. Opposition to him from universities and the Roman Catholic Church began to develop from the fact that his arguments appeared to contradict the Bible. In 1616 the Church declared Copernicanism "false and erroneous." Galileo and others were told that the Copernican theory could only be debated noncommittally as a mathematical supposition. For many years Galileo studied and wrote a book published eventually in 1632 as a "Dialogue." Individuals and groups of the Church, notably the Jesuits, convinced the Pope that the work was not in fact an objective appraisal of the Ptolemaic and Copernican theories, but a dangerous, destructive argument for Copernicanism. The Church developed a case to prosecute Galileo for "suspicion of heresy," and he was tried. He was found guilty of holding and teaching the Copernican theory and was ordered to recant. He did so, and the Pope ordered house arrest (rather than imprisonment) for him. He made further discoveries with the telescope until he became blind a few years before his death, and he continued his studies of the laws of motion until his death.

Gam(e)ster. *Noun*: gambler.

Gerson, Jean Charlier de (1363–1429). Mystic, reformer, Chancellor of the University of Paris, and reputed to be the author of *Imitation of Christ*.

Get. *Verb*: (1) to obtain or receive or acquire or earn; (2) to capture or win; (3) to beget, propagate.

Giddy. *Adjective*: (1) dizzy; (2) whirling rapidly; (3) easily excited, frivolous, inconstant.

Glass. *Noun*: (1) substance made by fusing sand and used for windows, vessels, containers; (2) a mirror; (3) hourglass.

Glide. *Verb*: Herbert's use in "THE FLOWER" is in the sense of slipping away imperceptibly—i.e., to pass away, to die, gently and imperceptibly, making the transition smoothly from this world to the next.

Go. *Verb*: (1) to move or travel; (2) to walk; (3) to be in a certain condition habitually; (4) to pass or happen; (5) to issue or result; (6) to depart, move away, leave; (7) to turn [to] or be transformed [into]; (8) to die.

Good Friday. The Friday before Easter, a day recalling the Crucifixion or PASSION of Christ.

Gordian. *Adjective*: referring to Gordius, King of Phrygia, who tied the yoke of a wagon to a pole with an intricate, complex knot. An oracle declared that the person who could untie the knot would rule all of Asia. No one could do so, but Alexander the Great, after failing to untie it, simply cut through it with his sword. The most common use of the adjective is in the phrase "Gordian knot," implying any complex problem. Herbert uses "Gordian knots" with heavy irony in "DIVINITY."

Gorse, John. MAGDALEN HERBERT's steward. His detailed accounts of her CHARING CROSS household afford us valuable information on guests, expenses, foods, entertainments, family members, and activities during this stage of George Herbert's life. (See "Mrs. Herbert's *Kitchin Booke*" by Amy M. Charles in "Selected Bibliography: Life.")

Goshen. Land in Egypt where the Israelites lived and where there was light in the dwellings during the plague of darkness brought over Egypt by Moses. See Exodus 8–10.

Greedy. *Adjective*: (1) excessively longing for food or drink, (2) excessively longing for wealth or material possessions, (3) excessively longing or desiring in general.

Grudge. *Verb*: (1) to complain, to grumble; (2) to be unwilling to give or allow, to begrudge; (3) to envy; (4) to trouble mentally.

H

Halt. *Verb*: to limp.

Hectique (hectic). *Adjective*: consumptive (i.e., as in pulmonary consumption, tuberculosis).

Herbert, Edward (1582 or 1583–1648). First child of RICHARD HERBERT and MAGDALEN HERBERT. Brother of GEORGE HERBERT. Married at EYTON in 1598 at the age of fifteen. Attended University College, Oxford. Knighted in 1603. Created 1st Baron of Cherbury in 1629 after having served as English ambassador at the French court from 1619 to 1624. Soldier, diplomat, poet, and philosopher. Wrote *De Veritate*, a philosophical work with rationalistic assumptions and usually seen as a precursor of deism in the next century. Regarded as one of the minor METAPHYSICAL poets, he is quite influenced by JOHN DONNE in the secular vein, especially in his intellectual complexity, compactness in style and language, and anti-Petrarchan love themes. He also wrote an autobiography (printed in 1770 as *The Life of Edward Lord Herbert of Cherbury Written by Himself*) in which he describes his brother George as an excellent scholar with perfections in "the Greek and Latin tongue, and all divine and human literature." He also refers to his brother's "most holy and exemplary life," with a reputation of being "little less than sainted," although he "was not exempt from passion and choler, being infirmities to which all our race is subject, but that excepted, without reproach in his actions" (pp. 12–13). In 1644 Lord Herbert surrendered his castle at MONTGOMERY to the Parliamentary/Puritan forces in order to save his library, a fact that caused the Royalists to loathe him as "treacherous."

Herbert, George (1593–1633). Poet, prose writer, and clergyman. See the section "Herbert's Life" early in this volume, as well as especially the entries for RICHARD HERBERT, MAGDALEN HERBERT, EDWARD HERBERT, HENRY HERBERT, and METAPHYSICAL.

Herbert, Henry (1595–1673). One of the younger brothers of GEORGE HERBERT. Son of MAGDALEN HERBERT and distant cousin to WILLIAM HERBERT and PHILIP HERBERT. He and George shared an interest in proverbs, such as those in *OUTLANDISH*

PROVERBS. In 1622 Henry Herbert leased the office of Master of Revels, giving him the authority to license productions and publications of plays. His income came from fees paid to the Master of Revels. He was knighted in 1623, thus becoming Sir Henry Herbert. He married a widow in 1625 and, through her dowry, acquired money and property. George Herbert probably stayed with his brother and family in one of their homes (Woodford) during a large part of 1626.

Herbert, Magdalen Newport (?–1627). Mother of GEORGE HERBERT. Married RICHARD HERBERT in 1581 and bore ten children by him. After his death in 1596, she lived with her children at EYTON, and then she moved to Oxford in 1599. In 1601 she again moved her household, this time to CHARING CROSS in London. During this period she was one of the patronesses of JOHN DONNE. Mrs. Herbert remarried in 1609, to Sir JOHN DANVERS, a man many years younger. In 1610 George Herbert wrote two sonnets to his mother: in them he vows that his poetic abilities will be consecrated to God, rather than to Venus. The household spent much time, especially in summers, in Sir John's beautiful home and gardens in CHELSEA. Donne spent several months in the latter part of 1625 in this home while there was an epidemic of plague in London. In June, 1627, Lady Danvers died, and Donne delivered a commemorative sermon for her on July 1 that was printed shortly after. George Herbert honored his mother after her death with his *Memoriae Matris Sacrum.*

Herbert, Philip, 4th Earl of Pembroke (1584–1650). Kinsman (distant cousin) of George Herbert. Son of MARY SIDNEY, Countess of Pembroke, and nephew of Sir PHILIP SIDNEY. Younger brother of WILLIAM HERBERT. Was Earl of Montgomery and a Knight of the Garter before succeeding to the Pembroke title in 1630 at the death of his older brother. The actor-editors of Shakespeare's *First Folio* dedicated it to Philip Herbert and his brother. Lived at WILTON HOUSE when George Herbert was installed and inducted as rector of BEMERTON. Married LADY ANNE CLIFFORD on June 1, 1630, a kind, cultured, and intelligent lady who maintained friendships of mutual respect with both DONNE and George Herbert.

Herbert, Richard (?–1596). Father of GEORGE HERBERT, EDWARD HERBERT, HENRY HERBERT, and seven other children. Prominent in MONTGOMERY, Wales, serving as sheriff, magistrate, and in Parliament. Married Magdalen Newport (see MAGDALEN HERBERT) in 1581. Died when George Herbert was three and one half years old.

Herbert, William, 3rd Earl of Pembroke (1580–1630). Kinsman (distant cousin) of GEORGE HERBERT. Son of MARY SIDNEY, Countess of Pembroke, and nephew of Sir PHILIP SIDNEY. Courtier during the latter part of the reign of Elizabeth I, through the reign of JAMES I, and in the early years of CHARLES I. Served as a privy councillor and as Lord Chamberlain under James I. Was Chancellor of Oxford, where Pembroke College was named for him in 1624. Was a patron of the arts (notably a patron of BEN JONSON). The actor-editors of Shakespeare's *First Folio* dedicated it to William Herbert and his younger brother PHILIP HERBERT. He is one of the possibilities for the identity of the young man of Shakespeare's *Sonnets*, but the "evidence" remains speculative and tenuous.

He lived at WILTON HOUSE at the time George Herbert was nominated for the position as rector of BEMERTON and indeed probably recommended him to King Charles I. William Herbert died shortly after, however, and George Herbert was installed and inducted after Philip Herbert succeeded as Earl of Pembroke.

George Herbert's "A Parody" specifically parodies a "Song" attributed to William Herbert that begins "Soul's joy, now I am gone."

Herbert's Remains. A book published in 1652 containing *THE COUNTRY PARSON* (or *A Priest to the Temple*), *OUTLANDISH PROVERBS* (or *Jacula Prudentum*), and some short minor pieces. The person who printed the volume and wrote a preface for it was BARNABAS OLEY. In 1671 Oley published a second edition of *The Country Parson* alone, with a new preface.

Hercules, Pillars of. See PILLARS OF HERCULES.

Hermogenes (2nd Century A.D.). Rhetorician who designated seven characteristics of good oratory and was influential in Herbert's time.

Heterogeneous ideas are yoked by violence together. See METAPHYSICAL CONCEIT.

Hierarchy, the heavenly. The supposed nine ranks or levels or orders of angels, especially as proposed by Dionysius the Areopagite, a Christian Platonist (more strictly, Neoplatonist) in the 5th century. His work *On the Heavenly Hierarchy* designated the highest division to be composed of Seraphs, Cherubs, and Thrones. The second division contains Dominations, Virtues, and Powers. The third has Principalities, Archangels, and Angels. The highest are the most contemplative, and the lowest are the most active. Those in the third division, in fact, mediate between man and the realm of God and the angels by delivering messages to man and carrying out God's bidding. The nine orders are also analogous to the nine SPHERES, and, in fact, these orders were believed to be the INTELLIGENCES that were assigned to the spheres, enabling the creation of the music of the spheres. Most of the angels that fell with Lucifer were of the Seraphs (Seraphim).

His. In many contexts, possessive pronoun for "its."

Honest. *Adjective*:   (1) honorable, respectable; (2) truthful, fair; (3) chaste, pure.

Humor (humour). *Noun*: (1) any fluid or juice of an animal or plant; (2) one of the four major fluids of the body, according to ancient and medieval physiology (primarily from GALEN): blood, phlegm, choler (red choler), and melancholy (black choler). The predominance of one humor over the others or the proportions in which the humors were mixed in the body were believed to determine a person's COMPLEXION—i.e., physical appearance, personality, and disposition (e.g., a dominance of choler causes anger). The healthy, well-balanced individual supposedly has all humors mixed equally. The four humors correspond to the four ELEMENTS (choler determines a choleric complexion and corresponds to fire with its hot and dry qualities; blood determines a sanguine complexion and corresponds to air with its hot and moist qualities; phlegm determines a phlegmatic complexion and corresponds to water with its cold and moist qualities; melancholy determines a melancholic complexion and corresponds to earth with its cold and dry qualities). To correct imbalance, one would take food or substances of the opposite qualities or decrease the one in excess; (3) the temperament or disposition exemplified by a person as a result of the proportion of the fluid humors within the body; (4) the particular style, tone, or spirit of a piece of writing or other artistic composition; (5) temporary mood or whim; (6) a disposition toward a certain action; (7) odd or quaint trait. (The common modern sense of the word as the quality of being, or the ability to be, comical or amusing or funny, or to perceive such comedy, does *not* occur in Herbert's writing.)

Hundred and Ten Considerations. See VALDÉS, JUAN.

Husbandry (husbandrie). *Noun*: (1) agriculture; (2) cultivation of crops; (3) economy, thriftiness, careful management of resources.

I

Immure. *Verb*: to confine or enclose.

Imp. *Verb*: in falconry, to put feathers from one bird into the damaged wing of another bird in order to mend it.

Impale. *Verb*: (1) to enclose with pales or posts, to fence in; (2) to thrust a pale or stake through.

Indear(e), endear(e). *Verb*: (1) to represent as valuable, lay stress upon, exaggerate [see "H. Scriptures (1)," line 10]; (2) to bind by obligations of gratitude [see *THE CHURCH MILITANT*, line 12].

Indifferent. *Adjective*: (1) impartial or unbiased; (2) unconcerned or apathetic; (3) of neutral quality, neither good nor bad; (4) unimportant or immaterial; (5) nonessential. Also see INDIFFERENT THINGS.

Indifferent things. A phrase originating in the late sixteenth century and increasingly common during the seventeenth century to refer to such matters of worship as various ceremonies, clerical vestments, discipline, order, and trappings that are not essential to salvation. Some writers prefer the phrase "things indifferent," and some use both phrases. The PURITANs, especially, wished to rid the English church of what they saw as unnecessary Roman Catholic elements.

Innocent. *Adjective*: (1) harmless, doing no harm; (2) free from moral wrong, sin, or guilt; (3) simple, unsuspecting, without guile, naive.

Instantly. *Adverb*: (1) persistently; (2) now, at this very moment; (3) immediately, at once.

Intellectual Soul. See TRIPARTITE SOUL.

Intelligence. *Noun*: an angel assigned to move one of the SPHERES, according to the PTOLEMAIC concept of the universe. See also HIERARCHY, THE HEAVENLY.

Invention. *Noun*: (1) finding out or selection of topics or arguments; (2) [in art and writing] the devising of a subject, idea, or method of treatment by use of the intellect or imagination.

Invest. *Verb*: (1) to dress or adorn; (2) to endow with attributes or qualities; (3) to install in an office or rank; (4) to endow with property, power, or authority.

J

Jacob. Son of Isaac and Rebekah who unfairly and cheaply bought the birthright of his older brother Esau and duped his blind father into giving him the patriarchal blessing that also should have been Esau's. His trick was to dress in animal skins to make Isaac think he was blessing Esau. "Jacob" means "supplanter." On a journey seeking a wife, Jacob had a dream at Bethel of a ladder extending from earth to heaven with angels ascending and descending on it. He eventually acquired Rachel as a wife by bargaining with her father Laban and then returned to Canaan. On his return trip he wrestled with an angel (Herbert's "struggle with Jacob" in "Decay") at Peniel and was renamed "Israel." Of his sons, JOSEPH was sold into slavery and then rose to high position in Egypt, where eventually Jacob was reunited with Joseph, and Jacob died in the land of GOSHEN. See Genesis 25–50.

Jacula Prudentum. See *OUTLANDISH PROVERBS.*

James I (1566–1625). King of England, 1603–1625. The son of Mary Queen of Scots of the Stuart family, he was James VI of Scotland prior to succeeding his cousin ELIZABETH I on the English throne. Well-educated and a lover of the arts, James himself wrote on religion, government, witchcraft, and demonology. He commissioned a group of English theologians and scholars to produce a new translation of the Bible that was published in 1611 as the Authorized Version, now more commonly called the "King James Bible." James argued for the divine right of kings and insisted on absolute power and abuse of privilege in some matters that increasingly alienated factions in Parliament. His dependence upon and granting of rewards and power to such favorites as Robert Ker, Earl of Somerset, and GEORGE VILLIERS, Duke of Buckingham, further alienated many of his subjects.

Herbert was Orator at Cambridge University, and he served briefly in Parliament during the latter years of King James. James died in 1625. Despite the statement by WALTON that Herbert's "court-hopes" died with King James, Herbert at this point had no wishes for a secular, governmental career. He had already determined for himself that he had only church-hopes.

Janus. Roman god with two faces looking in opposite directions. God of doorways, beginnings and endings, before and after, past and future.

Jeat. See JET.

Jeremy. The Old Testament prophet Jeremiah.

Jet, Jeat. Herbert's use of the word solely refers to black marble.

Johnson, Samuel. See METAPHYSICAL.

Jointure. *Noun*: (1) joining or union, (2) holding of an estate by two or more persons, (3) holding of property by both husband and wife, (4) estate settled upon a widow as her rights.

Jonson, Ben (1572–1637). Dramatist, actor, and poet. Jonson's turbulent life included some time as a soldier, imprisonment, and killing a man in a duel. After many years as a Roman Catholic, Jonson reverted to Anglicanism about 1610, draining the whole cup of wine at communion to signify his embracing of the state religion. Some of his best plays are *The Alchemist* and *Volpone*, satiric comedies. He published his plays, masques, and poetry in a volume of *Works* in 1616, containing his "Epigrams" (including epitaphs on some of his children and friends) and another group of poems in a section entitled "The Forest" (with the poem "To Penshurst" included). Jonson is the primary examplar of CLASSICAL ideals in Renaissance drama and poetry, both in content and style, and he influenced younger dramatists and poets (the "sons of Ben" and, later, "cavaliers") to follow his examples. King James granted Jonson a pension for life in 1616. Two years later Jonson spent some time in Scotland with WILLIAM DRUMMOND of Hawthornden, who recorded many of Jonson's comments on himself and others. In 1623 Jonson's tribute to the memory of his friend and fellow dramatist and poet William Shakespeare was published in the opening pages of the *First Folio* (Shakespeare's *Works*, his plays, collected and published seven years after his death.). Jonson suffered a paralytic stroke in 1628, with subsequent decline physically and artistically. He is buried in Westminster Abbey.

Some of Jonson's remarks made in his commonplace-book *Timber* and some of those reported by Drummond reflect the friendship and respect but also some differences in poetic principles between the CLASSICAL Jonson and the METAPHYSICAL DONNE. Jonson writes denigratingly of a "rough and broken" style, of farfetched metaphors that "hinder to be understood," and of "obscurity." It is, then, interesting that Drummond reports Jonson saying that Donne, in one poem, wanted to match Sir EDWARD HERBERT in "obscureness" and that Donne's work would not last because of not being "understood." Jonson also told Drummond that "Donne, for not keeping of accent, deserved hanging," the classicist's criticism of the metaphysical's irregular metrics. Ironically, some of the characteristics of these two become fused in such younger and later poets as GEORGE HERBERT, Thomas Carew, HENRY VAUGHAN, and ANDREW MARVELL.

"Jordan (1)." The title of both this poem and "JORDAN (2)" suggests several biblical references and possible meanings. It refers specifically to the river crossed by the Israelites upon entering the Promised Land after their wanderings in the wilderness. In Deuteronomy 27 Moses tells the people to erect a stone altar to God after they have crossed the Jordan. Elisha (in 2 Kings 5:10) tells Naaman to wash seven times in the Jordan and thus be cleansed of leprosy. In addition, Christ was baptized by John in the Jordan, so the Old Testament crossing of the Jordan is a type of New Testament baptism. Implications of turning from the old to the new, from the secular to the holy, from the worldly to the spiritual, then, are all suggested by crossing Jordan. In one sense it is baptismal cleansing, purification, and choosing spiritual salvation over old worldly values. In another sense it is the reflection of this choice in poetry—i.e., Herbert asserts his choice of the poetry of plain and simple Christian love, truth, and beauty over that of secular love and artificial truth and beauty. Related to this is the traditional contrast between the classical springs of Helicon (sacred to Apollo and the Muses) as a symbol of secular, pagan inspiration and poetry and the river Jordan as a symbol of Christian inspiration and poetry. He chooses Jordan and a baptized Muse for himself.

In the first stanza the speaker challenges the notion that only fictional matters and artificial, imagined beauty are appropriate for poetry. He asserts (by a rhetorical question) that there is beauty in truth: by implication, the truth of the Christian faith is the beauty that quite appropriately also may be embodied in poetry. The question in line 3 implies certainly that all "good structure" in poetry indeed does *not* lie in a "winding stair"—i.e., in a convoluted and artificially complex poetry that works only through the indirections and disguisings of plain truth through such means as the fictions of the pastoral convention or elaborate allegories. Lines 4 and 5 refer to the CHAIR OF GRACE, the royal chair of the sovereign. Literally, the lines of people passing by the chair must bow to it in respect for the authority of the sovereign. Metaphorically, Herbert uses "lines" for lines of poetry and "pass" for being recognized and approved as a thing of quality. So, the speaker here is raising the question of whether only that poetry is recognized as valid that uses only artificiality and fictions (bowing not to a "true" but to a "painted chair," a painting of a chair of grace).

Obviously, his implied answer to this rather humorous rhetorical question is a resounding "No." Implicit here is the assumption that earthly love, beauty, and truth are only mere reflections of heavenly or spiritual love, beauty, and truth. So, poetry of earthly matter is removed from, and ultimately inferior to, that of the heavenly. But, in addition, earthly matter couched in pastoral or allegorical trappings is removed even further from the direct and plain truth of the heavenly.

The second stanza continues the series of rhetorical questions. The "enchanted groves," "SUDDEN arbors," and "purling streams" are the stereotypes of pastoral love poetry. Obviously, the speaker ridicules the notion that these elements must be present in verse for it to be regarded as verse. In fact, he suggests that such a conventional pastoral poet may actually be attempting to hide ("SHADOW") his own poor artistry ("coarse-spun lines") under such hackneyed elements. The end of the stanza implies that certainly not all poetry must be so "veiled," so obscured by layers of fictions and pastoral and allegorical trappings that the reader must penetrate through to the truth by indirections and interpretations.

In the third stanza he gives the "shepherds" their due: these "shepherds" are the writers of such pastoral verse, and he grants their right to compose as they honestly see fit and valuable in their own secular poetry. But, at the same time, he wants his own right and freedom to compose plainly the kind of Christian truth that he sees also as most appropriate for poetry. The pastoral poets may "sing" their shepherds' songs, and the allegorists may continue to "riddle," to mask their matter in literary puzzles, as they "LIST," as they desire. As far as he is concerned, they may continue to "PULL FOR PRIME"—i.e., to achieve success in their own way. He feels no envy or resentment at their continually using the traditional, overworked "nightingale" and "spring" in such pastoral poetry. But he expects from such worldly poets his own freedom to write "rhyme" that relies on plainness and directness to express the love, truth, and beauty of his own "God" and "King." And he will simply "say" his lines, as opposed to the "shepherds" who "sing."

"Jordan (2)." For the implications of the title, see "JORDAN (1)." The speaker reflects upon his early writing of Christian poems, and, as he reflects, both he and the reader are aware of his pride in composing them. He notes their "luster," their shining brilliance (as he sees them), and he feels that they did so "excel." He sought "QUAINT" words— i.e., elaborate, ingenious ones. He also wanted impressive "INVENTION," the devising of subject matter for his artistic creations. His thoughts began to spread out ("burnish"), "sprout," and "swell" like plants, flowers. He beautified his "plain intention" by "curling" it with "metaphors," just as a hairdresser beautifies simple, natural hair. A sense of the artificiality and deceptiveness of it all is implied by the admission that he was "decking the sense" as if to "sell" it. In line 3 of this first stanza Herbert echoes lines 5–6 of the first sonnet of SIDNEY's *Astrophil and Stella*: "I sought fit words to paint the blackest face of woe, / Studying inventions fine, her wits to entertain." Both Sidney's and Herbert's speakers are proud, self-concerned, and artificial in their artistic endeavors to express love in poetry, secular love in Sidney's case and heavenly love in Herbert's.

Stanza 2 continues his frantic efforts to put on paper all of the "notions" presenting themselves in order to try to assure his poetic success, if one attempt was not successful ("not sped"). He revised his work by continually obliterating what he wrote ("blotted") and trying a better word or phrase, etc. He would blot out anything in his writing not lively ("quick") enough or that was "dead." He always tried for more "rich" language to describe the "sun," with a play on Christ the "Son." To describe the heavenly joys above the "sun" and "Son" with all the impressive language he could muster was the speaker's goal.

The third stanza makes obvious the speaker's present realization of his early poetic failure and its cause: he did "weave my self into the sense," committing pride and self-concern that stained work, supposedly pure and dedicated to God, with selfish interests and motives. His Adamic nature, with its tendency to temptation and fall through pride, subtly was bringing about his fall in Christian poetry. His rescue, however, again comes from Christ (who rescued humanity from Adam's fall) as Christ, the "friend" (see John 15:12–15 where Christ speaks of himself and humans as friends), whispers to the speaker the statements in the last three lines of the poem. (Herbert refers to Christ as "friend" in several poems.) Christ tells him that all of this "pretense," this pretentious and artificial writing is "wide" of the mark, completely off the target. In true "love," God's heavenly love, the simple sweetness is plainly already inherent and need only be copied out, with no need to expend energy and time trying to embellish it with human artificiality and pride in language. Again here Sidney's first sonnet of *Astrophil and Stella* is quite relevant and obviously alluded to by Herbert. The last line of Sidney's poem is as follows: "'Fool,' said my Muse to me, 'look in thy heart and write.'" So, just as Astrophil must simply look into his own heart and emotions to express his love for Stella in the simplest and most convincing terms, so must Herbert's speaker look into his heart for his love for God that only needs to be straightforwardly expressed.

Joseph. (1) In the Old Testament, son of Rachel and JACOB. He was loved by Jacob as his favorite child, and Jacob made Joseph a coat of many colors. Joseph's brothers hated him, and, when he came to them one day, they stripped him of his coat and sold him for twenty pieces of silver to the Ishmeelites to be taken as a slave to Egypt. The brothers then took Joseph's coat and dipped it in the blood of a kid goat they had killed. They took the coat to Jacob, who recognized it as Joseph's and assumed that he had been devoured by a wild animal. Jacob mourned a long time for Joseph. Joseph was sold in Egypt to Potiphar, one of the Pharaoh's officers. Joseph was adept at interpreting dreams and was called on to interpret some that the Pharaoh had. Joseph said that the dreams predicted seven years of plenty followed by seven years of famine in Egypt. He advised the Pharaoh to store grain during the bountiful years to use during the lean years. Joseph was appointed to oversee all of Egypt on behalf of Pharaoh. The years of plenty and famine did occur as Joseph had foreseen. Eventually Joseph was reconciled with his brothers and reunited with his father.   See Genesis 37–50. (2) In the New Testament, husband of MARY (Christ's mother). See accounts early in Matthew and Luke. (3) In the New Testament, Joseph of Arimathea, a wealthy man, secretly a follower of Christ, who took the body of Jesus after the crucifixion and placed it in his own new tomb. See Matthew 27:57–60 and John 19:38–42.

Julip (julep). A medical syrup used to lower fever.

K

Kepler, Johannes (1571–1630). German astronomer. Studied and extended the ideas of COPERNICUS. Corresponded with GALILEO and BRAHE, joining the latter in Prague for the last year of Brahe's life. Developed many of Brahe's observations more fully. Kepler argued that the planets revolve around the sun in elliptical orbits (thus contradicting the perfect, circular universe hitherto envisioned). Studied the planets, their moons, and comets with a telescope. Discovered some "new stars" in the heavens and published works significantly discrediting the older cosmology of PTOLEMY and developing the NEW PHILOSOPHY.

Knell. See DEATH BELL.

Know. *Verb*: (1) to recognize or distinguish; (2) to perceive; (3) to be acquainted with; (4) to have carnal experience with, be sexually intimate with, have sexual intercourse with.

L

Last Day. The Last Judgment, Judgment Day.

Late. *Adjective*: (1) occurring after the due or customary time, delayed or deferred in time; (2) recent in date, of recent times.

Lately. *Adverb*: (1) after or beyond the usual or proper time; (2) not long since, within recent times, recently.

Laud, William (1573–1645). Made Dean of Gloucester Cathedral in 1616 by King JAMES. After the accession of CHARLES, Laud held the following positions (among others): Bishop of Bath and Wells (1626), Privy Councillor (1627), Bishop of London (1628), Chancellor of the University of Oxford (1629), and Archbishop of Canterbury (1633). Laud enforced strict uniformity, orthodoxy, tradition, and royal authority in matters of the Church of England, criticizing and punishing deviations that favored PURITANISM and CALVINISM, particularly alienating some factions in the House of Commons rapidly gaining strength before and during the English Civil War. Laud was impeached in 1640 and executed by beheading in 1645.

   Laud ordained NICHOLAS FERRAR in 1626.

Leave. *Verb*: (1) to cease, stop, abandon, forsake an action, habit, or practice; (2) to depart from a place or person; (3) to cause or allow to remain; (4) to bequeath or transmit to heirs at death.

Leighton Bromswold. Location of the church of which Herbert was installed as prebendary in 1626. He found that this church had been deemed unfit for worship for twenty years and began plans and attempts to raise funds for its restoration. He contributed money himself for the work. Major restoration began in 1632 and was completed after Herbert's death through the efforts of ARTHUR WOODNOTH, HENRY HERBERT, and JOHN FERRAR. This is the church referred to by NICHOLAS FERRAR in his anonymous preface to *THE TEMPLE*: Ferrar says that God ordained Herbert as the "instrument for reedifying" of this church that had lain "ruinated almost twenty years."

Let. *Noun*: hindrance or obstruction. *Verb*: (1) to hinder or obstruct, (2) to permit or allow, (3) to cause.

Lethargickness, lethargy. *Noun*: (1) condition or state in which a person sleeps in a prolonged and unnatural way because of illness or physical deterioration, such as in a coma before death; (2) a condition of apathy or torpor.

Liberal(l). *Adjective*: (1) giving, bountiful, generous; (2) abundant, ample; (3) free from restraint.

Lie. *Verb*: (1) to recline for rest or sleep, (2) to be positioned on a bier or in a coffin or in a grave at death, (3) to be or remain in a condition of captivity or illness or misery, (4) to be in an unmoving position or at anchor, (5) to await in order to entrap, (6) to dwell or lodge temporarily, (7) to remain unworked, unused, or untouched, (8) to tell a falsehood.

Lincoln Cathedral. Cathedral of which Herbert was installed as canon by proxy on July 5, 1626. Herbert was nonresidentiary and agreed to either preach a sermon there on Pentecost each year or pay a deputy to do so.

Lion, the. See AMIENS.

List. *Verb*: (1) to desire or like, (2) to listen.

Little Gidding. See FERRAR, NICHOLAS.

Livery. *Noun*: a distinctive suit of clothes bestowed by a person upon his or her retainers or servants, thus serving as a means by which they may be recognized.

Llandinam. Village in MONTGOMERY. Herbert was granted a portion of the rectory here by Bishop JOHN WILLIAMS, thus giving Herbert some income shortly after he was ordained as deacon.

Lot. In the Bible, nephew of Abraham who was in Sodom when God sent two angels there appearing as men: God had told Abraham that He would not destroy the city if ten righteous men could be found there. Lot greeted the angels as they approached and invited them to stay as guests in his house. That night some men of the city came to Lot's house and told him to bring out his two guests so that they might "KNOW" them sexually. Lot refused, and the men threatened to break down his door. The two angels pulled Lot back into the house and blinded the men. The angels told Lot to gather his family and leave the city, for they planned to destroy it. The angels warned Lot and his family to flee to the mountain from this city in the plain and not to look back. God rained brimstone and fire upon both Sodom and Gomorrah, the cities of the plain, destroying them and their inhabitants. Lot's wife looked back as they were fleeing and was turned into a pillar of salt. Lot and his two daughters dwelled in a cave in the mountains. The two daughters decided that, since there were no other men that they could have sexual intercourse with and be impregnated by, they would have Lot drink wine and then lie with him in his drunken state. They both did so and became pregnant. The older daughter bore a son named Moab, and the younger had a son named Benammi (or Ammon). See Genesis 18 and 19.

"Love (3)." This is the last poem in *THE CHURCH* and follows "DEATH," "Doomsday," "Judgement," and "Heaven." This sequence echoes the following traditional "four last things" in the Christian world view: death, judgement, hell, and heaven. However, the true Christian's journey through the "church" (in its multiple senses) takes him not to hell, but through judgement to heaven and ultimately to the "Love" which is manifested in and indeed is God himself. Thus, the order of the sequence ending *The Church* is climactic and integral to Herbert's meaning, since it describes the reception of the soul into heaven.

In allegorical form the poem depicts Love and the soul as characters. The METAPHYSICAL CONCEIT is in the details of a social analogy, a social relationship that seems on the surface quite mundane and common, but which finally symbolizes the ultimate spiritual relationship between God and the soul. Love is the host, and the soul is the guest in this conceit.

Stanza 1 pictures the soul pulling away from Love's welcome: the soul feels "guilty," ashamed, unworthy. The soul feels guilty because of "dust and sin": on the literal level the "dust" would compare to the dust on the body and clothes of a traveller who comes inside from a journey on a dusty road, but symbolically the soul feels soiled by the dust of the journey through earthly life, death, and the grave as it arrives in heaven. In a sense, of course, the "dust" is "sin." But Love is the perfect host, perceptive of the nature of the guest and gracious in making the guest feel at ease. Love sees that the guest is "slack" (hesitant) as he enters and approaches the guest to ask if there is anything he needs to be made comfortable.

The soul's answer (in stanza 2) to Love's sweet question is that the soul lacks a guest worthy to be here: the soul does not feel that it is a worthy guest. But Love's reassuring answer is that the soul is indeed that worthy guest. But the soul still feels unworthy, recalling his own ingratitude and lack of love during his earthly journey. The soul's "Ah, my dear" continues the social situation, with social language. The soul feels unworthy even to "look" on Love. But the gracious host takes the hand of the guest and reassuringly smiles (again, the perfect host). Love's reply "Who made the eyes but I?" identifies Love with God the Creator: since Love (God) created the eyes, the soul can look on God.

Stanza 3 further makes explicit the identification of Love with God when the soul addresses the host as "Lord." But the soul persists in its sense of unworthiness, since he feels that he has "marred" those eyes that Love made—i.e., "marred" them with sinful uses. The soul's shame still is so great that he feels that he deserves damnation (feeling he "deserves" hell). But Love is still more insistent and persistent than the soul, reminding the soul that all sin has already been wiped away by the reminder that Love (God) "bore the blame": this identifies Love as not only God the Father (the Creator), but also as the Son, Christ, whose crucifixion was the ultimate expression of and granting of Love freely to the soul. The soul acquiesces only to the point that he "will serve." "My dear" continues the cultivated social tone for this spiritual relationship. But Love again insists that the soul be served and receive fully the Love of God. Finally the soul agrees to "sit and eat." The idea of Love as the host seems an implied pun on the common use of "host" as the consecrated bread of Holy Communion, exemplifying Christ's body. "Taste my meat" and "sit and eat" strongly echo the implications of Holy Communion, since the communicant partakes of the body and blood of Christ and thus tastes Christ's body as love expressed in his sacrifice for all. But earthly communion only foreshadows the final communion in heaven. Joseph H. Summers in *George Herbert: His Religion and Art* notes that the end of this climactic poem alludes to Luke 12:37 ("Blessed are those servants, whom the lord when he cometh shall find watching: verily I say unto you, that he shall gird himself, and make them to sit down to meat, and will come forth to serve them"). It is the Love of God that enables the soul to attain heaven, and the fullness of this love is exemplified by the final communion in heaven served by Christ.

Luther, Martin (1483–1546). Initiated the Protestant Reformation in his native Germany, leading to its later spread throughout Europe. Was an Augustinian monk in the Roman Catholic Church. Wanted to raise questions for debate on papal indulgences by nailing his *Theses* on a church door at Wittenberg in 1517. Eventually he was excommunicated, but he refused to recant. He left his monastic order, married, translated the Bible into German, and published the Augsburg Confession that called for a separate church. Luther's writings and arguments emphasize the doctrine of "justification" (salvation) by faith alone for the individual, lessening the importance of salvation through works, sacraments, priests, indulgences, and other means emphasized in the Roman Catholic Church. To an Augustinian monk like Luther, the writings of ST. AUGUSTINE were crucial in their emphasis on the importance of faith to salvation. Luther also disagreed with the Roman Catholic Church's insistence that there are seven true sacraments: Luther instead emphasized the two that are directly sanctioned by Christ, Holy Baptism and Holy Communion. (Compare and contrast the doctrines of CALVIN and Calvinism.)

M

Macarius. Christian hermit in Egypt in the 4th century.

Macrocosm. The "great world" or "large world," as opposed to the "little world" or MICROCOSM. In most contexts the concept refers to the universe, but in others it may refer to the earth or to any large whole or large world in itself (e.g., society or humanity). See MICROCOSM.

Magdalene. See MARY MAGDALENE.

Manna. *Noun*: (1) the miraculous food given by God to the Israelites in the wilderness, according to Exodus 16; (2) spiritual nourishment.

Mansuetude. *Noun*: gentleness.

Marvell, Andrew (1621–1678). One of the major METAPHYSICAL poets. Born in Yorkshire and educated at Cambridge. From 1650 to 1652 he served as tutor to Mary Fairfax, daughter of Lord Fairfax, a general for the parliamentary side in the English Civil War. During this time Marvell probably wrote "The Garden" and other major lyric poems. Was appointed Latin secretary to the Council of State. Later he was elected a Member of Parliament from Hull and served as such until his death. Marvell's influence early in the reign of Charles II secured John Milton's release from prison and probably saved him from execution.
    Marvell's use of the METAPHYSICAL CONCEIT, his love of paradox, his sometimes shocking images, and his wordplay qualify him as a metaphysical poet very much under the influence of DONNE and Herbert; however, one must note that the CLASSICAL strain and influences from JONSON are also strongly present in much of Marvell's poetry. The combination of influences can be seen in such a poem as his famous "To His Coy Mistress." Herbert and Marvell are similar to the extent that they both very much fuse the metaphysical and classical styles.

Mary. Mother of Jesus (Christ) and wife to Joseph. Virgin Mary.

Mary (Marie) Magdalene. A follower of Christ who was healed of demons by Christ (Luke 8:2), is commonly regarded as the repentant sinner or harlot who wept and washed Jesus's feet (Luke 7:37), and was once traditionally identified with Mary of Bethina (Bethany) who was the sister of Martha and Lazarus (Luke 10 and John 11, 12). She was later canonized as a saint.

Mean. *Adjective*: (1) of low degree, rank, or station; (2) inferior, poor in quality; (3) shabby. *Noun*: a condition, quality, disposition, or course of action that is equally removed from two extremes—i.e., a medium or that which is intermediate. *Verb*: (1) to have in mind as a purpose or intention, to purpose or to design; (2) to aim at, to direct one's way to; (3) to signify.

Measure. *Noun*: (1) size or quantity determined by measuring, (2) an estimate or opinion, (3) that by which anything is computed or estimated, (4) an extent or limit not to be exceeded, (5) proportion or symmetry, (6) moderation, (7) meter in poetry or music. *Verb*: (1) to determine the size or quantity of something, (2) to judge the value of something or someone, (3) to appraise by comparison with something else.

Meat. *Noun*: (1) food in general or nourishment or solid food; (2) the edible part of fruits or nuts, the pulp or kernel distinguished from the peel or shell; (3) the flesh of animals as food.

Meet. *Verb*: (1) to find, (2) to come face to face with, (3) to encounter or oppose in battle, (4) to unite or combine, (5) to agree, (6) to experience or undergo. *Adjective*: appropriate, fitting, suitable.

Memento mori. Latin phrase literally translated as "remember that you must die." In Herbert's time the phrase was used as a command to warn against death and was also used as an adjective. But most commonly the phrase was used as a *noun*: (1) a warning or reminder of death; (2) a "death's head," especially in the form of a skull or some representation of a skull, such as in a ring to be worn. See, for example, line 29 of "THE COLLAR."

Metaphysical. As used in this "Dictionary," "metaphysical" refers to the particular style and content of the poetry of JOHN DONNE and of those poets influenced by and/or similar to him in the 17th century. "Metaphysical" was first applied to the poetry of Donne by John Dryden quite late in the century, after all such poetry had been written: he said (in *A Discourse Concerning the Original and Progress of Satire*, 1693) that Donne "affects the metaphysics, not only in his satires, but in his amorous verses, where nature only should reign; and perplexes the minds of the fair sex with nice speculations of philosophy, when he should engage their hearts, and entertain them with the softnesses of love." He thus ridicules Donne and takes him to task for supposedly dwelling on philosophical speculations about the nature of reality and for pretentiously intellectualizing love, when he should be only emotional and romantic. Dryden, in his *MacFlecknoe* (1682), seems particularly to ridicule Herbert when he belittles "wild Anagram" and "Acrostick Land" and says, "There thou mayst Wings display, and Alters raise, / And torture one poor Word ten thousand ways." The denigration is apparently of Herbert's "Anagram of the Virgin Mary," "THE ALTAR," and "EASTER WINGS." Apparently taking his cue from Dryden, Dr. Samuel Johnson in the 18th century first called Donne and his followers in poetry the "metaphysical poets." Johnson's comments appear in his life of "Cowley" in his series *The Lives of the Poets* (1779). He describes with great hostility many of the characteristics of such poetry. The irony is that he very well describes the style and techniques of metaphysical poetry, but only to denigrate what many in the 17th and 20th centuries praise quite highly! What Johnson considers "bad," many consider "good" in Donne and his followers.

Johnson's label for Donne and his followers has been retained to the present time, and his comments serve as a way to define much of what metaphysical poetry and the metaphysical style indeed are. Johnson says that the metaphysical poets wrote verses with the "modulation . . . so imperfect that they were only to be found to be verses by counting the syllables." This does point to the use of irregular, distorted metrical patterns in some lines and poems, but in good metaphysical poetry such variation functions to convey specific feelings and meanings and thus is not in itself a flaw in poetry but can indeed be a virtue. Donne's contemporary, BEN JONSON, holding much earlier some of the same CLASSICAL assumptions as the later Dr. Johnson, comments to DRUMMOND that "Donne, for not keeping of accent, deserved hanging," thus also disagreeing with such irregular metrics. Similarly Ben Jonson says that "Donne himself, for not being understood, would perish," and Dr. Johnson complains of the metaphysical poets only wanting to "show their learning": it is a demanding, complex, intellectual poetry that is said to be obscure in thought and syntax at times, but it can be quite rewarding, despite the contrary view of its detractors. Ben Jonson also says (in his commonplace book titled *Timber*) that "metaphors far-fet hinder to be understood," and this perhaps anticipates Dr. Johnson's remark that these poets' "conceits were far-fetched": thus, another characteristic of metaphysical poetry is the use of the METAPHYSICAL CONCEIT (see the entry on it for fuller definition and for further comments by Dr.

Johnson about it). Dr. Johnson also notes the use of "hyperbole": exaggeration indeed is a characteristic of the works of Donne and his followers. Another characteristic of much metaphysical poetry is implied by a comment of one of Donne's admirers in the 17th century: Thomas Carew notes that Donne exiled the "goodly train of gods and goddesses" from noble poetry—i.e., Donne's work, as well as that of some of his followers, including Herbert, does not rely as much on classical allusions, themes, and forms as earlier Elizabethan and CLASSICAL poems do. T.S. Eliot, an admirer of metaphysical poetry in the 20th century, points out its unified "sensibility," the ability to fuse thought and feeling perfectly (see DISSOCIATION OF SENSIBILITY).

Although oversimplified, a working definition of "metaphysical" might be completed by the following characteristics (added to those six characteristics designated above as being extracted from the comments of Jonson, Johnson, Carew, and Eliot): (1) construction of many poems frequently irregular in style and structure—use of irregular divisions, stanzas, and lines; (2) use of the rhythms and pauses of natural speech; (3) use of informal, colloquial, everyday word choice and tone; (4) conveying a sense of unrestrained emotion in many lines and poems; (5) presentation of the poet and/or speaker primarily in a private, personal role writing to or speaking to a select, limited audience or hearer(s); (6) writing many poems in a deliberately anti-PETRARCHAN, anti-PLATONIC, anti-SPENSERian vein; (7) use of much paradox, other forms of irony, and wordplay; (8) reliance on argumentative form and content in many poems. (One should compare and contrast these characteristics with those designated as CLASSICAL.)

The "metaphysical poets" embrace a large number of poets, both secular and religious, in the 17th century. Scholars and critics have achieved no absolute agreement about the specific number, particular individuals, and even which are major and which are minor poets. Certainly four major ones are JOHN DONNE, George Herbert, ANDREW MARVELL, and HENRY VAUGHAN. Others that might be included as sharing "metaphysical" characteristics, however, are Thomas Carew, Henry King, Richard Crashaw, Thomas Traherne, Abraham Cowley, and perhaps other minor writers. In such a classification, however, one should be alert to how much *both* Donne (the "metaphysical") and Jonson (the "classical") influenced Herbert and other younger and later poets after Donne and Jonson: many combine "metaphysical" and "classical" characteristics in their poems.

Metaphysical   conceit.   One of the characteristics of METAPHYSICAL poetry is the frequent use of the metaphysical conceit, a lengthy, far-fetched, ingenious analogy developed in detail and relating unexpected or remote areas of experience or knowledge.

Such a conceit many times is developed over several lines or over several stanzas or even through an entire poem. In a famous essay (actually in his comments on Abraham Cowley in *The Lives of the Poets*) Samuel Johnson, in the 18th century, refers with hostility to the metaphysical poets using a "combination of dissimilar images" and of their "discovery of occult resemblances in things apparently unlike." He also says that in their poetry "the most heterogeneous ideas are yoked by violence together," that they wasted their intelligence on "false conceits," and that their "conceits were far-fetched." All of these remarks describe the metaphysical conceit; however, in the 17th and 20th centuries many poets and critics admire JOHN DONNE, George Herbert, and other followers of Donne for their employment of such conceits, valuing precisely what Dr. Johnson denigrates (see, for example, DISSOCIATION OF SENSIBILITY for some of T.S. Eliot's praises).

The most famous metaphysical conceit is the "compass" conceit in "A Valediction: Forbidding Mourning" by Donne. Herbert's poetry is so filled with metaphysical conceits that they can best be seen as specified and discussed in the individual entries on poems in this "Dictionary." However, a few excellent examples appear in "THE PULLEY," "THE WINDOWS," "VIRTUE," and "CHURCH-MONUMENTS."

Methusalem. See METHUSELAH.

Methuselah. Son of Enoch. He lived 969 years and is thus commonly taken as the epitome of long life and old age. See Genesis 5:21–27.

Microcosm. The "little world," as opposed to the "great world" or MACROCOSM. Writers of the Middle Ages and Renaissance usually employ the concept to refer to man (i.e., the individual human), and they depend upon the ideas of ARISTOTLE in this regard. But the word can in some contexts refer to or imply any kind of smaller world in itself that reflects in little the MACROCOSM: e.g., the state as a microcosm of the universe (the King or Queen like God presiding over all, with various ranks and types of people down the scale of being to the lowest, a structure that reflects the NATURAL ORDER or chain of being).

In its most frequent uses the microcosm or little world is believed to contain within it all of the elements and structural principles that are contained in the MACROCOSM that it reflects: for example, the individual human (the microcosm) was believed to have been created with elements and principles corresponding both to the earth (a MACROCOSM) and to the whole universe (a MACROCOSM). Man is composed, in his physical being, of the four ELEMENTS that make up everything on earth. His blood is analogous to the rivers of the earth, and his hair is like grass. Man's passions are like storms on earth (in Shakespeare's *King Lear,* Lear's raging in the storm illustrates the direct correspondence of microcosm and macrocosm). Man's spirit and intellect correspond to God in the universe. As discussed by writers of the time, the correspondences are seemingly endless. Herbert's uses of the individual as a microcosm are numerous: see, only as a few examples, "Man," "THE PULLEY," and "The Author's Prayer before Sermon" in *THE COUNTRY PARSON.*

Militant Church. See CHURCH MILITANT.

Mine(s). *Noun*: (1) place(s), excavation(s) in the earth from which metals and minerals are taken; (2) abundant source(s) of something; (3) mineral(s) or ore(s); (4) metaphor for the womb.

Mistress. *Noun*: (1) a woman who employs, cares for, has authority over others; (2) a woman who is loved and courted by a man—i.e., a sweetheart or a lady love; (3) a concubine or a woman used by a man for sexual pleasure in addition to or in place of a wife; (4) as a title or prefix, a term of respect; (5) a title of courtesy for a married woman; (6) a title of courtesy for an unmarried woman or girl. *Verb*: to dally with a mistress.

Montgomery. Shire in Wales associated with the Herbert family from the late fifteenth and early sixteenth centuries. Birthplace of GEORGE HERBERT. Also see RICHARD HERBERT, MAGDALEN HERBERT, and EDWARD HERBERT.

Mount Olivet. Mount of Olives, the location of the Garden of Gethsemane where Christ and his disciples went after the Last Supper. He went off a way from the disciples and prayed in agony and "his sweat was as it were great drops of blood falling down to the ground" (Luke 22:44). After praying, he found the disciples asleep, and Judas came with a crowd that arrested Christ, leading to his crucifixion. See "THE AGONY."

Move. *Verb*: (1) to change the position of something or someone; (2) to remove or shift; (3) to stir or disturb; (4) to put or keep in motion; (5) to excite, to stimulate, to stir up emotion or passion or anger; (6) to provoke some action or reaction; (7) to urge, exhort, incite, appeal, or propose.

Mule. In the only occurrence of the word in Herbert's works (line 204 of *THE CHURCH MILITANT*), two meanings are present in the pun: (1) a beast of burden, offspring of a horse and an ass; (2) a slipper for the foot.

Muse. *Noun*: (1) in Greek mythology, one of the nine goddesses who inspired learning and arts [including poetry and music] who frequently are called on [invoked] by a writer or artist for such inspiration; (2) loosely, a poet's inspiration or talent or particular style.

Music of the spheres. See SPHERE.

N

Natural order. The common concept of the Middle Ages and Renaissance that God created a perfect, ordered universe in which everything is placed in a particular position with an assigned function or purpose. As long as each entity's position and function are maintained, the universe operates smoothly and harmoniously. But if this God-given order, rank, or hierarchy is disrupted, chaos results and is destructive to each entity and to the whole universe. For example, God is at the top of order in the universe, followed by the ranks of angels, humans, animals, plants, and inanimate things. All elements in the cosmos (SPHERE, plant, sun, moon, etc.) have their specific places and functions that must be adhered to so that natural order is maintained.

The concept was easily extended to any MICROCOSM that reflects this MACROCOSM of the universe. For example, in each nation the proper king or queen is like God in the universe, and all subordinate ranks of people have their proper places and functions, being superior to some and inferior to others; therefore, political and social rebellion against proper authority could be viewed as rebellion against and sin against God, since God seemingly ordained natural order to be followed in every realm. The same reflection of natural order can be seen in the hierarchical structure of the church, family, and any group of humans. Indeed, within man as a MICROCOSM his own constituent elements ideally must adhere to natural order (e.g., controlled by his Godlike soul and reason, rather than the rebellious passions and senses), or chaos within the world or universe of himself will result.

Neo-Platonic. See PLATONIC.

Nestle. *Verb*: (1) to make a nest, (2) to settle in a nest or comfortable place.

Nethersole, Francis (1587–1659). University Orator at Cambridge, 1611–1619. George Herbert served as his deputy (1619) and then succeeded him in the post (1620).

New philosophy. The new science (or cosmology or astronomy) encompassing the theory of COPERNICUS that the earth is not the center of the universe (as the conception of PTOLEMY argued) but that the earth (as well as the rest of the solar system) revolves around the sun. The discoveries of BRAHE, KEPLER, GALILEO, and others verified and extended the arguments of Copernicus and became a part of the "new philosophy." This new science questioned the existence of the layers of ELEMENTS surrounding the earth, as envisioned in the Ptolemaic universe: especially questioned was the element of fire (asserted as nonexistent especially by Kepler and CARDAN). These astronomers argued for the existence of worlds other than earth in the universe, a proposal that (along with the contentions that earth is not the center and that the universe and solar system are not in perfect circles) raised disturbing questions about whether humanity and earth were indeed formed and placed by God as central in his perfect, harmonious creation. What formerly had been assumed to be a perfect and unchanging universe was now being challenged in many ways. Herbert's reflection of and treatment of these concerns may be seen in such poems as "THE AGONY," "Vanity (1)," and "The Temper (2)": in this last poem occurs the line "Though elements change, and heaven move."

"New Year Sonnets." See "SONNETS 1 AND 2."

Nilus. The Nile River in Egypt.

Noah's vine. Literally referring to Noah's planting of a vineyard: see Genesis 9:20. Metaphorically referring to Christ as the vine and the crushed grapes, with his sacrificial blood as the wine.

Noisome. *Adjective*: (1) harmful, noxious; (2) ill-smelling; (3) unpleasant.

Nor . . . nor. Correlative conjunctions sometimes used by Herbert and other writers of the 16th and 17th centuries: gradually being replaced in Herbert's time by the modern "neither . . . nor."

O

Observe. *Verb*: (1) to notice, remark, perceive; (2) to treat with attention; (3) to treat with ceremonious respect or reverence.

Octave. See SONNET.

Oley, Barnabas (1602–1686). Royalist clergyman. Taxor and Proctor at Cambridge University. Responsible for safely bringing the university plate to the headquarters of CHARLES I in 1642, so that it might be used for financing his expenses of war. With the rise to power of Cromwell and Parliament, Oley was ejected from his fellowship, lost personal and landed property, and forced out of his benefice. Wandered around England for years in poverty. Restored to his fellowship and made prebendary of Worcester Cathedral in 1660.

Oley edited *Herbert's Remains* in 1652, the volume containing Herbert's prose works *THE COUNTRY PARSON* (or *A Priest to the Temple*) and *JACULA PRUDENTUM*. This volume contains an anonymous "Prefatory View of the Life and Virtues of the Author, and Excellencies of this Book," later acknowledged as his by Oley when he brought forth a second edition of *The Country Parson* in 1671, with a new preface published with the old one reprinted. WALTON drew heavily on Oley's comments for his *Life of Herbert*. Oley's 1652 preface is responsible to a great extent for creating the royalist view of Herbert as the model Anglican priest, to be held and esteemed as the opposite of those found in the Puritan Cromwellian church. In the 1671 preface Oley says that it was EDMUND DUNCON who had Herbert's manuscript of *The Country Parson* and presented it for publication.

Olivet. See MOUNT OLIVET.

Optic(k). *Noun*: a telescope.

Order, idea of. See NATURAL ORDER.

Order(s). See HIERARCHY, THE HEAVENLY.

Ordinary (Ordinarie). *Adjective*: (1) regular, usual ["in ordinary": occurring as a regular custom or practice]; (2) conformable to order or rule; (3) not distinguished by rank or position; (4) common, plain. *Noun*: (1) a prescribed or customary course or procedure; (2) a book containing the established order for divine service in the church; (3) a regular daily meal; (4) a public meal regularly provided at a fixed price in an eating-house or tavern; (5) an eating-house or tavern in which public meals are provided at a fixed price; (6) a variety of kersey, a plain, coarse cloth woven from wool.

Outlandish. *Adjective*: foreign.

Outlandish Proverbs. Also see *HERBERT'S REMAINS* and BARNABAS OLEY. This collection of foreign proverbs put into English by Herbert first appeared in 1640, was printed again in 1651 under the title *Jacula Prudentum*, and again in *Herbert's Remains* of 1652. For the complex bibliographical facts and problems associated with this work, see Hutchinson's discussion in his *The Works of George Herbert*. It is generally agreed that most of the proverbs were selected and translated by Herbert from primarily French, Italian, and Spanish sources.

Ovid (43 B.C.–A.D. 18). Roman poet whose Latin name is Publius Ovidius Naso and who sometimes is referred to as "Naso." Studied rhetoric, travelled, and eventually decided to be a poet. His most famous and influential works are *Amores*, *Ars amatoria*, and *Metamorphoses*. Ovid is regarded as an entertaining storyteller and writer of amorous and erotic verse. Herbert alludes to *Ars amatoria* in "The Thanksgiving" (see "art of love" in lines 45–47).

Oxymoron. *Noun*: a form of paradox in which two apparently contradictory terms occur in conjunction—one example is "soul's blood" in line 13 of "PRAYER (1)."

P

Paracelsus (1493–1541). Physician whose full name was Philippus Aureolus Theophrastus Bombast von Hohenheim. Herbert was aware of and influenced by some of his ideas and terms concerning ALCHEMY and medicine. Paracelsus attempted to discredit GALEN and the HUMORS. He saw God as the ultimate alchemist who derived the creation out of chemical processes. Paracelsus also popularized the terms MICROCOSM and MACROCOSM. He comments on such matters as the QUINTESSENCE and BALM.

In medical treatment, Paracelsus and the chemics (or chemiques) disagreed with the methods of Galen and the GALENISTS. Instead of correcting imbalances of HUMORS with foods of opposite qualities, the chemics tried to purge from the body the essence of the disease by using an antagonistic medicine.

Partition-wall. Reference to the "middle wall of partition" between Jews and Gentiles that St. Paul says is broken down by Christ (see Ephesians 2:14).

Parts. *Noun*: a special meaning, common in Herbert and other writers of the time, refers to a person's natural or acquired attributes, qualities, talents, or abilities.

Passing Bell. Bell tolled softly and slowly as a person is dying (passing away) in order to secure prayers for the soul. Compare DEATH BELL and FUNERAL BELL.

Passion, the. The suffering of Christ on the cross. Also used to designate GOOD FRIDAY.

Patriark, Patriarch. *Noun*: (1) one of the twelve sons of JACOB, from whom the tribes of Israel descended; (2) one of the forefathers of the race from Adam through Abraham, Isaac, and Jacob. In his "Notes" to VALDESSO's *Considerations*, Herbert refers to Abraham as "the great Patriark" ("To the 62 Consid."). See SARA(H).

Pattern poems. Also called "shaped verses." Poems in which the visual arrangement of lines and stanzas in written and printed form create shapes and symbols related to the content and/or title of the poem. Herbert and other writers of the 17th century wrote a few of these poems in the body of their work. See "THE ALTAR" and "EASTER WINGS" for examples in Herbert. Such poems were popular in classical Greek poetry, and another English poet employing the type in Herbert's century was Robert Herrick, the major follower of BEN JONSON. Herbert's affinity with the CLASSICAL strain from Jonson is thus enforced by his use of the form.

"Pearl, The." In his original manuscript Herbert includes beside the title a reference to Matthew 13:45. One finds that Matthew 13:45–46 says, "Again, the kingdom of heaven is like unto a merchant man, seeking goodly pearls: Who, when he had found one pearl of great price, went and sold all that he had, and bought it." Thus, the "pearl" is heaven, and all worldly riches must ultimately be forsaken to gain it. The speaker of the poem is knowledgeable about and appreciates worldly values, but he recognizes and accepts the spiritual as superior.

The poem is carefully organized with CLASSICAL progression, balance, and symmetry in four stanzas of ten lines each. "I know the ways of learning" (line 1), "I know the ways of honor" (line 11), and "I know the ways of pleasure" (Line 21) set up in impressive parallelism the three large realms of secular, worldly values (learning, honor, and pleasure) that he is intimately familiar with. Then the opening line (31) of the final stanza summarizes them with parallel style ("I know all these"), only ultimately to turn to the spiritual realm of God's love anticipated by the refrain of each of the first three stanzas ("Yet I love thee").

In each of the first three stanzas the speaker gives a lengthy catalog of the worldly things he knows, impressive just in the sheer enumeration of them coming so rapidly at the reader in sequence. It overwhelms one with the sense of the speaker's knowledge of and involvement in the world. But then the reader is brought up short by that very short line at the end of each stanza ("Yet I love thee"). The power of the phrase is made great by its undercutting all the length and fullness of development preceding it. Its short, simple spiritual affirmation conveys the overpowering love of God, and it becomes the simple goal achieved at the end of each stanza after working through the entangling complexities of the worldly realm enumerated in each stanza. Beyond the worldly temptation indicated in the bulk of each stanza is the escape into the simple love and salvation at the end. In fact, each of the first three stanzas mirrors the larger structure of the entire poem: just as the last line of each represents spiritual salvation beyond the worldly interests represented in the previous nine lines, so does the last stanza of the poem represent that salvation beyond the worldly values represented in the first three stanzas. Effective also is the symmetrical contrast between "know" in the first line of each of the first three stanzas and "love" in the last line of each. The love of God overpowers all worldly knowledge, an idea inherent in the structure of the first three stanzas that is fully explicated in the last stanza. Certainly significant also is the fact that all four stanzas (and thus the poem itself) ends with "thee": i.e., "thee" is God who is equated with the kingdom of heaven, the ultimately chosen "pearl."

In the first stanza the focus is on the speaker's knowledge of the "ways of learning." Scholars and critics have tried to determine what Herbert means by the "head and pipes that feed the press, and make it run." It has been suggested that there may be a reference to an olive press or printing press. Hutchinson's edition (see my "Selected Bibliography") suggests that "the *head* is the fountain of knowledge, the universities, and the *pipes* are those who mediate that knowledge to the world in the learned professions." He cites OLEY's reference in *Herbert's Remains* to "those Horns of Oyl, the Two Universities." Certainly these suggestions could include the printing press as one means used by the learned professions to disseminate that knowledge. In the context of the "ways of learning" these suggestions by Hutchinson seem most logical and appropriate. The speaker goes on to say that he knows what truths human reason has arrived at by the observation of nature. Also, with a tinge of satirical humor, the speaker says that he knows what human reason has spun out of itself (i.e., divorced from "nature") into human laws and policy (i.e., statecraft, political matters): the comparison of reason to a "good housewife" at the spinning wheel connotes a practicality in human reason applied to political matters, whether true or only the image fostered by statesmen themselves. It is interesting, however, that the view of human reason spinning something "of itself" closely resembles the analogy used by Herbert's friend FRANCIS BACON in *The Advancement of Learning* when he compares the mind of the SCHOOLMEN to a spider spinning out "laborious webs of learning." Bacon also argues at the same point that if the "wit and mind of man" work upon "matter" which he calls "the contemplation of the creatures of God" (i.e., of nature), then it is "limited thereby" (in a good sense, to Bacon). But he says that if the mind works "upon itself, as the spider worketh his web, then it is endless, and brings forth indeed cobwebs of learning, admirable for the fineness of thread and work, but of no substance or profit." Thus, subtly suggested in Herbert's echo of Bacon here may be the fact that the proud knowledge of human reason divorced from God's creation holds the seeds of its own destruction or, at least, rejection. The speaker's transcending it to a realm more important than this knowledge is foreshadowed at this point, certainly, with the Baconian echo of its futility. In addition, the Baconian image of a maze of learning that is "spun" (as cobweb or as thread) certainly is relevant to the context of Herbert's poem: each of the first three stanzas, in fact, become a kind of maze of human knowledge through which the speaker works to emerge to the love of God. And, again, each stanza mirrors the whole poem in this regard. The speaker proceeds (line 5) to assert that he knows astrological theories about how the stars influence earthly matters ("what the stars conspire"). He also knows what science has learned from mere observation of nature and what it has tried to force by the "fire" of laboratory experiments (probably thinking of the attempts of ALCHEMY). Taken literally, line 7 indicates that the speaker knows of geographical discoveries from ancient times to his own time. Metaphorically the "old discoveries" could be any discoveries in any realm of learning in the past, and "new-found seas" could be new discoveries in any realm. Line 8 is a classically balanced line that summarizes all of learning that he has mastered, both "stock" (i.e., "cause") and "surplus" (i.e., "history"— effects that have resulted from the causes). (Hutchinson cites Beeching's contention that "stock" is the learning we inherit and "surplus" is what we add to it.) In fact, the "stock" could refer to the "old discoveries" and the "surplus" to the "new-found seas." The speaker already knows the "ways of learning" or knows how to find them out (line 9). But beyond all of this he still loves God.

In the second stanza he turns to "ways of honor." These are the ways of court, courtesy, society, and politics. Certainly there is caustic satire on "honor," since what is depicted as its "ways" are rather hypocritical, unethical, and vicious—generally lacking the integrity and morality of "honor" in its truest sense. The speaker knows the requirement of maintaining witty repartee and how to judge which individual or faction wins in contests of doing favors for some powerful political entity in order to achieve the desired ambitious goal and to win the world (lines 12–17). Lines 15–16 picture the courting of a powerful political figure (king or nobleman, etc.) as if it were the wooing of a lover, with a lover's artificial expressions and a lover's token (a knotted ribbon) of supposedly true love ("true-love-knot"). The speaker knows the cost to his own integrity to attain rich worldly goals: he knows how many "drams of spirit" it costs him, playing on "spirit" as liquor to be drunk, but also with the sense of his soul to be sold. But he still loves God beyond this worldly knowledge.

The third stanza turns to the "ways of pleasure." Here Herbert uses musical metaphors combined with sexual ones to convey the idea of physical, sensuous pleasures. The use of musical terms has best been explained by Douglas Brown, pp. 136–37 of his edition, and by Gareth Reeves, p. 143 of his edition (see my "Selected Bibliography"). They comment that the (1) "strains," (2) "lullings," (3) "relishes," and (4) "propositions" are specific musical terms referring to (1) melodies or tunes or portions of a movement; (2) soothing songs or refrains;

(3) musical ornaments or embellishments in performing in song or on lute, viol, or virginal; and (4) leading parts or themes opening a fugue. Of course, terms such as "sweet" and "relishes" also reverberate with suggestions of taste, food. And the transition from musical to sexual imagery is made explicitly in "propositions of hot blood and brains," where the "propositions" clearly apply to sexual propositions made by a lover in the heat of passion. And the sexual drive's power is enforced by the sudden emphasis on plosive *p* and *b* sounds in "propositions," "blood," and "brains," all made even more telling with heavy metrical stresses. He says in line 26 that he "knows the projects of unbridled store": many editors gloss "store" here as *wealth* or "unbridled store" as *unlimited wealth*. But this seems inconsistent with the context of passion and physical temptation and pleasure. More likely is the implication of "STORE" as simply a stock or supply of something accumulated for later use, and here it is a stock of passion. And "unbridled store" echoes PLATO's image of passion as a runaway horse that should be controlled by the bridle of reason. The likelihood that the speaker is referring to accumulated passion running rampant seems supported by his next statement that "My stuff is flesh": he is subject to bodily temptations, and his "senses live." The fact that he calls his flesh "stuff" suggests that he is aware of its inferiority to the spirit which he ultimately endorses over the body. He is aware of the continual body/soul conflict in the microcosm of the human: his five senses complain that they are controlled by the soul ("he that curbs them"), even though there are five senses to only one soul.

In the last stanza the speaker says that he "knows" all these "ways" cataloged in the first three stanzas and that they are all available to him as ways of life that he could choose of his own free will. However, he consciously chooses the way of God instead: he seeks God with "open eyes." In "seeled" (some editions have "sealed") Herbert is using a term from falconry: see SEEL and SEAL. Unlike the eyes sewn shut of the young falcon in training, the speaker's eyes are "open," and he thus can "fly" to God with full awareness of all available to him and yet choose God as his ultimate goal and caretaker. The mercantile imagery of lines 34–36 return to the biblical passage suggested in the title: the speaker, like the merchant, well understands what he loses and what he profits in this selling and buying to gain the ultimate pearl, the kingdom of heaven. Lines 37–40 make an effective climax to the idea of the speaker successfully emerging from the "labyrinths" of worldly values and ways, a maze that has been reflected both in the structure and syntax of each individual stanza and of the poem as a whole. In the image of the "silk twist let down from heaven" Herbert fuses allusions to both classical and Christian elements. It suggests the cord by which Ariadne led Theseus out of the labyrinth after he had killed the minotaur. Also,

Homer in the *Iliad* (Book 8) pictures Zeus with a golden chain or rope extending from heaven. But it also suggests the image of God (seen in many contemporary illustrations of the PTOLEMAIC universe found in books of Herbert's time) with his hand extending from a cloud holding to a rope or chain, sometimes connected to the goddess Nature and then to man on earth. Some editors also see a reference to JACOB's ladder (Genesis 28:10–17), taken as a TYPE of Christ's cross. Probably most important is the fact that the beautiful cord of twisted silk represents God's grace, God's love, which is freely provided and which directs man to love of God: this is the "way" of God and to God, in contrast to any use of man's own "WIT" (intellect).

Pembroke, Countess of. See SIDNEY, MARY, and CLIFFORD, LADY ANNE.

Pembroke, Earl of. See HERBERT, WILLIAM, and HERBERT, PHILIP.

Perirrhanterium. Greek term designating an instrument for sprinkling holy water. See *THE CHURCH-PORCH*, where it is used as a subtitle.

Pestilence. *Noun*: plague. Herbert, however, uses the word metaphorically in Chapter 9 of *THE COUNTRY PARSON* to mean "carnal impurity," as he explains in brackets following its occurrence.

Petrarch. See PETRARCHAN.

Petrarchan. Francesco Petrarca (1304–1374), better known as Petrarch, was an Italian poet most famous for his lyrics concerning his love for Laura, either a real or imagined lady. According to Petrarch, she was indeed a real lady who was married. By his account he met her in 1327, and she died in 1348. His lyrics portray his love for her, doomed to lack physical response and fulfillment. Among these lyrics those in the SONNET form give Petrarch his lasting fame and influence.

　　As an adjective "Petrarchan" can be found in reference to the particular sonnet form that Petrarch used (also called the "Italian") that was introduced into English by Sir Thomas Wyatt, eventually being employed and adapted by later Renaissance poets. See SONNET.

　　"Petrarchan," however, also refers to the content of these sonnets, particularly to the assumptions about love, women, and the relationship between men and women. The "Petrarchan love convention" is a particular set of literary assumptions, descriptions, and techniques that stem from Petrarch's sonnets to Laura that were continued and developed further by poets up to Herbert's time (especially by SIDNEY and SPENSER). In a poem (or poems) employing this convention, the speaker typically is a man talking to or about the extremely beautiful woman he wishes to win as his love. This "Petrarchan lady" is beautiful, but she also is proud and disdainful. Usually she cruelly rejects the man's overtures to her. The man is her humble subject and worshipper in a kind of idealized and spiritualized love-religion, with the lady as a goddess (or, at least, presented as if on a pedestal above the lowly man). The lady ordinarily is blonde (the ideal) and is described with stereotypical characteristics and comparisons such as cheeks like roses, lips like cherries, teeth like pearls, eyes like suns or stars or crystals, breath like perfume, and hair like fine golden wire. With her goddesslike power, she has the ability to grant the man mercy ("pity") and life (by accepting him) or suffering and death (by rejecting him). She typically will not respond to the man, and this plunges the man into despondency and disillusionment. Despite his tears (like rain) and sighs (like winds), she cruelly rejects him: his passion causes him to "burn" with desire, but her rejection causes him to "freeze." The man sometimes must turn to other concerns and activities (going to war, reading philosophy, writing poetry, etc.) to purge him of his grief and to occupy his mind after this great disappointment in love. Many times the poet will use a "Petrarchan conceit," a lengthy, detailed analogy comparing the love or the lady or the man to something else (e.g., the love relationship to a journey at sea or a declaration of love to a military campaign). Cupid, with his "darts" (arrows), at times is portrayed as helping the lady to tempt, capture, tantalize, and torture her victims.

Herbert writes with full knowledge of this convention when he scorns, satirizes, and adapts its elements for his own concern with the larger beauties and loves of God, Christ, and the spiritual in general.

Philippus Aureolus Theophrastus Bombast von Hohenheim. See PARACELSUS.

Philosophers. Herbert's use of the term in "THE AGONY" primarily, but not exclusively, refers to scientists, including astronomers, geographers, and mathematicians. Also see PHILOSOPHY and NEW PHILOSOPHY.

Philosopher's stone. See ALCHEMY.

Philosophy. *Noun*: (1) the love of wisdom; (2) advanced knowledge and study of natural, moral, political, and metaphysical matters; (3) science [natural philosophy]. Also see NEW PHILOSOPHY.

Phisick. See PHYSIC.

Phlegm. See HUMOR. The dominance of phlegm over the other three humors was believed to cause a person to lack energy and to be lazy, slothful.

Phlegmatic(k). See HUMOR.

Physic, Phisick, Physicke. *Noun*: (1) medical science, medicine; (2) the medical profession; (3) medical treatment. *Adjective*: medical or medicinal.

Physicke. See PHYSIC.

"Pilgrimage, The." This allegory portrays the Christian's journey through life: the physical landscape symbolizes psychological and spiritual matters.

In stanza 1 the speaker sees in the distance "the hill" that he regards as his ultimate goal, destination, "expectation." Line 3 ("A long it was and weary way") employs alliteration of *w*, a sound that takes a long time to pronounce and thus adds length in its reading: this time of pronunciation and the repetition itself convey the very sense of the long and weary journey referred to. The Christian must avoid the extremes of spiritual despair and pride. Despair here is presented as a gloomy cave, full of darkness for one's spirit. On the other hand, pride is allegorized as a rock, appropriate because of the unfeeling, aloof, unresponsive, stubborn nature of pride.

In stanza 2 the speaker has progressed on the road of life to "Fancy's Meadow." This suggests a pleasant period of life in which one can enjoy fine things of the world, especially through the power of imagination in art and in matters of love (see FANCY). This stage of the pilgrimage through life, this period, suggests youth, carefree and unfettered by worries and responsibilities. The speaker would gladly (see FAIN) have liked to remain here ("made abode"), but he was "quickened" by his "hour": in other words, he was suddenly conscious of and urged on by his limited life span (seeming to be only an "hour," compared to the whole of time before and after). He then proceeds to "Care's Copse": the image is of a group of trees ("copse") through which one must wind and make his or her way. This is the period of worry and responsibility that succeeds carefree youth: this more

worrisome, restricted period is thus contrasted to tripping through
flowers in an open meadow.

Stanza 3 proceeds to the next stage, the "Wild of Passion." The
"Wild" essentially connotes a wilderness, a wasteland. Alternatively, he
calls it "Wold" in the next line: such uncultivated areas in England
indeed were called "Wild," "Wold," and "Weald." Many editors and
critics see a pun on "Wold," suggesting *would*: certainly this well relates
it to "Passion," since "passion" here suggests worldly temptations,
emotions, desires, and succumbings of all sorts resulting from yielding
to the *will*, worldly self-serving wishes. The speaker seems caught up,
then, in worldly ambitions and desires, a state which explains the
paradox in calling this a "wasted place, but sometimes rich." It is a
period of accumulating worldly riches and success, but it is spiritually
lacking. The ultimate futility of this stage of life and of its concomitant
worldly riches is emphasized by the fact that here he "was robbed of
all" his "gold," except for "one good angel." Herbert here is making a
METAPHYSICAL pun on "ANGEL": there was a gold English coin
called this because it had the image of the Archangel Michael slaying the
dragon of Revelation. But the only "angel" that the speaker has left
seems to be the small remaining sense of the spiritual that remained with
him while he was accumulating the literal coins called angels. It is the
small inkling of his spiritual origin and spiritual destiny that still has
remained with him, despite the extent to which it has been ignored and
forgotten in the midst of worldliness. Significantly, "a friend" had tied
it to his side: as in many of Herbert's poems, the "friend" is Christ, with
Herbert here echoing a passage from John [see "JORDAN (2)"].

Stanzas 4 and 5 portray the speaker's arrival at the "Gladsome
Hill," the one he had originally seen from a distance and had regarded
as his ultimate goal: he calls it his "expectation" in stanza 1, and in
stanza 4 he says that he had regarded it as having his "hope" and
"heart." But he is surprised to find the opposite at the top of the hill—
only a "lake of brackish waters." These waters suggest "tears," on one
level, since in stanza 5 he asks God if both the "way and end be tears."
But then he sees that he was deceived: this hill is not the true destination.
Editors and critics have been silent, puzzled, or contradictory
concerning these two stanzas. These two do present the most difficult
interpretative problem in the poem. Possibly the speaker has focused on
a false goal, on something he thought would provide him salvation and
reward but did not do so. Finding stagnant water, rather than cleansing
and purifying water, supports this implication. Possibly the speaker has
been deceived by the doctrine of good works or living a holy life with a
sense of one's own holiness and dedication to the gaining of salvation by
one's own efforts. Significantly, I think, the speaker does not gain his
perception that he was "deceived" until *after* he falls to his knees and

cries to God, his "King." Perhaps this reminder of God's grace, not man's efforts, was needed.

In stanza 6, then, he sees the true "hill" in the distance: more of the "pilgrimage" remains. And this true hill can only be gained by death, physical death, at the end of life's pilgrimage: he hears a cry saying, "None goes that way / And lives." He must die to the things of this world and die physically in order to gain spiritual salvation through God's grace granted with the physical death of Christ, God himself. Certainly the "hill" may suggest the hill of Calvary upon which Christ died: each Christian ultimately must follow Christ and his "way" through physical death to resurrection. The speaker at the end is prepared for this final stage of the pilgrimage, since he sees that the journey through this world and life is "foul" and makes death paradoxically "FAIR" (beautiful), because of the spiritual life it grants one. And death is "but a chair": i.e., death is only a chair. Death here is seen as a comfortable means of transportation from this life into the next: the "chair" is a sedan chair, one used to carry someone from one place to another. Men would hold poles supporting this chair on a platform, usually with curtains surrounding it. Herbert is associating the "chair" with the means by which one in a coffin is carried to be placed on a bier and then buried. For example, in "Mortification" (lines 29–30) Herbert says, "A chair or litter shows the bier, / Which shall convey him to the house of death."

Pillars of Hercules. Sometimes called the "old Pillars." The two mountains across from each other (in Spain and North Africa) at the western entrance to the Mediterranean Sea from the Atlantic Ocean. Between the two mountains is the Strait of Gibraltar, supposedly marking the western limit of the Old World.

Pink, Pinke. *Verb*: to puncture or pierce.

Plato (about 427–about 347 B.C.). Greek philosopher. Influenced by Socrates. Established a school (the Academy) in Athens about 387 B.C. and taught there until he died. His most famous and influential works are the dialogues, including the *Symposium*, the *Republic*, the *Timaeus*, and the *Laws*. For some of his and his followers' basic ideas, see PLATONIC.

Platonic. In its strict use, referring to the beliefs of PLATO, but, more generally and loosely, to the beliefs and later developments of his philosophy as pursued by followers such as Plotinus (3rd century A.D.) and Dionysius the Areopagite (the philosophy of these followers is more properly called "Neo-Platonic"). Most writers of Herbert's time generally do not make sharp distinctions between the doctrines of Plato himself and those of the Neo-Platonists. (Generally throughout this "Dictionary" the term "Platonic" is used in senses that embrace concepts from both Platonism and Neo-Platonism.)

Plato argues that each physical entity in this world is a mere shadow or imitation of the original or real Idea (or Form) of that kind or class of creature that exists in an external and unchanging realm beyond time and physical space. Since the soul knew these Ideas in its previous state of existence, human reason tries to recollect them. The ultimate Idea is the Idea of the Good. The greatest wisdom of man, as well as the greatest goal for man, is contemplation of and striving toward this Good. The soul and intellect, therefore, are valued as real, while the body and senses are comparatively unreal. From the value placed on the soul, it follows that true beauty is spiritual and that true love is spiritual. Union of spirits, then, is "Platonic love" and is a reality beyond mere physical union of lovers. A lover is severely limited if he or she contemplates only the beauty of a single individual when one should ascend to beauty of the many in physical bodies and then higher to intellectual beauty and then higher to the beauty of the Idea.

Neo-Platonism suffuses Plato's thought with mystical and/or Christian concepts, effecting a reconciliation of philosophies. Plotinus developed the precise argument that the "Absolute" or "One" (source of all beauty, truth, and goodness) generates everything material and spiritual in the world. Since God is easily identified as the "One," Plotinus's arguments fostered development of more specifically Christian Neo-Platonism by AUGUSTINE, medieval Christian philosophers, and such Renaissance Christian humanists as CASTIGLIONE. They saw God at the top of that stair of love ascended by one's soul through the help of reason. The beauty of the body gives only an external hint of the beauty and goodness of the soul within, and that soul in turn reflects its divine origin. In ideal love conventions (expressed most memorably for the writers of the Renaissance in Sir Thomas Hoby's translation of Castiglione's *THE COURTIER*) the ideal courtier (or lover) resists the temptations of the senses and physical attraction through passion by asserting his reason to overcome passion. His angelic and Godlike reason leads him up the ladder of love to a sense of spiritual beauty in the one woman, in all women, over everything beautiful in the world, and ultimately to a ravishment with heavenly beauty as the soul ascends the ladder into a union with God. See also HIERARCHY, THE HEAVENLY.

Play. In some contexts the word means to manage, direct, or deal with.

Pleasure. *Noun*: (1) enjoyment, delight; (2) sensuous, physical enjoyment; (3) sensual, sexual enjoyment; (4) the source of or object that gives enjoyment; (5) wish or will.

Plotinus. See PLATONIC.

Pope's mule. See MULE.

Pose. *Verb*: to puzzle, confuse, perplex.

Possess. *Verb*: (1) to reside in or occupy; (2) to hold as property, to own; (3) to have [as an attribute or quality]; (4) to seize or take; (5) [of a demon or spirit] to occupy, dominate, and control a body or other entity; (6) to have another person sexually, to have sexual intercourse with.

Post. *Verb*: to ride or travel or leave with haste.

"Prayer (1)." A poem from *THE TEMPLE*. It is a SONNET in the English form, with the variation of *effe* as the rhyme scheme of the third quatrain. The poem essentially is a series of metaphors for prayer with no verb, no "is," following the initial word "Prayer." Prayer as a kind of food, sustenance, refreshment recurs in the poem, with its beginning in "church's banquet." "Banquet" suggests a sumptuous feast, but in Herbert's time it could also refer to a serving of sweets and wine or to a dessert. So, prayer is a spiritual food, giving an abundance of sustenance to the believer, and/or is a pleasing, sweet dessert added to other means of worship. Prayer has "angels' age," something eternally and timelessly present and giving temporal humans a taste or foreshadowing of infinity. Line 2 alludes to God's breathing of life into Adam (see Genesis 2:7): prayer is man's way of recognizing the source of his life in breathing forth God's own gift in prayer. "Soul in paraphrase" presents prayer as a kind of explication of the soul: the soul explains itself to God by expressing itself in a fully developed verbal form. Prayer sends the human heart on a pilgrimage to heaven to worship God, and it also is like a lead weight ("plummet") on a line to "sound" or measure the depth of both heaven and earth (thus revealing the individual's place within each realm). Herbert probably intends here also, however, the idea of prayer as a clock's "plummet," the weight that must be sufficient for the clock to strike accurately. Thus, prayer is "sounding" or ringing out aloud the individual's awareness of or perceptions about both heaven and earth.

The second quatrain introduces some images more violent in nature. "Engine" (line 5) is an instrument of warfare, a weapon: prayer becomes a means by which one wages war with God, to have God capitulate to one's wish. Prayer might be seen as a battering ram to break down walls, gates, and fortifications around God or as a cannon to threaten even more powerfully to importune God. A secondary meaning perhaps suggested also is an "engine" of torture, another common use in Herbert's time. Perhaps prayer at times is employed by man as a rack upon which he places God to try to force agreement. "Sinners' tower" also suggests a military tower, with the individuals trying to attain and maintain a military advantage in the "war" with God. Also, at the same time, there is a suggestion of the Tower of BABEL, constructed by men who wanted its top to reach heaven. Man also tries to sound ominous, threatening, and powerful by making prayer like God's thunder in reverse (line 6). The sense of man's use of prayer as a weapon or threat, with the implication that prayer may even be displeasing to God at times, is increased by "Christ-side-piercing spear": prayer may be the most powerful weapon against God that the human has at his disposal, but the individual praying being compared to the soldier who pierced Christ's side with a spear (see St. John 19:34) seems rather unflattering. The aggressive power inherent in the phrase is enforced by the four heavily stressed syllables in it, and the harshness is conveyed by the recurring "s" (and "c") sibilants in it. Line 7 lessens the aggressive violence, but still continues the idea of prayer's great power: it is so powerful that just one hour of prayer can transform ("transpose") the world that took God six days to create. But another meaning implied is that it can change the everyday six-day week for the individual, as well. Herbert, however, intends another meaning here in "transpose": in music, to "transpose" is to write or perform a composition in a key other than that of the original. Thus the ordinary world is transposed from the mundane to one of heavenly harmony on a spiritual plane. The music metaphor leads, then, into line 8 in which prayer is a "kind of tune."

The third quatrain opens with a line that, after the first two syllables, falls into perfectly regular iambic meter. The regularity, smoothness, and repetition in "and peace, and joy, and love, and bliss" convey the harmony just implied in the previous quatrain and connote the pleasantness inherent in all that he lists and is transferring to prayer itself. "Manna" continues the motif of spiritual food from the first line ("church's banquet"). The specific biblical allusion is to the manna of Exodus 16:14–15, but, in addition to prayer as a food given by God, here it is also given back to God: "exalted" manna is returned to heaven, just as "God's breath in man" (line 2) is returned to the origin. Picturing prayer as "Heaven in ordinary" (line 11) has been interpreted in various ways by editors, scholars, and critics. It may carry multiple meaning and fit with various motifs of the poem. It is seen by some as referring to a regular daily meal set out in a public eating-house, and this suggests that it is a part of the motif of food. Others also see a reference to the Eucharist, the consecrated bread and wine (for example, see Bonnell in my "Selected Bibliography" under critical studies of the individual poems of "The Church"). Greenwood (see "Selected Bibliography") suggests that "ordinary" refers to the divine service and that it could refer to such courtly phrases as "chaplain in ordinary." These may be relevant, but the primary level seems to refer to ordinary, everyday clothing: one notes the contrast in the same line to "man well dressed." (For my specific argument about this, see Ray, Robert H., "Herbert's 'Prayer I,'" *The Explicator* 51 (1992–93): 215–16.) Paradoxically, then, by prayer heaven comes to man on earth in plain, humble, everyday form, and man elevates himself in prayer's spiritual dignity to appear to God.

The last line of the third quatrain and the couplet climax the images of ascension that have earlier been touched upon in several lines. Prayer as the "milky way" suggests a road of stars to heaven. The "bird of Paradise" was thought to be constantly in the air, elevated above earth. Then prayer becomes church bells heard even beyond the air and the stars, heard indeed in heaven by God. Earthly symbols of worship (church bells) are heard in the spiritual world. "Soul's blood" is an oxymoron insisting on prayer as man's communion wine offered to God in return for the bodily blood offered by Christ: this image and that of "land of spices" echo the food imagery from earlier lines. The final "something understood" suggests that prayer not only is like church bells "heard" by God, but, more important, it is "understood" by God. Ultimately, of course, "something" is quite ironic, since this vague term for prayer comes after so many vivid images for it. Prayer can never be precisely or fully defined in its multifaceted nature, through metaphor or otherwise. The human is incapable of understanding it completely, but the important thing, after all, is that God understands it.

Prefer. *Verb*: (1) to advance in status or promote; (2) to offer, present, recommend; (3) to hold one thing or person before others in esteem, to like better.

Prerogative. *Noun*: (1) an exclusive right or privilege, (2) precedence or superiority.

Press(e). *Noun*: (1) apparatus of torture with which a person is subjected to heavy weights placed on the body; (2) apparatus for extracting juice out of something—e.g., a wine press or olive press; (3) a machine to impress type upon paper—i.e., a printing press.

Pretend. *Verb*: (1) to profess or claim; (2) to declare falsely in order to deceive; (3) to aspire.

Prevent. *Verb*: (1) to anticipate or prepare for; (2) to arrive before, to precede, to outrun; (3) to outdo or surpass; (4) to forestall by precautionary measures; (5) to cut off or preclude someone or something from an action; (6) to stop or hinder; (7) to frustrate or defeat.

Priest to the Temple, A. See *THE COUNTRY PARSON*.

Prime. For special use, see PULL FOR PRIME.

Prime Mover. See FIRST MOVER.

Primero. See PULL FOR PRIME.

Primum Mobile. See FIRST MOVER.

Prince Henry. See STUART, HENRY.

Profaneness(e). *Noun*: (1) quality of being secular, common, civil, not sacred; (2) quality of being unholy, of desecrating something that is holy or sacred; (3) quality of being irreverent, blasphemous, impious.

Prove. *Verb*: (1) to test or try, (2) to find out or learn, (3) to experience, (4) to establish something as true, (5) to show the existence or reality or validity of something.

Ptolemaic. Referring to Ptolemy and/or his concept of the universe. See PTOLEMY.

Ptolemy (Claudius Ptolemaeus). Greek astronomer, mathematician, and geographer in Alexandria, Egypt, during the 2nd century. Formulated (by building on earlier observations) the basic concept of the universe generally known as the "Ptolemaic" view, although many of its ideas were, in the Middle Ages, fused with some from ARISTOTLE. Ptolemy argued that the universe is geocentric— i.e., earth is its center. He argued that the earth itself does not move. The other created entities (moon, sun, planets, and stars) revolve around the earth in concentric, solid, transparent SPHERES. The FIRST

MOVER is the outermost sphere that gives the first motion to all of the spheres and maintains their harmony, resulting in the MUSIC OF THE SPHERES. His view of the universe was accepted from his own century without serious question until the early 16th century when COPERNICUS proposed the heliocentric view. Ptolemy's ideas were increasingly challenged and discredited by other scientists of the NEW PHILOSOPHY. Terms, ideas, and metaphors from the Ptolemaic astronomy are numerous in Herbert's works.

Puling. *Adjective*: whining.

Pull for prime (pulling prime). Draw a winning card or cards in the game of primero.

"Pulley, The." As numerous editors point out, Herbert adapts a version of the classical myth of Pandora for his own Christian purposes: Jupiter gave Pandora a box containing the blessings of the gods, but, when she opened it, all the blessings escaped, except for hope. From this CLASSICAL foundation, however, Herbert fashions a quite METAPHYSICAL poem, showing explicitly the strong influence from DONNE. The poem centers upon the METAPHYSICAL CONCEIT of the "pulley," a word mentioned only in the title. The "pulley" is that which pulls man back to God, specifically "rest" in the sense of peace of mind, spiritual rest or repose. In this idea about rest Herbert echoes a concept common at least as far back as AUGUSTINE who says in his *Confessions* (I.i) that "our heart is restless until it finds rest in Thee [i.e., in God]." Herbert possessed St. Augustine's works, and he bequeathed them to NATHANAEL BOSTOCKE in his will. Although the Christian concept of rest was commonplace, it was not common to picture it in a farfetched analogy as a mechanical pulley. In addition to this conceit, other metaphysical traits are seen in the wordplay, puns, and colloquial language of the poem.

In stanzas 1 and 2 God the Creator is portrayed as pouring all blessings and riches into man. The world's riches are contracted into a "SPAN," an image suggesting the idea of man as a MICROCOSM. So man is given strength, beauty, wisdom, honor, and pleasure. When almost all of the blessings had been poured out of God's glass, he then "made a stay"—i.e., God paused. God saw that only "rest" still lay in the bottom of the glass. This is spiritual rest, spiritual peace of mind.

Stanzas 3 and 4 picture God deciding that he will not pour out this kind of rest on his "creature" (i.e., man as God's creation). The reason for this decision is that if man were given this rest, then man would adore God's "gifts" instead of God himself, the source of those gifts: God fears that man would be satisfied with the world, with Nature, and would feel no need to turn back to God. Man would "rest" in the creation and not return for rest to the Creator. In that case "both" (i.e., both man and God) would be "losers." Man would lose God (and salvation), and God would lose his "creature," man. God decides to let man keep the "rest," here playing on the word, since now it refers to the *remainder* of the blessings (those other than "rest" in the sense of spiritual peace). But man will have all of those other blessings with an inherent "repining restlessness," a state that will have him always pining for God's love and peace that are not found in the blessings and things of this world. Paradoxically, man will be "rich and weary" ("rich" with those blessings and worldly gifts God has granted him but "weary" because God has retained ultimate rest for man to be found only in God). "Weariness" will "toss" man to God through the action of the "pulley," that "rest" which pulls man to God.

Puritan. *Noun*: (1) a type of Protestant beginning during Queen ELIZABETH's reign who wished to "purify" the Church of England by further ridding it of what were regarded as corrupt practices and forms of worship remaining from the Roman Catholic Church, such as some of the hierarchical organization, ceremonies, emphasis on beautiful forms of worship, clerical vestments, etc.; (2) later loosely applied to one who separated from the Church of England for worship; (3) one who is, or wishes to be seen as, extremely precise and scrupulous in morality, religion, and manners, etc.

For implied criticisms of facets of the Puritans' views toward beauty and external form in worship, see, for example, "THE BRITISH CHURCH," "CHURCH MUSIC," and "THE WINDOWS."

Puritanism. The doctrines and practices of the Puritans. See PURITAN.

Q

Quaint. *Adjective*: (1) skilled, clever, ingenious; (2) ingeniously designed or made with art, elaborate; (3) beautiful or fine or dainty.

Quatrain. See SONNET.

Queen of Bohemia. See STUART, ELIZABETH.

Quick. *Adjective*: (1) characterized by the presence of life, alive; (2) vivid, lifelike; (3) live, burning [coal]; (4) lively, sprightly; (5) rapid. *Noun*: the tender, sensitive flesh in any part of the body (such as under the nails) or the tender part of a sore or wound.

Quicken. *Verb*: (1) to give or restore life; (2) to stimulate, excite, inspire; (3) to give speed to.

Quintessence. See ALCHEMY.

R

Ragged. *Adjective*: Herbert's one use (in "REDEMPTION") of this word is in its special sense applied to sounds—i.e., harsh or discordant.

Rational Soul. See TRIPARTITE SOUL.

Receipt(s). *Noun*: a prescription or list of ingredients in a medicine.

"Redemption." This SONNET is in the English form, with the variation *effe* as the rhyme scheme of the third quatrain. The major METAPHYSICAL CONCEIT is the analogy of the relationship between a landlord and a tenant as comparable to the relationship between God and the speaker (or humanity in general). In fact, in reading the first quatrain, one receives no suggestion of Christian doctrine: it seems to describe an earthly relationship only. But, with the second quatrain and the word "heaven," one begins to see that this worldly relationship stands for a spiritual, Christian relationship, with the seeming earthly lord actually being the Lord God.

In the first quatrain the speaker reveals that he has been "tenant" for a long time to a "rich lord" (who, we later see, is really God who owns the entire universe). The tenant (man or everyman or every human) feels that he is not "thriving": in worldly terms this would be *economic* "thriving," but in terms of the entire poem it turns out to be *spiritual* thriving. So, he desires to make a "suit" to the lord: he wants to ask him for a more profitable "lease," one with a smaller rent so that he can make a better profit on his returns. "AFFORD" here primarily means to *grant* (i.e., for God to grant), but it seems also to play on the idea that the speaker wants something much more economically feasible for himself. But at this point, in light of the poem's major import, we should see that "new small-rented lease" and "old" lease are highly significant in the poem's spiritual allegories. The "old" lease certainly suggests the old covenant, the Old Testament law (God's agreements with Abraham and Moses) under which humanity lived from the fall of Adam to the coming of Christ. So, the speaker would represent humanity before the crucifixion of Christ. It is the crucifixion of Christ that gives humanity the "new small-rented lease," the new covenant, the New Testament grace that does not demand as much in strict obedience to laws and emphasis on works from the individual as did the Old Testament law. The new grace relies on faith and love, rather than on works and law.

In the second quatrain the speaker relates that he sought the "lord" at his "manor" (i.e., God in heaven). At this point the reader begins to perceive that the speaker is not only humanity *before* Christ's crucifixion, but he also represents anyone *since* then: any individual weighed with sin and guilt may seek God in heaven through prayer. The "land" owned by God is not only earth but also humanity. God owned this "land" before Adam's fall and repossesses it with Christ's crucifixion: the fact that he had "dearly bought" this land "long since on earth" suggests the death of Christ occurring in the past for every human of the present, but it implies that each one has to discover Christ's sacrifice on an individual level. Just as Christ died to save pre-crucifixion fallen humanity, so has he died to save each sinful, fallen individual in the continuing present. The history of the human race from a Christian perspective is repeated in the life of the individual. So, the poem at this point has become a double allegory.

The third quatrain and couplet portray the speaker immediately ("STRAIGHT") returning to find his lord. The speaker naively assumes that he will find such a high-born individual in beautiful, elegant, prestigious, and impressive places where people gather. His search of the many such places is conveyed by the cataloguing of them in line 11. Then he is surprised to find him among harsh and discordant ("RAGGED") noise and laughter of "thieves and murderers": Christ was crucified with two "thieves," and the "murderers" were the Jews and Romans who arrested, tried, and crucified him. In addition, Christ was always humbly working among the lowly thieves, prostitutes, and poor during his life, in contrast to the pompous, proud existence that the speaker apparently assumed: in other words, his discovery of Christ is a complete discovery of the true nature of the New Testament God of humility, service, love, grace, and forgiveness in both his life and death. The ultimate surprise in the poem is that Christ says to the speaker, "Your suit is granted," even before the speaker can ask anything. This can be seen as God knowing the heart of man, anticipating his request, and then dying to fulfill it. However, it is deliberately ambiguous to suggest that it is *already* granted, has *already* been granted, for each individual of the present in Christ's sacrifice centuries ago: it simply is a matter for each person to discover for himself that he *already* has been provided for by the New Covenant. The statement made by Christ in the poem may also be an allusion to Christ's actual words on the cross, "It is finished." It is God's work of *redemption* that was and is already finished and available for all of fallen humanity at the time of Christ's death and for every human since.

The title "Redemption" relates directly to the economic and legal conceit of the poem. "Redemption" literally is buying back something formerly owned or paying for something claimed by another. It was especially common in the Middle Ages and Renaissance for Christian works to refer to Adam being bound in a bond to Satan. Christ redeemed this bond, buying back mankind who had, through sin, fallen into Satan's possession. Christ paid the price for man's sin—i.e., "dearly bought" mankind with his own life. At the Last Supper Christ said, "For this is my blood of the new testament, which is shed for many for the remission of sins" (Matthew 26:28). Through this payment by Christ every human (i.e., the speaker of the poem) has a new "lease" to thrive spiritually.

Remove. *Noun*: the act of changing one's place, departure to another place. *Verb*: (1) to move from out of an occupied place; (2) to withdraw from a place, to go away; (3) to transfer a cause or person for trial from one court of law to another; (4) to dismiss; (5) to dispose of; (6) to take away from.

Repair(e). *Verb*: (1) to go [to a place], (2) to restore to a sound condition, (3) to furnish or provide with, (4) to replace decayed or damaged parts, (5) to renew or restore by making up for previous decay or loss.

Respective. *Adjective*: respectful.

Rest. A special use of the word is in the card game primero and refers to the stakes kept in reserve: the game ends when these stakes in reserve are lost.

Rise. *Verb*: (1) to get up from sitting, lying, resting, sleeping; (2) to recover from sin, from a spiritual fall; (3) to come back from death or the grave, to experience resurrection; (4) to take up arms for battle; (5) to move above the earth's horizon [said of the sun and other heavenly bodies]; (6) to ascend; (7) to be elated with joy or hope; (8) to appear, spring up, come into existence.

S

Sad. *Adjective*: (1) serious, somber; (2) sorrowful, mournful.

St. Albans, Viscount. See BACON, FRANCIS.

St. Andrew's Church. The chapel of Bemerton St. Andrew. See BEMERTON.

St. Augustine. See AUGUSTINE, SAINT.

St. John Chrysostom. See CHRYSOSTOM, SAINT JOHN.

St. Thomas Aquinas. See AQUINAS, SAINT THOMAS.

Salisbury. City in WILTSHIRE and site of Salisbury Cathedral. The cathedral is about two miles from St. Andrew's Church and the rectory where George Herbert lived in BEMERTON. Herbert would attend the cathedral twice a week and play with musical gatherings after the services: WALTON says that Herbert would "sing and play his part at an appointed private music meeting." Walton also relates some incidents (whether fact or fiction, we do not know) that occurred on Herbert's walks to Salisbury that illustrate Herbert's piety and compassion. Herbert supposedly gave one man some rules for "practical piety" in a loving manner, conversed with another minister about the improvement of the clergy and the restoration of catechizing, and helped a poor man whose horse had fallen under the burden of his large load. In the cathedral today Herbert is memorialized in one of the stained glass windows.

Sallet. Salad.

Sam(p)son. Son of Manoah of the Danites who was so strong that he killed a lion with his hands. Married a Philistine woman who betrayed Sampson: she talked him into revealing the solution to a riddle he had posed to the Philistines about the lion's carcass with honey in it, and she then told it to her people. After his father-in-law kept Sampson from his wife and gave her to another man, Sampson tied firebrands on the tails of three hundred foxes and let them run through the Philistines' fields of grain, thus burning their crops and vineyards. The Philistines later tried to hold Sampson bound in cords, but he burst them and then killed one thousand of them with the jawbone of an ass. Eventually he loved a woman named Delilah who, for silver offered her by the Philistines, finally had Sampson tell her that the secret of his strength lay in his uncut hair. She took the money from the Philistines and had Sampson shaved while he slept. When he awoke, his strength was gone. The Philistines took him, blinded him, and put him in prison in Gaza. His hair grew while he was imprisoned; therefore, when thousands of Philistines gathered and brought Sampson there in order to mock him, he was able to push apart the two pillars his hands were touching and to destroy the building, the Philistines, and himself. Herbert alludes to this in "Sunday" when he says that "Sampson bore the doors away." See Judges 13–16.

Sara(h). Half-sister and wife of Abram (Abraham). When a famine drove them into Egypt, they did not reveal that they were husband and wife. Pharaoh heard of her beauty, took her into his family, but God sent plagues on Pharaoh because he had Abram's wife. Therefore, he returned her to Abram with gifts of servants and cattle. When she was old and far past the normal childbearing stage, God promised her a son. She did become pregnant, and Isaac was born, to her great joy. See especially Genesis 12 and 16–21.

Herbert, in his "Notes" to VALDESSO's *Considerations*, refers to Sara's and Abraham's deception as a "weakness in the great Patriark [i.e., in Abraham]."

Schismatic(k). *Noun*: a person who breaks with a specific church or faith or who promotes any breach (schism) in unity.

School. *Noun*: (1) place for instruction; (2) a group of people holding similar beliefs and principles; (3) a body of teachers and scholars.

Schoolmen. The scholastic philosophers—medieval European university teachers, philosophers, theologians, and writers who followed and developed the ideas of ARISTOTLE and early Christian writers in minute and profuse speculations: one of the Schoolmen was AQUINAS.

Sconce, sconse. *Noun*: a fort or earthwork defense.

Seal. *Noun*: (1) a design pressed into a piece of wax attached to a letter or other document to attest to its authenticity; (2) a piece of wax bearing the impression of a design or other symbol of authentication on a document; (3) a symbol of a covenant or confirmation, especially in a theological context; (4) the impression of a signet ring on something to claim ownership or to authenticate; (5) an impressed mark as a sign on anything; (6) a piece of wax that holds something closed; (7) a sign or symbol of a high office. *Verb*: (1) to impress, affix, symbolize authenticate, or close something with a seal (as defined above under uses as a noun); (2) in some contexts, possibly a variant spelling of "SEEL," meaning to sew shut a bird's eyes, a term from falconry.

Security. *Noun*: (1) condition of being protected from danger; (2) confidence and freedom from doubt or care; (3) something which makes secure; (4) property pledged to assure fulfillment of an obligation or payment of debt.

Seel. *Verb*: to sew shut a bird's eyelids during its training—from falconry.

Seize. *Verb*: (1) to take hold of, to grasp; (2) [in legal use] to take possession of (property).

Sensibility. See DISSOCIATION OF SENSIBILITY.

Sensible Soul. See TRIPARTITE SOUL.

Sensitive Soul. See TRIPARTITE SOUL.

Session-day, Session(s). Sessions usually refer to judicial proceedings held by a Justice of the Peace or other legal official, and session-day is the day on which such proceedings or trials are held. More generally, the terms may refer to any meeting or conference of any deliberative body.

Sestet. See SONNET.

Set. A special adjectival meaning in *THE CHURCH MILITANT*, line 51, is "defeated."

Seven Virtues. See VIRTUES.

Severall, sev'rall, several. *Adjective*: (1) separate, distinct; (2) distinctive, particular; (3) various, diverse.

Shadow. *Verb*: (1) to screen from blame or attack, (2) to protect or shelter from the sun, (3) to cover or obscure with a shadow, (4) to conceal, (5) to prefigure or symbolize, (6) to portray or to paint a picture. *Noun*: (1) darkness caused by a body intercepting the light of the sun or other luminous element, (2) a symbol or prefiguration.

Shaped verses. See PATTERN POEMS.

Sharp. *Adjective*: (1) having a keen cutting edge or fine point; (2) intellectually discerning, perceptive, clever.

Showl, shoal. *Noun*: (1) a large number of persons thronging together or classed together, (2) a crowd.

Shrowd, shroud. *Noun*: (1) protection or temporary shelter; (2) winding sheet for a corpse, a death shroud.

Sidney, Mary (1561–1620). Countess of Pembroke and sister of Sir PHILIP SIDNEY. After her brother's death she published many of his works and completed the translation of the *Psalms* that her brother had begun. She translated other works and was well-known as a patroness of writers. She was the third wife of Henry Herbert, 2nd Earl of Pembroke, and was the mother of both WILLIAM HERBERT, 3rd Earl of Pembroke, and PHILIP HERBERT, 4th Earl of Pembroke, who married Lady ANNE CLIFFORD.

Sidney, Philip (1554–1586). Sir Philip Sidney was a poet, prose writer, translator, courtier, and literary patron during the reign of ELIZABETH I. His *Arcadia* was written for his sister MARY SIDNEY, Countess of Pembroke, while he stayed at WILTON HOUSE. He began a translation of the *Psalms* that his sister completed after his death. Sidney's *Astrophil and Stella* sonnet sequence is the first important such cycle in English, influencing SPENSER, Shakespeare, DONNE, Herbert, and all succeeding writers of sonnets. His use of the PETRARCHAN convention is quite important for the background of secular love poems of Herbert's time, compared to Herbert's own emphases. The closest echo of and apparent influence from Sidney is in the ending of "JORDAN (2)": a "friend" (apparently Christ) whispers to the poet-speaker some advice parallel to that of Astrophil's "Muse" at the end of the first sonnet of *Astrophil and Stella*. Sidney was regarded as the ideal of a courtier and died of a wound from battle in 1586. He was buried in St. Paul's Cathedral.

Silly, sillie. *Adjective*: (1) happy, lucky; (2) innocent, naive, harmless; (3) pitiable, helpless, defenseless; (4) insignificant, poor; (5) foolish, simple.

Simples. *Noun*: (1) medicines made from one herb or plant, (2) plants or herbs used to prepare medicines.

Sink. *Noun:* cesspool or sewer.

Sirens. In mythology, sea nymphs who, with enchanting singing, lured sailors to their death on the rocks. CIRCE warned Odysseus of them, so he closed the ears of his sailors with wax and had himself tied to the mast of the ship. When they failed with Odysseus, the sirens killed themselves. They were also referred to as "mermaids." Herbert alludes to them in "Self-condemnation."

Six and seven. A gambling phrase (from rolling dice) meaning carelessly to risk everything. See line 401 of *THE CHURCH-PORCH*.

Size. *Noun:* (1) the bigness, quantity, or magnitude of anything; (2) status of anything; (3) quality of anything; (4) shortened form of "assize," a judicial session held for a given period in each county of England at which traveling judges sit to hear and administer cases.

Snuff. *Noun:* wick of a candle or portion of the wick that is already burned and blackened and must be removed to again light the candle effectively.

Sodom. See LOT.

Sonnet. In its strictest definition, a 14-line lyric poem in iambic pentameter meter. The two major forms of the sonnet in English are (1) the Italian or PETRARCHAN and (2) the English or Shakespearean. The Italian or Petrarchan form was used in Italian poetry by Petrarch and others before the English Renaissance, and Sir Thomas Wyatt introduced it into English verse with his translations of some of Petrarch's poems and in the writing of some of his own. Such a sonnet typically divides into two parts, the octave (lines 1–8) and the sestet (lines 9–14): usually there are changes of sorts between the two divisions (in imagery, tone, attitude, etc.). Most commonly the octave asks a question, poses a problem, or presents some situation or experience to which the sestet provides an answer, solution, or response. The rhyme scheme of the octave is *abbaabba*, but the scheme of the sestet varies. The English or Shakespearean form was developed by Wyatt's younger contemporary the Earl of Surrey (Henry Howard) and divides into three quatrains (a set of four lines) and a couplet (two rhyming lines) with the rhyme scheme *abab cdcd efef gg*.
   Other variations in form of such 14-line sonnets have been developed with poets' experimentations in line length, meter, rhyme scheme, etc., but these two primary forms remain the bases for

variations from the hands of such experimenters as Sir PHILIP
SIDNEY, EDMUND SPENSER, and others.

Herbert wrote sixteen sonnets, two to his mother and fourteen in
THE TEMPLE. They are as follows: "SONNETS 1 AND 2" (those to
his mother), "REDEMPTION," "Holy Baptism (1)," "Sin (1),"
"PRAYER (1)," "Love (1)," "Love (2)," "The Holy Scriptures (1),"
"The Holy Scriptures (2)," "Avarice," "Christmas," "The Holdfast,"
"Joseph's Coat," "The Sonne," and "The Answer." All are essentially in
the English form, the major variation being that, in ten of them, the
rhyme scheme of the third quatrain is *effe*, rather than *efef*.

"Sonnets 1 and 2." I am designating, for convenience, the two
sonnets sent by Herbert to his mother (MAGDALEN HERBERT) as
"Sonnet 1" and "Sonnet 2." These were sent to her in a letter of "New
Year, 1609/10," shortly after Herbert entered Cambridge and just
before his seventeenth birthday. In the letter Herbert says, "I need not
their [the Muses'] help, to reprove the vanity of those many Love-
poems, that are daily writ and consecrated to Venus; nor to bewail that
so few are writ, that look towards God and Heaven. For my own part,
my meaning (dear Mother) is in these Sonnets, to declare my resolution
to be, that my poor abilities in Poetry, shall be all, and ever consecrated
to God's glory." They were first published in WALTON's *Life of
Herbert* in 1670. The two sonnets are in the English form (see
SONNET), with the exception of the *effe* rhyme scheme in the third
quatrain: this variation is employed later by Herbert in many of the
sonnets in *THE TEMPLE*.

"Sonnet 1" bemoans the loss of complete dedication and
willingness to sacrifice all to God, such spiritual passion ("heat") as the
martyrs once did feel. The first three lines introduce the sonnet's
primary motif of heat and burning, seen in "heat," "burn," and
"flames." A truly METAPHYSICAL touch here is the added
implication that many of the martyrs were literally burned, executed by
flames, in return for their inner passion devoted to God. Line 6 refers
to poems being sacrificed on God's altar ("burnt"), line 12 to "fire," and
line 13 to "fuel." Lines 3–4 also present an analogy of Poetry as a
servant of Venus, wearing the clothing ("LIVERY") worn by all of her
servants. Herbert proposes that God's love should be able to move the
human spirit to praise as well as any "she," any woman, can move a man
to praise. In a clever analogy/contrast, Herbert then says that God's
"Dove" (the Holy Spirit) can easily exceed the flight of winged Cupid,
Venus's son and God of Love: thus, (1) love of God is superior to the
earthly, physical love symbolized by Venus and Cupid, and (2) poetry
inspired by and written about the Holy Spirit is superior to and more
elevated than that inspired by and written about Cupid (and all he

symbolizes). The seriousness is combined with humor here in a way typical of METAPHYSICAL poetry, since doves were also traditionally regarded as sacred to and associated with Venus. A brief METAPHYSICAL CONCEIT appears in lines 10–11 in the comparison of verse that concerns God with a deep stream: both are "smooth" on the surface with a mass of real substance inherent beneath. The final question posed in lines 12–14 is why the "fire" of love placed within each human breast by God chooses to be fueled by, to feed upon, the earthly and physical beauty of a woman, mortal beauty that eventually will decay and be so loathsome that even the worms of the grave may refuse to eat it! This latter image in its grotesque humor has affinities with several found in the poetry of DONNE. Herbert also seems to be playing with some of the meanings of "BRAVE" in his time: here the primary emphasis is on "worth" or "excellence," but "courageous" and "beautiful" also fit the context of the individual daring to go against the easy, conventional way of secular poetry and choosing the true, divine, spiritual beauty of God over that of the false, ephemeral, earthly beauty of a "she."

"Sonnet 2" continues slightly the motif of "fire" from "Sonnet 1." The lowly secular poets praising only women's beauty are said to have "fire" that is "wild" (line 10): their passion is like a wildfire, a fire out of control blazing across earthly ground, rather than ascending "upward" to praise God. Their "poor INVENTION" in their low intellect "burns" (line 9): as poets, they only repeat the most worn of stereotypes from PETRARCHAN poetry, such as comparing women's eyes to crystal (line 8). True content could be shown by looking afresh at true beauty in God and describing it. Lines 6–7 imply that use of the old conventional Petrarchan analogies of a lady's cheeks like "roses and lilies" in color is a perversion of the true symbolism of roses and lilies: their beauty should lead one to their Creator, not to a woman. Also, the rose is associated with the Biblical Rose of Sharon and with the redness of Christ's sacrificial blood. The lily connotes purity and suggests Christ and the Virgin Mary in various Christian contexts. Herbert, then, argues from his opening conceit (lines 1–4) that God's majesty pervades the universe, and it is manifested in beauty that true poets should praise in their ink. In the "Deluge" (the Old Testament Flood) sin was purged from the earth: the flood of God's majesty over the earth and poems that let this majesty flow through their ink will obliterate the sin of those verses of earthly passion. The last three lines (in Donnelike imagery) drive home the point that beneath the surface of the earthly woman's face is only filth, but beneath the surface beauty of God (the Creator of the physical universe) is even greater beauty, true beauty in the spiritual realm. Herbert seems to want more than one meaning of "DISCOVERY" to apply here, primarily connoting both the literal uncovering of this true beauty and the surprising revelation upon uncovering it.

Soul, Feminine. The soul is referred to as feminine in Castiglione's *THE COURTIER* and in countless other writers of the Renaissance. Uses abound in Herbert. For overt references see, for example, "Nature" and "CHURCH MONUMENTS." But suggestions of God or Christ as the lover of the soul assume this concept in other poems.

Souls, Tripartite or Three. See TRIPARTITE SOUL.

Span. *Noun*: (1) distance from the tip of the thumb to the tip of the little finger or from the tip of the thumb to the tip of the forefinger of a fully extended hand: this distance averaging nine inches was used as a measure of length; (2) a very small space or length; (3) a short space of time, frequently referring to the short time of a human's life. *Verb*: (1) to grasp or seize; (2) to measure by an outstretched hand; (3) to measure out or set a limit; (4) to form an arch across or over, to stretch or extend over in an arch, to cross from side to side; (5) to reach or extend over either space or time.

Speed. *Verb*: (1) to succeed or prosper; (2) to attain one's purpose or desire; (3) to make progress; (4) to hasten; (5) to make haste.

Spell. *Verb*: (1) to read letter by letter; (2) to discover by close study or observation; (3) to decipher, comprehend, understand; (4) to contemplate, consider.

Spenser, Edmund (1552?–1599). English poet. Educated at Cambridge. Served in the Earl of Leicester's household in 1579 and thereby met Sir PHILIP SIDNEY. Wrote *The Shepherd's Calendar* and dedicated it to Sidney. Appointed secretary to Lord Grey of Wilton in 1580, serving him in Ireland. Spenser lived in Ireland until very near the end of his life. After he was forced to flee Ireland following an insurrection in 1598, he died the following year in London in near-poverty. Robert Devereux, Earl of Essex, paid for his funeral. He was buried in Westminster Abbey, and Lady ANNE CLIFFORD erected a monument for him there about twenty years later.

Spenser's masterpiece is *The Faerie Queene*, dedicated to Queen ELIZABETH, and portraying her as Gloriana, on one of the many allegorical levels in the long epic poem. Spenser also wrote *Four Hymns*, specifically reflecting the heavy influence from PLATONIC thought on Spenser. Among several other works, also important are his PETRARCHAN sonnet sequence entitled *Amoretti* that concerns his courtship of Elizabeth Boyle and his *Epithalamion* that depicts their marriage. Christian Platonism suffuses all of Spenser's major works.

Herbert was well aware of Spenser's works, since Spenser's contribution to English PETRARCHAN poetry, along with that of SIDNEY, is very much in the background when Herbert deliberately directs his praise of beauty and love to Christian figures and values. See especially "SONNETS 1 AND 2" in which Herbert asks if poetry only serves Venus's turn and ridicules poets' emphases on women's cheeks as roses and lilies and their eyes as crystals.

Sphere(s). *Noun*: (1) commonly in Herbert's work, refers to one of the solid, transparent globes in which all of the known planets, the sun, the moon, and the stars are placed, according to the system envisioned largely by PTOLEMY. These Ptolemaic spheres were thought to number either 9, 10, or 11. Some contended that angels or INTELLIGENCES managed each separate sphere. It was believed that, as the spheres revolved, they created a perfect music known as the music of the spheres. Adam and Eve could hear the music before their fall, but no human after the fall can hear it. The speaker of Herbert's "ARTILLERY" says, "I, who had heard of music in the spheres." (See also HIERARCHY, THE HEAVENLY); (2) the circular, visible outer limit of space; (3) heaven; (4) domain in which one lives and acts; (5) a round body or ball.

Spittle. *Noun*: (1) hospital; (2) spit, saliva.

Spouse. Frequently refers to the Church (the Church as the bride of Christ).

Staff(e). *Noun*: (1) a stick carried to help in walking or climbing; (2) a stick with a hooked end, used by a shepherd to tend sheep; (3) a rod to measure distances and heights; (4) distaff of a spinning wheel.

Standing Majesty. The sovereign's throne in its usual, permanent royal residence (the "standing house"). See CHAIR OF GRACE.

Stay. *Verb*: (1) to stop or halt or stand still; (2) to cease carrying out some activity; (3) to remain in a place, rather than leaving; (4) to remain unmoving in position or unchanging in condition; (5) to tarry, linger, delay; (6) to reside in a place for a time; (7) to wait, to be inactive; (8) to detain or hold back or stop someone or something; (9) to support, sustain, hold up, comfort. *Noun*: (1) a delay; (2) a stop or pause; (3) a cessation; (4) a support.

Stew(s). *Noun*: brothel(s), house(s) of prostitution. So called because of their development from some heated public bathhouses.

Still. *Adverb*: ever or always or continually. *Adjective*: motionless or silent. *Verb*: to quiet or to calm.

Stock(s). *Noun*: (1) trunk of a tree or stem of a plant; (2) a fund, a sum of money; (3) a store, accumulated supply or wealth; (4) [put into the] stocks: instrument of punishment and public ridicule made of a wooden frame with holes into which the ankles (and sometimes the wrists) could be locked.

Store. *Noun*: (1) sufficient or abundant supply; (2) a person's accumulated goods or money; (3) a treasure; (4) a stock of anything laid up for future use.

Stour. *Adjective*: sturdy, solid, unmoving.

Stowre. See STOUR.

Straight. *Adjective*: (1) not crooked; (2) direct, undeviating; (3) honest, proper. *Adverb*: (1) immediately, without delay; (2) in a direct course, by the shortest way.

Stuart. Family ruling England for most of the seventeenth century. See JAMES I and CHARLES I.

Stuart, Charles. See CHARLES I.

Stuart, Elizabeth (1596–1662). Daughter of King JAMES. Married FREDERICK, Elector Palatine, on February 14, 1613. She became Queen of Bohemia in 1619 when Frederick accepted the election as King Frederick V. She was nicknamed "the Winter Queen" (in the role of Queen only from November, 1619, until November, 1620, when Frederick was defeated by the Catholic League). Driven out of their country, they lived in exile. Her husband died in 1632. She returned to England in 1661 and died there in 1662. "To the Queen of Bohemia" concerns her and is a poem attributed to George Herbert.

Stuart, Henry (1594–1612). Son of King JAMES. Prince of Wales who was popular with the people and a future king of great hope. His death of typhoid fever stunned and greatly saddened the nation, and the death was followed by many written tributes, including JOHN DONNE's "Elegy upon the Untimely Death of the Incomparable Prince

Henry" and one by EDWARD HERBERT. JONSON told DRUMMOND that Donne claimed to have written his own poem on Prince Henry "to match Sir Edward Herbert in obscureness." George Herbert wrote two Latin elegies on the Prince's death. The death of Henry meant that CHARLES would succeed to the throne.

Stuart, James. See JAMES I.

Style. *Noun*: a distinguishing title or designation. *Verb*: (1) to give a name or style to, (2) to call by a name or style.

Sublimate. *Noun*: mercuric chloride, a poison derived from mercury.

Sublunary. *Adjective*: below the moon—referring to the realm of the created universe below the SPHERE of the moon, according to the PTOLEMAIC concept of the universe; this area includes the earth and the layers of the other three ELEMENTS (water, air, and fire). Anything in the sublunary realm is associated with the worldly, earthly, and physical, and is subject to time, change, decay, and death.

Subtil, subtile, subtill, subtle. *Adjective*: (1) impalpable, fine, or delicate; (2) involving discrimination or fine points, abstruse, difficult; (3) clever or sly.

Sudden, suddain. *Adjective*: (1) happening without warning, (2) hasty or rash, (3) prompt or immediate, (4) brief or momentary.

Superliminare. Means "above the threshold." Herbert uses the word for a short poem placed between *THE CHURCH-PORCH* and *The Church* (see *THE TEMPLE*), suggesting the threshold, the transition from one to the other.

Sweets. *Noun*: perfumes, sweet fragrances.

T

Temple, The. Herbert's major body of poems was published under this title in a book of 1633, several months after Herbert's death. The full title in the first edition is *The Temple: Sacred Poems and Private Ejaculations.* An unsigned preface ("The Printers to the Reader") was written by NICHOLAS FERRAR (attribution is made to him by his brother JOHN FERRAR, by BARNABAS OLEY, and by IZAAK WALTON). As Amy Charles points out (see her *A Life of George Herbert*, pp. 184–86), Nicholas Ferrar, in the manuscript copied at Little Gidding and from which the first edition was published, apparently gave the work the title *The Temple* (without the subtitle) and also added the epigraph from Psalms 29:8 ("In his Temple doth every man speak of his honour"). It is most likely, then, that Herbert himself did not give his poems this general title under which they were published.

The major section titles, however, are Herbert's. The first section is the long poem titled *THE CHURCH-PORCH.* The second section is the largest, most important one and is titled *The Church*: here are the many lyrics of varying length that are Herbert's poetic masterpieces and for which he is most famous. The final section is another long poem, this one titled *THE CHURCH MILITANT.*

The entire work is made up of either 164 or 170 poems, depending upon whether or not one regards some of the poems that were copied and printed as single poems in 1633 as actually properly being separate poems. For this whole problem, one should see the 1980 essay by Shawcross cited in my "Selected Bibliography" under "*The Temple*: In General and Its Unity." In this "Dictionary" there are separate entries for *The Church-Porch* and *The Church Militant.* In addition, approximately one-sixth of the poems of *The Church* are given separate entries: those so entered are some that are most frequently found in anthologies and/or deemed to be Herbert's best, most representative, and most famous poems. The content of all poems of *The Temple*, however, has been examined for elements to make up other entries.

The subjects of seemingly endless speculation have been and continue to be such matters as the principles of structure and/or unity in both *The Temple* and *The Church.* The basic principle proposed is an architectural one, emphasizing entering *The Church* only after proper preparation in *The Church-Porch.* The individual poems then become the building blocks or parts of Herbert's Church (or "Temple"—

remembering, however, that this is Ferrar's word) erected to the glory of God. Obviously supporting this overall architectural analogy are poems named after physical parts of a church, such as "THE ALTAR," "CHURCH MONUMENTS," "The Church Floor," and "THE WINDOWS." Herbert's treatment of these physical elements become symbolic of many other matters beyond the literal level, however. Another view is that the "Church" is the universal church and that the individual progresses through it from birth to death and salvation, beginning the trek with what Christ has already done for the individual through his crucifixion for and redemption of humanity (see several of the opening poems of *The Church*). Many other principles of unity for the whole "Church" and/or "Temple" and for sequences and patterns within Herbert's work have been and are still being proposed by critics: some see reflections of the church calendar, of catechetical instruction, of the Book of Common Prayer, of commonplace books and the psalter, of the use of TYPEs, of the heart as the "church," and many other possible structural bases. One should especially examine the critical works included in my "Selected Bibliography" under "*The Temple*: In General and Its Unity" to begin to grasp the complexity and multiplicity of theories proposed for Herbert's structural principles in the body of his poems. A "Dictionary" of this nature cannot do justice to the patterns of Herbert's work as a whole, but necessarily must focus on the nature of individual, representative poems that reflect part of the larger patterns.

Tentation. Temptation.

Tertullian (Quintus Septimus Florens Tertullianus) [about 155–225]. Early Christian convert and writer in Carthage who defended Christianity against pagans, Jews, and heretical sects. Influential in his expression of the doctrine of the TRINITY; his arguments for the true birth, death, and resurrection of Christ; his arguments against pagan and heretical concepts of the soul; his writings on the history of baptism; his exposition of the Lord's Prayer; and his discussion of idolatry. One of the earliest and most important Christian writers in Latin, Tertullian is referred to by Herbert in Chapter 34 of *THE COUNTRY PARSON*.

Then. Common spelling of modern "than."

Things indifferent. See INDIFFERENT THINGS.

Thorough. Common spelling for modern "through."

Thorow. Common spelling for modern "thorough."

Three Books of God. See BOOKS OF GOD.

Three Souls. See TRIPARTITE SOUL.

Throughly. Common spelling of modern "thoroughly."

Tincture. *Noun*: (1) color or dye; (2) stain or blemish; (3) in ALCHEMY, a spiritual principle or immaterial substance, the quality of which can be infused into things; (4) an active, physical principle that can be extracted from a substance; (5) an essence of a substance [such as gold] that supposedly can be extracted and used to change other substances.

Tire. *Noun*: (1) attire, attiring, apparel, clothing; (2) ornament for the head.

Touch. *Verb*: special senses in Herbert's time are (1) to use a "touchstone," a black stone used to test the quality of gold or silver by the color they leave when rubbed on this stone; (2) figuratively applied to testing the value or authenticity of anything.

Toy. *Noun*: a trifle, a trivial thing.

Trace. *Verb*: (1) to follow the footprints of or to pursue, (2) to determine the course of something.

Transubstantiation. *Noun*: in theological usage, this is the miraculous change of the bread and wine of the Eucharist (or Holy Communion) into the body and blood of Christ, a belief primarily associated with Roman Catholicism. It is the source of much debate among Protestant factions regarding the extent to which the body and blood are really present or only symbolically so in the bread and wine.

Travel. *Verb*: (1) to afflict or trouble, (2) to labor or work hard, (3) to journey.

Tree. Herbert frequently employs the noun in special biblical and Christian senses: (1) the Tree of Knowledge (of good and evil) in Eden, the fruit from which Adam and Eve were forbidden to eat (also referred to as the "forbidden tree," "fruitful tree," and "Adam's tree") [see Genesis 2 and 3]; (2) the Tree of Life in Eden that held immortality for humanity [see Genesis 2 and Revelation 22]; (3) the cross on which Christ was crucified, Christ's cross (one of the three "trees") on Calvary or Golgotha (the hill near Jerusalem where Christ was crucified). Also referred to as "Christ's tree." An old Christian belief held that Christ's cross was made of the wood from the Tree of Knowledge and that Christ was crucified on the very site on which the Tree of Knowledge grew in Eden. Also, the Tree of Life has been interpreted as a symbolic foreshadowing of Christ and his granting of immortality again to humanity through his "tree"; (4) "David's tree" refers to that mentioned in one of the Psalms (attributed to David)—"And he shall be like a tree planted by the rivers of water, that bringeth forth his fruit in his season; his leaf also shall not wither; and whatsoever he doeth shall prosper" (Psalms 1:3).

Trencher. *Noun*: a plate on which food is served, frequently ornamented with moral sayings, lessons.

Trinity. The Christian concept that God or the Godhead is made up of three unified and indivisible divine figures or "persons": the Father (God the Creator), the Son (Jesus Christ), and the Holy Spirit (Holy Ghost). Frequently the Father is associated with wrath and power; the Son with love, mercy, and light (the "sun" and "son"); and the Holy Spirit with ever-present grace (biblically, symbolically, and artistically represented as a dove, fire, and breath).

Trinity College. The college at Cambridge University attended by George Herbert. He matriculated here in 1609, took his Bachelor of Arts degree in 1612, was elected minor fellow in 1614, was elected major fellow and took his Master of Arts degree in 1616. Subsequently he became a sublector, then Praelector in Rhetoric in the University (1618), then deputy for the University Orator (1619), and eventually the University Orator (1620). Many of Herbert's extant letters, as well as the two sonnets sent to his mother (see MAGDALEN HERBERT and "SONNETS 1 AND 2"), were written during his years at Cambridge. It is also likely that Herbert wrote *THE CHURCH-PORCH* and *THE CHURCH MILITANT*, as well as some other poems (or early versions of poems) that eventually became parts of *THE CHURCH* section of *THE TEMPLE*. Most of Herbert's Latin verse probably was written during the Cambridge years.

His Cambridge positions meant that Herbert served at times as tutor, as lecturer, as writer and deliverer of orations, and as composer of official university correspondences of various sorts. All the while Herbert was increasingly studying and buying books concerning theology to prepare for his service in the church eventually. In one of his letters to Sir JOHN DANVERS written from Cambridge, Herbert speaks of wanting books desperately because "I am now setting foot into Divinity, to lay the platform of my future life. . . ."

Tripartite Soul. A concept inherited from Scholastic Philosophy (see SCHOOLMEN) and ARISTOTLE that was still commonly alluded to in Herbert's time. The "soul" many times was assumed actually to consist of three souls or three parts of the soul. The vegetative (or vegetable) soul is possessed by plants, animals, and humans, and it is responsible for growth and reproduction. The sensitive (or sensible) soul is possessed by animals and humans, and it is responsible for the functioning of the five senses. The rational (or intellectual) soul is possessed by humans, and it is responsible for reason, understanding, and free will. This third soul distinguishes humans from plants and animals, places humanity just below the angels and God in the hierarchy of creatures (see NATURAL ORDER), and makes humans potentially angelic and godlike. Herbert specifically refers to this concept in Chapter 9 of *THE COUNTRY PARSON*: "Other temptations he has, which, like mortal enemies, may sometimes disquiet him likewise; for the human soul being bounded, and kept in, in her sensitive faculty, will run out more or less in her intellectual."

Triumphant Church. See CHURCH TRIUMPHANT.

True. *Adjective*: (1) steadfast, loyal, faithful; (2) consistent with fact, agreeing with reality; (3) exact, accurate, correct; (4) proper, legitimate; (5) real, genuine, not imaginary.

Try. *Verb*: (1) to separate, choose, select; (2) to search by examination; (3) to determine; (4) to examine and determine judicially; (5) to test or prove the strength or goodness or truth of something; (6) to experience or undergo; (7) to attempt to do or perform.

Tuberculosis. The apparent cause of George Herbert's recurring illness, weakness, and eventual death. Called "consumption" in the seventeenth century (e.g., in WALTON).

Tudor, Elizabeth. See ELIZABETH I.

Tullie. See CICERO.

Tully. See CICERO.

Two Books of God. See BOOKS OF GOD.

Type. *Noun*: (1) a symbol or emblem; (2) a person, object, or event of the Old Testament that prefigures or foreshadows a person, thing, or event of the New Testament.

U

Uncouth. *Adjective*: (1) strange or unknown, (2) crude, unrefined, unpleasant.

Use. *Verb*: (1) to follow as a custom, (2) to be usual or customary, (3) to carry on an occupation or profession or function, (4) to spend time in a certain way, (5) to put into practice or carry into action, (6) to employ something for a certain purpose, (7) to make use of land by working or tilling or occupying, (8) to take or partake of as food or drink, (9) to do a thing customarily or by habit. *Noun*: (1) act of employing a thing for any purpose; (2) spending; (3) habit or custom; (4) distinctive ritual, liturgy, service, or worship in a particular church or ecclesiastical division.

Usurer. *Noun*: a person who lends money at interest, especially large or excessive interest.

V

Vain. *Adjective*: (1) having no value, worth, or significance; (2) having no effect or power, futile, fruitless, useless; (3) empty; (4) foolish, silly, thoughtless. This word did *not* have the meaning of "proud" or "displaying personal vanity" in Herbert's time.

Valdés, Juan (about 1510–1541). Born in Spain of a noble family. Under the influence of the works of Erasmus, he seriously questioned facets of orthodox Roman Catholicism. In the face of the Spanish Inquisition, he went to live in Italy. Died in Naples. While in Naples he wrote *The Hundred and Ten Considerations* in Spanish. Later it was published in Italian. NICHOLAS FERRAR translated it into English as the *Considerations* by Valdesso (the Italian form of his name). Herbert sent to Ferrar some of his opinions about the work in the form of a letter to Ferrar and some "Brief Notes" commenting on facets of Valdesso's arguments. Some of Herbert's own theological inclinations may thus be gleaned from these: on this matter, see especially the essay by Ilona Bell cited in the "Selected Bibliography" under "Miscellaneous and More Than One Type of Prose Work."

Valdesso, John. See VALDÉS, JUAN.

Vaughan, Henry (1621–1695). One of the major METAPHYSICAL poets. Born in Wales. After apparently studying law for a time in London, he returned to Wales where he eventually settled into a medical practice. His early works are secular and reflect more the influence of JONSON and the CLASSICAL strain in both subject matter and style. But about 1648–50 illness, war, death, and a reading of the poetry of Herbert led to a spiritual transformation in Vaughan. Thereafter he wrote the religious poetry on which his poetic reputation rests. The influences of both DONNE and Herbert are quite apparent in Vaughan, and generally METAPHYSICAL CONCEITs, colloquialisms, wordplay, and paradox dominate his work, although some of the classical style remains. Like Herbert and MARVELL, then, he is primarily metaphysical, but not exclusively. The quality of his poetry varies from poem to poem and line to line, and he is generally regarded as ranking fourth in the line of quality behind Donne, Herbert, and Marvell, as far as the major metaphysicals are concerned. Influences from ALCHEMY and mysticism combine with Christianity in Vaughan to create some unique spiritual beliefs and poems. His major book of poetry is *Silex*

Scintillans (1650, expanded in 1655), and two of his best and most famous poems are "The Retreat" and "The World." Vaughan acknowledges his poetic debt to Herbert. He chose to emphasize, ultimately, Christian poetry over secular. He uses many of Herbert's titles for titles of his own poems, and he employs many of Herbert's lines or close versions of them in his own poems. Other echoes of Herbert in words, phrases, images, and style permeate Vaughan's work.

Vegetable Soul. See TRIPARTITE SOUL.

Vegetative Soul. See TRIPARTITE SOUL.

Venus. In mythology, Roman name for the Greek goddess of love, Aphrodite. Known also as the goddess of beauty. Married to Vulcan (god of fire) but was unfaithful to him in having many lovers, resulting in many children by her. One of her sons was Cupid, god of love. Although primarily symbolic of physical beauty, love, and passion, she also is seen in some contexts as the principle of fertility and generative love.

Vertue. See VIRTUE.

Verulam, Baron. See BACON, FRANCIS.

Villiers, George (1592–1628). Prepared by his family to be a courtier. Introduced to King JAMES in 1614 and given the office of cupbearer. The resentment and jealousy of Robert Ker, Earl of Somerset, toward Villiers increasingly alienated the King and hastened the rise of Villiers as the new favorite of James. In 1615 James made Villiers gentleman of the bedchamber and knighted him. In 1616 he became Viscount Villiers and Baron Waddon, with an impressive grant of land. In 1617 he was made Earl of Buckingham. He later secured the unquestioned endorsement of King James when the King stated, "You may be sure that I love the Earl of Buckingham more than any else" and "Christ had his John, and I have my George." Further titles, privileges, and income accumulated for Buckingham, including his appointment as Lord High Admiral, responsible for the navy. In 1623 he was created Duke.

By the time James died, Buckingham was controlling foreign policy and continued to do so in the early years of the reign of CHARLES. His role as favorite (and practically king himself) increasingly disturbed the House of Commons, with England becoming involved in incompetent attempts at alliances and battles. Parliament impeached Buckingham in 1626, but Charles dissolved Parliament to prevent a trial. Misunderstandings with France increased, and by early 1627 war with France resulted. Buckingham's leading of ships and men at the Isle of Rhé failed miserably with a loss of thousands of English soldiers. Parliament, in a remonstrance, designated Buckingham's power as the cause of England's troubles. He was condemned and hated publicly after this, a mood leading to his assassination in 1628 by a discharged naval officer who felt that his own act served England by ridding it of a tyrant.

   In a letter from CHARING CROSS dated December 26, 1618, Herbert comments that Buckingham came to chapel an hour before prayers began on Christmas day. As University Orator, Herbert delivered the oration at York House on July 13, 1626, at the completion of the installation ceremonies for Buckingham as the new Chancellor of Cambridge University.

Virtue. *Noun*: (1) conformity of life and conduct with principles of morality; (2) physical strength, force, or energy; (3) courage, valor; (4) particular power, efficacy, or good quality inherent in such things as plants, medicines, or precious stones.

"Virtue." This poem illustrates very well the influences on Herbert from both the METAPHYSICAL and CLASSICAL strains of poetry, from both DONNE and JONSON. Some of the analogies are, in essence, metaphysical conceits, but the structure, symmetry, and parallelism are of the classical style.

   Stanza 1 addresses the day as something pleasing, with the speaker admiring and appreciating the coolness, calmness, and brightness of it. The perfectly regular iambic tetrameter of the first line conveys the harmony and calmness that he associates with the day. The day is called the "bridal of the earth and sky": it is the wedding, the marriage of earth and sky, the union of the best characteristics of both. But this elevated feeling turns at the stanza's mid-point with the conceit of "dew" as tears that will "weep" for the "fall" (the death) of the day with the coming of night. The short last line of the stanza curtly insists on the inevitable mortality of the day: the line's shortness perfectly conveys the sense of physical life cut off abruptly by death, as well as the shortness of the life of the day. The "sweet day," then, is developed as a symbol of anything mortal and beautiful in this life. Despite its beauty and pleasantness, it is doomed to die. The "dew," then, is like tears expressing sadness at the death of mortal beauty. Thus, the speaker has great appreciation for mortal beauty, but recognizes its inevitable death. The heavily stressed "die" at the end of the stanza serves to enforce this point. One notes also that the first word of this stanza is "sweet," and the last word is "die": this is true also of stanzas 2 and 3, and the clear implication is that, despite the sweetness of physical beauty embodied in the day, rose, and spring, the result is their death.

Stanza 2 begins to establish the classical parallelism and symmetry of the poem: "Sweet rose" parallels the beginning of the previous stanza ("Sweet day"), the turn toward death occurs again at the mid-point of the stanza, and the short last line virtually duplicates that of the first stanza. The "rose" in this stanza becomes the symbol of mortal beauty: it is personified as having an "angry" (i.e., red) face, and it is "BRAVE," suggesting both *handsome* and *bold*. It is so brilliantly beautiful, in fact, that it causes someone who suddenly looks at it ("rash gazer") to have tears well up in his eye so that he has to wipe them away. In other words, the brilliance of the rose is like the brilliance of the sun in causing a physical response in that tears flow with a sudden glance at it. But certainly Herbert also implies symbolically the sadness foreshadowed in the inevitable death of this extremely beautiful mortal entity. And the image of tears and sadness subtly echoes and ties in with the dew as tears in the previous stanza. The turn toward the grim origin and destination of this beautiful rose in the third line of this stanza supports the need for tears and sadness. The root of the rose is still grounded in the earth from which it came and to which it is destined to return: the earth from which it came will be the grave to which it will return. This, of course, is the destiny of all mortal beings and things. "Ashes to ashes, dust to dust" is very much suggested at this point.

By the third stanza, Herbert has us expecting another phrase parallel to those beginning each of the first two stanzas, and with "Sweet spring" we are not disappointed. Another symbol of appealing and beautiful physical life is placed before us. However, very cleverly Herbert has now brought all three symbols together with "full of sweet days and roses." The spring season contains days and roses, and all of these symbolize mortal life. The speaker, in a conceit, calls spring a "box where sweets compacted lie." "Sweets" are perfumes, so spring is like a box of perfumes, with the perfumes being "days" and "roses." The evocation of pleasing smell and color of perfumes again conveys how much the speaker appreciates mortal beauty. But again the mid-point turn faces up to the inevitable death of this beauty: the speaker sees in the conclusions of musical phrases ("CLOSES") that everything of worldly beauty has its end. The short last line carries the same sense of life's brevity, but here the speaker says, "And all must die." Significantly, the emphasis is on "all," rather than the single "thou" of the two previous stanzas. In other words, the implication first is that all of these three ("day," "rose," and "spring") must die, but, on a much larger level, "all" refers to all earthly, physical, mortal entities whatsoever that these three simply symbolize.

Once Herbert has set up the pattern that we expect to be repeated in each stanza, then he surprises us with the deviation from it in the fourth stanza. Here we do not find "Sweet" as the first word and some entity as the second word. Rather, we have "Only" as the first word and the entity is not specified until the end of the first line ("soul"). But, of course, this structural and stylistic change perfectly embodies the argument, the content, of his poem. The "soul" is *not* parallel to "day," "rose," and "spring" because the soul is *immortal*, rather than *mortal*. Its uniqueness as a spiritual entity, rather than a physical one, is implied by "Only" and by the different beginning line. The soul is unique and is given a unique stanza in this poem in order to set it off against the things of mortality in this world. And the last line of this stanza ends in "lives," not in "die" as the previous three stanzas. The soul is the only thing that will live beyond this world and this mortal life. The soul is called "virtuous," echoing the poem's title. Herbert here is playing on two meanings of VIRTUE common in his time: one suggests proper moral conduct that resists worldly temptation, but the other is simply *strength*. And the strength, the endurance of the soul beyond the physical world, is expressed in a conceit by Herbert: the "virtuous soul" is like "seasoned timber" that "never gives"—i.e., the soul is like wood treated to endure beyond ordinary wood that decays. It never "gives" in two senses: it never gives way to worldly temptation, and it never gives in to mortal decay. In fact, when the "whole world" (this physical earth) is destroyed by the fire ("turn to coal") predicted by the Bible for the earth's destruction at the end of time, then the soul "chiefly lives." The soul has its prime (chief) existence in its life beyond its more restricted existence within this physical and temporal prison of the world. It will be released from all mortal trammels and will endure after all days, roses, springs, and everything mortal and temporal that they represent have been destroyed. Despite his appreciation of mortal beauty, then, the speaker recognizes that the soul is superior in its endurance and beauty, in its "virtue."

Virtues, the. The Cardinal Virtues are justice, prudence, fortitude, and temperance. The Seven Virtues add faith, hope, and love to the Cardinal Virtues. Also see AQUINAS.

Vizard. *Noun*: mask.

W

Walton, Izaak (1593–1683). The evidence of Walton's trade(s) is a bit confusing: he may have been an ironmonger (a dealer in hardware) at one time (he belonged to the Ironmongers' Company), and he almost certainly was a linen draper (dealing in cloth and clothing), since there is evidence that he had such a shop in London. Later in life he was a writer of prose. Living on Fleet Street, he was a parishioner of St. Dunstan's-in-the-West while JOHN DONNE was its vicar. Became a friend and admirer of Donne, as well as an acquaintance of other writers and clergymen of the time. Wrote the first biography of Donne, published in 1640 with Donne's *LXXX Sermons*. He added to it and published his *The Life of John Donne* separately in 1658. Then it was revised further and included as one of the *Lives* in 1670 and 1675 volumes, containing also those of George Herbert, Henry Wotton, and Richard Hooker. Walton also wrote *The Compleat Angler* (first published in 1653), a book concerning fishing—but with comments on nature, pastoral ideals, theology, poets, and poetry mingled in it.

Although Walton's biographies have been severely challenged on many points of facts, chronology, accuracy of quotations, and completeness of character (see, for example, Novarr's *The Making of Walton's "Lives"* and Charles's *A Life of George Herbert*, as well as others in the "Selected Bibliography"), he did write from some firsthand experiences and knowledge gathered from friends and letters. All later biographers of Herbert are indebted to Walton, even though modern research has discovered facts and records that correct many of his assertions. To some extent Walton imposed order and simplicity on his *The Life of Mr. George Herbert* (and on his other lives, as well) by picturing his subject as the epitome of holiness and as symbolic of the best that the Church of England in its traditional and Royalist loyalties could offer, especially since Walton wrote through the decades in which the English Church was being attacked and changed by the PURITANs and Nonconformists.

Walton went to CHELSEA, witnessed Donne's memorial sermon for MAGDALEN HERBERT, and bought a copy after its publication. Although Walton saw George Herbert, he was not really acquainted with him (as Walton himself clearly states in his "Introduction" to the biography). He did have access to some of Herbert's letters. His most reliable eyewitness accounts of Herbert were given to Walton many years after Herbert's death by EDMUND DUNCON and ARTHUR WOODNOTH. Walton's general purpose in creating Herbert as a touchstone for both a Christian and an Anglican is best seen in the following statement from his penultimate paragraph: "Thus he lived, and thus he died like a Saint, unspotted of the World, full of Alms-deeds, full of Humility, and all the examples of a virtuous life. . . ."

Want. *Verb*: to lack or be without. *Noun*: (1) deficiency, shortage, or lack of something; (2) poverty or destitution.

Waste. *Verb*: (1) to devastate or ruin; (2) to use up, diminish; (3) to employ uselessly; (4) to expend needlessly or to squander; (5) to spend or to pass unprofitably or idly.

Water. *Noun*: (1) one of the four ELEMENTs; (2) the liquid of which oceans, seas, lakes, ponds, and rivers are made; (3) liquid that falls as rain; (4) drink that sustains life; (5) in some contexts, liquid for washing, cleansing; (6) in some contexts, water of baptism that cleanses the spirit; (7) in some contexts, a reference to tears.

Westminster School. Grammar school attended by George Herbert. He probably entered during 1604 while LANCELOT ANDREWES was still the Dean of Westminster Abbey. Here Herbert was firmly grounded in grammar, logic, rhetoric, Latin, Greek, and music. From this school Herbert proceeded in 1609 to TRINITY COLLEGE, Cambridge.

Williams, John (1582–1650). Lord Keeper, Dean of Westminster, and Bishop of Lincoln who ordained Herbert as deacon in 1624 and granted Herbert a portion of the rectory of Llandinam, MONTGOMERY. In 1626 he also made Herbert a canon of Lincoln Cathedral.

Wilton House. Ancestral home of the Earls of Pembroke in WILTSHIRE. George Herbert was kinsman to the 3rd Earl, WILLIAM HERBERT, and to his brother the 4th Earl, PHILIP HERBERT. Wilton House is quite close to Fugglestone St. Peter and to the chapel of Bemerton St. Andrew, for both of which George Herbert served as rector from April, 1630, to his death (see BEMERTON). During the time that LADY ANNE CLIFFORD was Countess of Pembroke, George Herbert visited her at Wilton House. It was CHARLES I's favorite home to visit, and he came there every summer. The home still stands today, and one may tour it and the beautiful grounds. Van Dyck portraits of Charles I and his family, as well as of the Herbert family, hang in the Double Cube Room which was designed by Inigo Jones.

Wiltshire. County in southwestern England in which Herbert resided for the last five years of his life. See DAUNTESEY HOUSE, BAYNTON HOUSE, BEMERTON, SALISBURY, and WILTON HOUSE.

"Windows, The." This is a poem that fits well the structural principle of the physical "Church" (see THE TEMPLE). But the title actually points to the METAPHYSICAL CONCEIT that is developed through the entire poem: holy preachers are compared to stained-glass windows.

In the first stanza the speaker seems astonished that God would give a mere man such an overwhelming task to preach God's "eternal word," implying a contrast between "man" and "eternal word." Man is finite and feeble, and it seems impossible that he can convey the "word" (in the senses of both divine revelation and Christ). Line 2 begins the conceit by comparing finite man to a "brittle, crazy glass": "CRAZY" here means *cracked* or *flawed*. One would think that such glass would give a distorted, dim reflection of the word and would not convey God's light clearly. But, surprisingly, God uses man to serve as just such a "window" of glass in God's "temple" to admit God's light and word to those within. The preacher serves this function to those in the congregation in a church (or, on a larger level, the "temple" of God is the whole world). It is through God's "grace" that mere man has this glorious, privileged, elevated position granted to him by God (see "AFFORD"). A literal window is physically elevated in a church, but the preacher as a window is spiritually elevated above his nature as a mere physical human.

The second stanza further develops the conceit ingeniously. God does "ANNEAL" in glass God's own "story": in other words, the preacher is like a stained-glass window with the colors fixed into it by a heating process, and thus is the window impressively beautiful. But also a stained-glass window has stories from the Bible portrayed in it ("Thy story"), most frequently events from the life of Christ. So, the life of Christ is portrayed in impressive colors with God's light shining through the windows: in the case of the "holy" preacher as such a window, he is one who exemplifies the nature and doctrines of Christ in his own life. His own life is Christlike ("Making Thy life to shine within / The holy preachers . . ."). This impressive "window" with Christ's life in all of its beauty visually apparent is a contrast to "crazy," uncolored glass. A holy preacher has attained his own Christlike life through a tempering, heating process of trial and struggle in his own life. The Christlike preacher "more doth win": he wins more souls than does the preacher who only talks about Christ and does not himself live like Christ. Herbert in "More reverend grows" surely is playing on two meanings of "reverend," one an adjective, the other a noun: the holy preacher is more *revered*, but also becomes a true *reverend*! A clear window, not infused with colors and pictures of God's story, is only "waterish, bleak, and thin": this is analogous to a preacher who is not truly "holy," who does not have Christ's life in his own actions. This preacher cannot "win" as many souls as can the "holy" one who is like a stained-glass window.

The third stanza begins by asserting that "one" who has "doctrine and life, colors and light" brings a "strong regard and awe": "doctrine" is symbolized by the "light" shining through the window, and "life" is symbolized by the "colors" showing Christ's life in the window, then. The "holy preacher" has not only words about Christ, but also Christ's actions in his own life to illustrate the words. This is in contrast to one who has "speech alone"—i.e., one who has only the words and not the actions has little lasting effect upon others. This kind of preacher spouts words that are only "flaring" things: their "light" ("doctrine" in words) only impresses one briefly and then disappears like a brief flash of light. For an impression upon others to last, the preacher must practice what he preaches, must have the actions to back up the words, must have the "colors" ("life") to support the "light" ("doctrine"). The last line of the poem asserts that words will only echo in the "ear," the external part of a person, from which the sound disappears easily and quickly, in contrast to words supported by actions that will penetrate to the "conscience," the internal part of a person.

Herbert's careful artistry may be appreciated by noting what he does with sounds in the poem. The number of nasal (*m* and *n*) sounds increase with each stanza (from 12 to 16 to 23). In addition, in the first stanza there are no nasal sounds in the words ending the lines, in the second stanza there are three of the five ending words with nasals, and in the last stanza every ending word has nasals. And, significantly, the last word of the poem is "ring," with a nasal that climaxes the very ringing sound building through the poem. So, one of the effects created by Herbert is that early in the poem there is no impressive ringing when man's apparent inability to preach the "eternal word" is discussed, but, by the end of the poem, one hears very impressively the lasting sounds penetrating into one's internal being that are the effect of the "holy preacher" with both Christlike words and actions. (For my fuller and more specific arguments on Herbert's technical artistry in this poem, see Ray, Robert H., "Spatial and Aural Patterns in 'The Windows,'" *George Herbert Journal* 1, no.2 (1978): 38–43.)

Wink. *Verb*: to close the eyes (*not* the modern sense of to close and then rapidly open one or both eyes).

Wit. *Noun*: (1) intelligence or understanding; (2) cleverness or mental quickness; (3) talent for brilliant and amusing statement; (4) quality of speech and writing that aptly associates thoughts, usually in a surprising or unexpected way.

Woodnoth, Arthur. A cousin of NICHOLAS FERRAR. He was a goldsmith, as well as a purchasing agent for Ferrar's household at Little Gidding. He also served as a business manager for Sir JOHN DANVERS, at one point (in late 1631) asking George Herbert's advice on whether or not to continue this position or to enter the church. Woodnoth wrote many letters to Ferrar, and he visited Herbert at BEMERTON. Woodnoth was present outside the church when Herbert was inducted there. He also accompanied Herbert on a visit to LADY ANNE CLIFFORD at WILTON HOUSE. Woodnoth described Herbert's death in a letter to Ferrar and apparently provided WALTON with his account of Herbert's death. Herbert appointed Woodnoth as the executor of his will, a duty that Woodnoth took quite seriously and carried out conscientiously.

Word, the. (1) Christ, (2) the Bible or a part of it, (3) God's will.

Worm. *Noun*: (1) maggot [especially the "worm" of the grave]; (2) segmented earthworm; (3) larva or grub or caterpillar that destroys vegetation; (4) intestinal parasite; (5) metaphorically, a thought that symbolically "devours"; (6) metaphorically, a human as a miserable, lowly, weak, or pitiable creature.

Y

Yeeld, yield. *Verb*: (1) to give in, submit, surrender; (2) to grant or concede.

Z

Zone, the. *Noun*: the Torrid Zone, the area of high temperature on the earth's surface around the equator between the tropics of Cancer and Capricorn.

SELECTED BIBLIOGRAPHY

I. WORKS [All of Herbert's works are listed by editor.]

A. Poetry

Brown, Douglas, ed. *Selected Poems of George Herbert*. London: Hutchinson Educational, 1960.

Charles, Amy M., ed. *The Williams Manuscript of George Herbert's Poems*. Delmar, New York: Scholars' Facsimiles & Reprints, 1977. [Facsimile reproduction, with introduction by Charles]

Charles, Amy M., and Mario A. Di Cesare, eds. *The Bodleian Manuscript of George Herbert's Poems: A Facsimile of Tanner 307*. Delmar, New York: Scholars' Facsimiles & Reprints, 1984. [Facsimile reproduction, with introduction by Charles and Di Cesare]

McCloskey, Mark, and Paul R. Murphy, eds. *The Latin Poetry of George Herbert: A Bilingual Edition*. Athens, Ohio: Ohio University Press, 1965. [Herbert's Latin and Greek poems, with McCloskey's and Murphy's English translations on facing pages]

Patrides, C.A., ed. *The English Poems of George Herbert*. London: J.M. Dent & Sons, 1974.

Pebworth, Ted-Larry. "George Herbert's Poems to the Queen of Bohemia: A Rediscovered Text and a New Edition." *English Literary Renaissance* 9 (1979): 108–20.

Reeves, Gareth, ed. *Selected Poems of George Herbert*. London: Heinemann, 1971.

Summers, Joseph H., ed. *George Herbert: Selected Poetry*. New York and Toronto: New American Library, 1967.

B. Poetry and Prose

Grosart, Alexander B., ed. *The Complete Works in Verse and Prose of George Herbert.* London: Robson, 1874. 3 vols.
Hutchinson, F.E., ed. *The Works of George Herbert.* Oxford: Clarendon Press, 1941 (revised 1945; many reprints since 1945). [The standard edition]
Martz, Louis L., ed. *George Herbert and Henry Vaughan.* Oxford: Oxford University Press, 1986. [Contains *The Temple,* some poems from the Williams manuscript, poems from Walton's *Life of Herbert,* and *A Priest to the Temple, Or The Country Parson*]
Palmer, George Herbert, ed. *The English Works of George Herbert.* Boston and New York: Houghton Mifflin, 1905. 3 vols.
Tobin, John, ed. *George Herbert: The Complete English Poems.* Harmondsworth, Middlesex, England: Penguin Books, 1991. [Despite the title of this volume, it also contains a selection of Herbert's Latin verse, his prose work *A Priest to the Temple, Or The Country Parson,* and Walton's *Life of Herbert*]
Wall, John N., Jr., ed. *George Herbert: The Country Parson, The Temple.* 1981. Reprint. New York, Ramsey, Toronto: Paulist Press, 1985. [Reprint corrects the printer's errors of the original. Modernized texts, with introduction by Wall]

II. BIBLIOGRAPHIES, CONCORDANCES, AND OTHER RESEARCH TOOLS

Di Cesare, Mario A., and Rigo Mignani. *A Concordance to the Complete Writings of George Herbert.* Ithaca and London: Cornell University Press, 1977.
Mills, Jerry Leath. "Recent Studies in Herbert." *English Literary Renaissance* 6 (1976): 105–18.
Patrides, C.A. *George Herbert: The Critical Heritage.* London: Routledge and Kegan Paul, 1983. [A selective survey (74 excerpts) of Herbert's reputation from 1615 to 1936. Unfortunately, the user of this work should be cautioned about accepting many of its assertions and transcriptions without verifying, without checking against reliable research tools or the original works themselves. Some examples selected only from the portion concerning the seventeenth century are as follows: (1) the poetic fragment attributed to Codrington (pp. 4 and 63) actually is in the handwriting of a "J.H." in the original manuscript, and the fragment is incorrectly transcribed in Patrides's volume; (2) Archbishop Leighton quotes only once from Herbert, not "frequently" (p. 11); (3) rather than three lines

of "Virtue," the entire poem is quoted in Hall's work of 1676
(p. 11); (4) Flatman's allusion first appeared in 1679, not 1686
(p. 13); (5) Walton says that *Edmund Duncon*, not Arthur
Woodnoth, was asked by Herbert to deliver the manuscript to
Nicholas Ferrar (p. 58); (6) Daniel's 1648 ode on *The Temple*
was first published in 1878, not 1959 (p. 70); (7) the quoted
passage from Dryden's *MacFlecknoe* does not correspond in
either spelling or wording to the 1682 edition cited (p. 137);
(8) the uses of Herbert in Thomas White's work are more
extensive than indicated (p. 145). For other errors to be noted
and warnings to be heeded by the potential user, one should also
read the review of this volume by Fram Dinshaw in *The Review
of English Studies* (36: 566–68 [November, 1985]).]

Ray, Robert H. *The Herbert Allusion Book: Allusions to George
Herbert in the Seventeenth Century*. Chapel Hill, North Carolina:
Texts and Studies series of *Studies in Philology* (83:4) and the
University of North Carolina Press, 1986. [Guides one to writers,
books, and manuscripts of the 1615–1700 period that allude to
Herbert. Also, an annotated bibliography presents the most
important books and articles (through 1983) that note and discuss
seventeenth-century allusions to Herbert.]

Ray, Robert H. "Recent Studies in Herbert (1974–1986)." *English
Literary Renaissance* 18 (1988): 460–75.

Roberts, John R. *George Herbert: An Annotated Bibliography of
Modern Criticism, Revised Edition, 1905–1984*. Columbia:
University of Missouri Press, 1988.

III. LIFE

Benet, Diana. "Herbert's Experience of Politics and Patronage in 1624."
George Herbert Journal 10 (1986–87): 33–45.

Charles, Amy M. "Herbert and the Ferrars: Spiritual Edification." In
Like Season'd Timber: New Essays on George Herbert, edited by
Edmund Miller and Robert DiYanni, 1–18. New York: Peter
Lang, 1987.

Charles, Amy M. *A Life of George Herbert*. Ithaca and London:
Cornell University Press, 1977. [The standard biography.
Challenges and corrects Walton and many early biographers]

Charles, Amy M. "Mrs. Herbert's Kitchin Booke." *English Literary
Renaissance* 4 (1974): 164–73.

Doerksen, Daniel W. "Magdalen Herbert's London Church." *Notes and
Queries* 34 (1987): 302–305. [Illustrates that St. Martin-in-the-
Fields was the church regularly attended by Magdalen Herbert
and her family while living at Charing Cross]

Held, George. "Herbert and His Brothers: Brother Poets: The Relationship between George and Edward Herbert." In *Like Season'd Timber: New Essays on George Herbert*, edited by Edmund Miller and Robert DiYanni, 19–35. New York: Peter Lang, 1987.

Huntley, Frank L. "The Williams Manuscript, Edmund Duncon, and Herbert's Quotidian Fever." *George Herbert Journal* 10 (1986–87): 23–32. [Proposes that Duncon's delivery of Herbert's manuscript of poems occurred in 1626, that it was the early version of *The Temple*, and that Arthur Woodnoth actually delivered the final version to Nicholas Ferrar in 1633]

Jordan, Richard Douglas. "Herbert's First Sermon." *Review of English Studies* 27 (1976): 178–79.

Maycock, A.L. *Nicholas Ferrar of Little Gidding*. 1938. Reprint. Grand Rapids, Michigan: William B. Eerdmans Publishing Co., 1980. [Valuable to understand the spiritual and literary affinities between Herbert and Ferrar]

Mayor, J.E.B. *Nicholas Ferrar: Two Lives by His Brother John, and by Dr. Jebb*. Cambridge: Cambridge University Press, 1855. [Especially valuable for John Ferrar's account, that of a contemporary witness to the literary relationships and friendships of Herbert with Nicholas Ferrar, Arthur Woodnoth, Edmund Duncon, and others]

Miller, Edmund. *George Herbert's Kinships: An Ahnentafel with Annotations*. Bowie, Maryland: Heritage Books, 1993. [Traces ancestors of Herbert to the tenth generation; notes relationships with literary, religious, and historical figures; and includes several indexes]

Novarr, David. *The Making of Walton's "Lives"*. Ithaca: Cornell University Press, 1958. [Essential to understand facts and fictions in Walton's treatment of Herbert]

Reiter, Robert E. "George Herbert and His Biographers." *Cithara* 9 (1970): 18–31.

Walton, Izaak. *The Lives of John Donne, Sir Henry Wotton, Richard Hooker, George Herbert, and Robert Sanderson*. The World's Classics. London: Oxford University Press, 1927. [Classic, original *Life of Herbert*. Published first in 1670 and then again in revised form in 1675. The 1675 publication is the version reproduced in this 1927 edition.]

IV. REPUTATION AND INFLUENCE

Anselment, Raymond A. "Seventeenth-Century Adaptations of 'The Church-porch.'" *George Herbert Journal* 5 (1981–82): 63–69.

Armbrust, Crys. "Nineteenth-Century Re-Presentations of George
Herbert: Publishing History as Critical Embodiment." *Huntington
Library Quarterly* 53 (1990): 131–51.

Banzer, Judith. "'Compound Manner': Emily Dickinson and the
Metaphysical Poets." *American Literature* 32 (1960–61): 417–33.

Bell, Ilona. "Herbert and Harvey: In the Shadow of the Temple." In
Like Season'd Timber: New Essays on George Herbert, edited by
Edmund Miller and Robert DiYanni, 255–79. New York: Peter
Lang, 1987. [Discusses Christopher Harvey's *The Synagogue*, a
seventeenth-century imitation of Herbert's *The Temple*]

Brittin, Norman A. "Emerson and the Metaphysical Poets." *American
Literature* 8 (1936–37): 1–21.

Broderick, John C. "The Date and Source of Emerson's 'Grace.'"
Modern Language Notes 73 (1958): 91–95. [Proposes that the
source is Herbert's "Sin (1)"]

Bump, Jerome. "Hopkins, Metalepsis, and the Metaphysicals." *John
Donne Journal* 4 (1985): 303–29. [A major portion of this article
examines the extent to which Gerard Manley Hopkins was
influenced by Herbert.]

Charles, Amy. "Touching David's Harp: George Herbert and Ralph
Knevet." *George Herbert Journal* 2, no. 1 (1978): 54–69.

Clements, A.L. *The Mystical Poetry of Thomas Traherne*. Cambridge,
Massachusetts: Harvard University Press, 1969. [Discusses aspects
of Herbert's influence on Traherne]

Coleridge, Samuel Taylor. *Coleridge on the Seventeenth Century*.
Edited by Roberta Florence Brinkley. 1955. Reprint. New York:
Greenwood Press, 1968.

D'Amico, Diane. "Reading and Rereading George Herbert and Christina
Rossetti." *John Donne Journal* 4 (1985): 269–89.

DiYanni, Robert. "Herbert and Hopkins: The Poetics of Devotion." In
Like Season'd Timber: New Essays on George Herbert, edited by
Edmund Miller and Robert DiYanni, 369–88. New York: Peter
Lang, 1987.

Doerksen, Daniel W. "Nicholas Ferrar, Arthur Woodnoth, and the
Publication of George Herbert's *The Temple*, 1633." *George
Herbert Journal* 3 (1979–80): 22–44.

Duckles, Vincent. "John Jenkins's Settings of Lyrics by George
Herbert." *Musical Quarterly* 48 (1962): 461–75.

Duncan, Joseph E. *The Revival of Metaphysical Poetry: The History of
a Style, 1800 to the Present*. Minneapolis: University of
Minnesota Press, 1959.

Duncan-Jones, Elsie. "Benlowes's Borrowings from George Herbert."
Review of English Studies 6 (1955): 179–80.

El-Gabalawy, Saad. "Two Obscure Disciples of George Herbert." *Notes and Queries* 24 (1977): 541–42. [Allusions to Herbert by Knevet and Goodman]

Eliot, T.S. *George Herbert*. London: Longmans, Green and Co., 1962.

Eliot, T.S. "What Is Minor Poetry?" *Welsh Review* 3 (1944): 256–67. Reprinted in *On Poetry and Poets* (New York: Farrar, Straus, and Cudahy, 1957), 34–51. [Sees Herbert as a major poet and *The Temple* as a unified major work]

Gottlieb, Sidney. "Allusions to George Herbert in Robert Overton's *Gospell Obseruations, and Religious Manifestations*." *Studies in Philology* 90 (1993): 83–100.

Gottlieb, Sidney. "Eliot's 'The Death of Saint Narcissus' and Herbert's 'Affliction' (I)." *George Herbert Journal* 9, no. 2 (1986): 54–56.

Griffin, John R. "Herbert and the Oxford Movement: His Character and Rule of Holy Life." In *Like Season'd Timber: New Essays on George Herbert*, edited by Edmund Miller and Robert DiYanni, 329–43. New York: Peter Lang, 1987.

Harrison, Antony H. "Reception Theory and the New Historicism: The Metaphysical Poets in the Nineteenth Century." *John Donne Journal* 4 (1985): 163–80.

Hester, M. Thomas. "'broken letters scarce remembred': Herbert's *Childhood* in Vaughan." *Christianity and Literature* 40 (1990–91): 209–22.

Howell, A.C. "Christopher Harvey's *The Synagogue* (1640)." *Studies in Philology* 49 (1952): 229–47. [Notes some of the ways in which Harvey imitated Herbert]

Idol, John L., Jr. "George Herbert and John Ruskin." *George Herbert Journal* 4, no. 1 (1980): 11–28.

Idol, John L., Jr. "Herbert and Coleridge: He Grows in My Liking." In *Like Season'd Timber: New Essays on George Herbert*, edited by Edmund Miller and Robert DiYanni, 317–28. New York: Peter Lang, 1987.

Johnson, Thomas H. "Edward Taylor: A Puritan 'Sacred Poet.'" *New England Quarterly* 10 (1937): 290–322. [Comments particularly on Herbert's influence]

Johnson, Wendell Stacy. "Halfway to a New Land: Herbert, Tennyson, and the Early Hopkins." *Hopkins Quarterly* 10 (1983–84): 115–24.

Joselyn, Sister M., O.S.B. "Herbert and Hopkins: Two Lyrics." *Renascence* 10 (1957–58): 192–95. [Compares Herbert's "Affliction (1)" and Hopkins's "Carrion Comfort"]

Kennedy, Richard F. "Allusions to Herbert in John Spencer and Edward Benlowes." *George Herbert Journal* 12, no. 1 (1988): 45–47.

Kennedy, Richard F. "John Swan's Adaptation of George Herbert's 'Man.'" *George Herbert Journal* 6, no. 1 (1982): 31–33.

Kinnamon, Noel J. "The Psalmic and Classical Contexts of Herbert's 'Constancie' and Vaughan's 'Righteousness.'" *George Herbert Journal* 8, no. 1 (1984): 29–42.

Köppl, Sebastian. *Die Rezeption George Herberts im 17. und 18. Jahrhundert.* Heidelberg: Carl Winter, 1978.

Leach, Elsie A. "John Wesley's Use of George Herbert." *Huntington Library Quarterly* 16 (1952–53): 183–202.

Leach, Elsie. "More Seventeenth-Century Admirers of Herbert." *Notes and Queries* 7 (1960): 62–63.

Leitch, Vincent B. "Herbert's Influence in Dylan Thomas's 'I See the Boys of Summer.'" *Notes and Queries* 19 (1972): 341.

Malpezzi, Frances M. "Dead Men and Living Words: Herbert and the Revenant in Vaughan's 'The Garland.'" *George Herbert Journal* 15, no. 2 (1992): 70–78.

Matar, N.I. "*The Temple* and Thomas Traherne." *English Language Notes* 25, no. 2 (1987): 25–33.

Nethercot, Arthur H. "The Reputation of the 'Metaphysical Poets' During the Age of Johnson and the 'Romantic Revival.'" *Studies in Philology* 22 (1925): 81–132.

Nethercot, Arthur H. "The Reputation of the 'Metaphysical Poets' During the Age of Pope." *Philological Quarterly* 4 (1925): 161–79.

Nethercot, Arthur H. "The Reputation of the 'Metaphysical Poets' During the Seventeenth Century." *Journal of English and Germanic Philology* 23 (1924): 173–98.

Oberhaus, Dorothy Huff. "Herbert and Emily Dickinson: A Reading of Emily Dickinson." In *Like Season'd Timber: New Essays on George Herbert*, edited by Edmund Miller and Robert DiYanni, 345–68. New York: Peter Lang, 1987.

Patrides, C.A. *George Herbert: The Critical Heritage.* London: Routledge and Kegan Paul, 1983. [A selective survey (74 excerpts) of Herbert's reputation from 1615 to 1936. Unfortunately, the user of this work should be cautioned about accepting many of its assertions and transcriptions without verifying, without checking against reliable research tools or the original works themselves. Some examples selected only from the portion concerning the seventeenth century are as follows: (1) the poetic fragment attributed to Codrington (pp. 4 and 63) actually is in the handwriting of a "J.H." in the original manuscript, and the fragment is incorrectly transcribed in Patrides's volume; (2) Archbishop Leighton quotes only once from Herbert, not "frequently" (p. 11); (3) rather than three lines

of "Virtue," the entire poem is quoted in Hall's work of 1676
(p. 11); (4) Flatman's allusion first appeared in 1679, not 1686
(p. 13); (5) Walton says that *Edmund Duncon,* not Arthur
Woodnoth, was asked by Herbert to deliver the manuscript to
Nicholas Ferrar (p. 58); (6) Daniel's 1648 ode on *The Temple*
was first published in 1878, not 1959 (p. 70); (7) the quoted
passage from Dryden's *MacFlecknoe* does not correspond in
either spelling or wording to the 1682 edition cited (p. 137);
(8) the uses of Herbert in Thomas White's work are more
extensive than indicated (p. 145). For other errors to be noted
and warnings to be heeded by the potential user, one should also
read the review of this volume by Fram Dinshaw in *The Review
of English Studies* (36: 566–68 [November, 1985]).]

Petry, Alice Hall. "Herbert and Emerson: Emerson's Debt to Herbert."
In *Like Season'd Timber: New Essays on George Herbert,* edited
by Edmund Miller and Robert DiYanni, 297–315. New York:
Peter Lang, 1987.

Pettet, E.C. *Of Paradise and Light: A Study of Vaughan's 'Silex
Scintillans'.* Cambridge: Cambridge University Press, 1960.
[Herbert's influence on Vaughan is discussed throughout this
book, but especially in Chapter 3.]

Pritchard, Allan. "Additional Seventeenth-Century Allusions to George
Herbert." *George Herbert Journal* 11, no. 2 (1988): 37–48.

Ray, Robert H. "Henshaw, Venning, and Bates: Quoters of the Bible or
of Herbert?" *George Herbert Journal* 6, no. 1 (1982): 34–36.

Ray, Robert H. *The Herbert Allusion Book: Allusions to George
Herbert in the Seventeenth Century.* Chapel Hill, North Carolina:
Texts and Studies series of *Studies in Philology* (83:4) and the
University of North Carolina Press, 1986. [Compiles 849
allusions to Herbert from about 243 books and manuscripts of the
1615–1700 period (written by about 175 individuals). Indexes
guide one to authors and titles of books and manuscripts and to
Herbert's works. An annotated bibliography presents the most
important books and articles (through 1983) that note and discuss
seventeenth-century allusions to Herbert.]

Ray, Robert H. "Herbert's Seventeenth-Century Reputation: A Summary
and New Considerations." *George Herbert Journal* 9, no. 2
(1986): 1–15.

Ray, Robert H. "Herbert's Words in Donne's Mouth: Walton's Account
of Donne's Death." *Modern Philology* 85 (1987–88): 186–87.

Ray, Robert H. "Two Seventeenth-Century Adapters of George
Herbert." *Notes and Queries* 27 (1980): 331–32.

Reese, Harold. "A Borrower from Quarles and Herbert." *Modern
Language Notes* 55 (1940): 50–52.

Rickey, Mary Ellen. "Vaughan, *The Temple*, and Poetic Form." *Studies in Philology*, 59 (1962): 162–70.

Roberts, J. Russell. "Emerson's Debt to the Seventeenth Century." *American Literature* 21 (1949–50): 298–310.

Rygiel, Mary Ann. "Hopkins and Herbert: Two Meditative Poets." *Hopkins Quarterly* 10 (1983–84): 45–54.

Shawcross, John T. "Additional Seventeenth- and Eighteenth-Century Allusions to George Herbert." *George Herbert Journal* 15, no. 1 (1991): 68–72.

Shawcross, John T. "An Allusion to 'The Church Militant' in Howell's *An Institution of General History*." *George Herbert Journal* 6, no. 2 (1983): 49.

Shawcross, John T. "Two Herbert Allusions." *George Herbert Journal* 9, no. 2 (1986): 57–58.

Shields, David S. "Herbert and Colonial American Poetry: Then Shall Religion to America Flee." In *Like Season'd Timber: New Essays on George Herbert*, edited by Edmund Miller and Robert DiYanni, 281–96. New York: Peter Lang, 1987.

Sloane, William. "George Herbert's Reputation, 1650–1710: Good Reading for the Young." *Notes and Queries* 9 (1962): 213.

Smith, Eric R. "Herbert's 'The 23d Psalme' and William Barton's *The Book of Psalms in Metre*." *George Herbert Journal* 8, no. 2 (1985): 33–43.

Smith, Nigel. "George Herbert in Defence of Antinomianism." *Notes and Queries* 31 (1984): 334–35.

Symes, Gordon. "Hopkins, Herbert and Contemporary Modes." *Hibbert Journal* 47 (1948–49): 389–94.

Thompson, Elbert N.S. "*The Temple* and *The Christian Year*." *PMLA* 54 (1939): 1018–25. [Comparison of Herbert's and Keble's works]

Thota, Anand Rao. *Emily Dickinson: The Metaphysical Tradition*. New Delhi: Arnold-Heinemann, 1982.

Treglown, Jeremy. "The Satirical Inversion of Some English Sources in Rochester's Poetry." *Review of English Studies* 24 (1973): 42–48. [Argues that Rochester refers to Herbert's "Love (3)" in one poem]

Wilcox, Helen. "'Heaven's Lidger Here': Herbert's *Temple* and Seventeenth-Century Devotion." In *Images of Belief in Literature*, edited by David Jasper, 153–68. New York: St. Martin's Press, 1984. [Notes, with examples cited, that Herbert's work in the seventeenth century was regarded as "a model for practical devotion"]

Wilcox, Helen. "Puritans, George Herbert and 'Nose-Twange.'" *Notes and Queries* 26 (1979): 152–53.

Wilcox, Helen. "'The Sweet Singer of the Temple': The Musicians'
Response to Herbert." *George Herbert Journal* 10 (1986–87): 47–
60.
Williamson, Karina. "Herbert's Reputation in the Eighteenth Century."
Philological Quarterly 41 (1962): 769–75.
Yoder, R.A. "Toward the 'Titmouse Dimension': The Development of
Emerson's Poetic Style." *PMLA* 87 (1972): 255–70. [Notes some
of Emerson's allusions to Herbert and influences of Herbert on
Emerson's style]

V. CRITICAL STUDIES

A. Background

Baker, Herschel. *The Wars of Truth: Studies in the Decay of Christian
Humanism in the Earlier Seventeenth Century.* Cambridge,
Massachusetts: Harvard University Press, 1952.
Bald, R.C. *Donne's Influence in English Literature.* 1932. Reprint.
Gloucester, Massachusetts: Peter Smith, 1965.
Chambers, A.B. *Transfigured Rites in Seventeenth-Century English
Poetry.* Columbia: University of Missouri Press, 1992.
[Liturgical approach, with discussions of Herbert scattered
throughout]
Church, Margaret. "The First English Pattern Poems." *PMLA* 61
(1946): 636–50. [Discusses origins and traditions preparative to
such pattern poems as those of Herbert]
Clarke, Elizabeth. "Silent, Performative Words: the Language of God in
Valdesso and George Herbert." *Literature and Theology* 5
(1991): 355–74.
Eliot, Thomas Stearns. "The Metaphysical Poets." *[London] Times
Literary Supplement*, October 20, 1921, pp. 669–70. [A famous
and influential essay, reprinted frequently in collections of essays
and in anthologies]
Ellrodt, Robert. "Scientific Curiosity and Metaphysical Poetry in the
Seventeenth Century." *Modern Philology* 61 (1964): 180–97.
Freeman, Rosemary. *English Emblem Books.* London: Chatto &
Windus, 1948.
Galdon, Joseph A., S.J. *Typology and Seventeenth-Century Literature.*
The Hague and Paris: Mouton, 1975.
Halewood, William H. *The Poetry of Grace: Reformation Themes and
Structures in Seventeenth-Century Poetry.* New Haven and
London: Yale University Press, 1970. [Chapter 4 is on Herbert.]
Higgins, Dick. *George Herbert's Pattern Poems: In Their Tradition.*
West Glover, Vermont: Unpublished Editions, 1977.

Husain, Itrat. *The Mystical Element in the Metaphysical Poets of the Seventeenth Century*. Edinburgh and London: Oliver and Boyd, 1948. [Chapter 3 discusses the mystical element in Herbert.]

Johnson, Samuel. *Johnson's Lives of the Poets: A Selection*, ed. J.P. Hardy. Oxford: Oxford University Press, 1971. [Contains the "Life of Cowley," a famous and influential commentary on metaphysical poetry that was originally published in 1779]

Lewalski, Barbara Kiefer. "Typological Symbolism and the 'Progress of the Soul' in Seventeenth-Century Literature." In *Literary Uses of Typology from the Late Middle Ages to the Present*, edited by Earl Miner, 79–114. Princeton, New Jersey: Princeton University Press, 1977.

Mahood, M.M. *Poetry and Humanism*. 1950. Reprint. New York: W.W. Norton & Company, 1970. [Chapter 2 is "Two Anglican Poets," in which Herbert and Christina Rossetti are discussed.]

Martines, Lauro. *Society and History in English Renaissance Verse*. Oxford: Basil Blackwell, 1985.

Nicolson, Marjorie Hope. *The Breaking of the Circle: Studies in the Effect of the "New Science" upon Seventeenth-Century Poetry*. Revised ed. New York: Columbia University Press, 1960.

Otten, Charlotte F. *Environ'd With Eternity: God, Poems, and Plants in Sixteenth and Seventeenth Century England*. Lawrence, Kansas: Coronado Press, 1985.

Parfitt, George. *English Poetry of the Seventeenth Century*. London: Longman, 1985.

Parry, Graham. *Seventeenth-Century Poetry: the Social Context*. London and Dover, New Hampshire: Hutchinson & Company, 1985. [Chapter 3 is "George Herbert and the Temple of Anglicanism."]

Peterson, Douglas L. *The English Lyric from Wyatt to Donne: A History of the Plain and Eloquent Styles*. Princeton, New Jersey: Princeton University Press, 1967.

Rivers, Isabel. *Classical and Christian Ideas in English Renaissance Poetry: A Students' Guide*. London: George Allen & Unwin, 1979.

Ross, Malcolm Mackenzie. *Poetry and Dogma: The Transfiguration of Eucharistic Symbols in Seventeenth Century English Poetry*. New Brunswick, New Jersey: Rutgers University Press, 1954. [Chapter 6 is "George Herbert and the Humanist Tradition."]

Roston, Murray. "Herbert and Mannerism." *John Donne Journal* 5 (1986): 133–67.

Swardson, H.R. *Poetry and the Fountain of Light: Observations on the Conflict between Christian and Classical Traditions in Seventeenth-Century Poetry*. Columbia: University of Missouri

Press, 1962. [Chapter 3 is "George Herbert's Language of Devotion."]

Tuve, Rosemond. *Elizabethan and Metaphysical Imagery: Renaissance Poetic and Twentieth-Century Critics.* Chicago: University of Chicago Press, 1947.

Veith, Gene Edward, Jr. "The Religious Wars in George Herbert Criticism: Reinterpreting Seventeenth-Century Anglicanism." *George Herbert Journal* 11, no. 2 (1988): 19–35.

Veith, Gene Edward, Jr. "Teaching about the Religion of the Metaphysical Poets." In *Approaches to Teaching the Metaphysical Poets*, edited by Sidney Gottlieb, 54–60. New York: The Modern Language Association of America, 1990.

B. General: Poetry and Prose

Bottrall, Margaret. *George Herbert.* London: John Murray, 1954. [General biographical and critical study, emphasizing Herbert's themes and craftsmanship]

Doerksen, Daniel W. "Things Fundamental or Indifferent: Adiaphorism and Herbert's Church Attitudes." *George Herbert Journal,* 11, no. 1 (1987): 15–22.

Hodgkins, Christopher. *Authority, Church, and Society in George Herbert: Return to the Middle Way.* Columbia: University of Missouri Press, 1993.

Hovey, Kenneth Alan. "Holy War and Civil Peace: George Herbert's Jacobean Politics." *Explorations in Renaissance Culture* 11 (1985): 112–19.

Kyne, Mary Theresa. *Country Parsons, Country Poets: George Herbert and Gerard Manley Hopkins as Spiritual Autobiographers.* Greensburg, Pennsylvania: Eadmer Press, 1992.

Miller, Edmund. *Drudgerie Divine: The Rhetoric of God and Man in George Herbert.* Salzburg: Institut für Anglistik und Amerikanistik, Universität Salzburg, 1979. [Emphasizes Herbert as a Christian writer]

Miller, Edmund, and Robert DiYanni, eds. *Like Season'd Timber: New Essays on George Herbert.* New York: Peter Lang, 1987.

Nardo, Anna K. *The Ludic Self in Seventeenth-Century English Literature.* Albany: State University of New York Press, 1991. [Concerns theme of play in literature. Chapter 5 is "George Herbert Pulling for Prime."]

Schoenfeldt, Michael C. *Prayer and Power: George Herbert and Renaissance Courtship.* Chicago and London: University of Chicago Press, 1991. [Examines Herbert as poet and parson in the context of courtesy, emphasizing the use of courtly supplication to command God's allegiance in *The Temple*]

Sessions, William A. "Bacon and Herbert and an Image of Chalk." In *"Too Rich to Clothe the Sunne": Essays on George Herbert*, edited by Claude J. Summers and Ted-Larry Pebworth, 165–78. Pittsburgh: University of Pittsburgh Press, 1980. [Discusses the respect of Bacon and Herbert for one another and some influences of Bacon on Herbert's poetry and prose]

Stewart, Stanley. *George Herbert*. Boston: Twayne Publishers, 1986.

Summers, Claude J., and Ted-Larry Pebworth, eds. *"Too Rich to Clothe the Sunne": Essays on George Herbert*. Pittsburgh: University of Pittsburgh Press, 1980.

Summers, Joseph H. *George Herbert: His Religion and Art*. Cambridge, Massachusetts: Harvard University Press, 1954. [Emphasizes Herbert's religion and the Anglican traditions, ceremonies, and symbols that create Herbert's careful art. Also surveys Herbert's life, reputation, and influence]

Veith, Gene Edward, Jr. *Reformation Spirituality: The Religion of George Herbert*. Cranbury, New Jersey: Associated University Presses, 1985. [Argues that many Lutheran and Calvinistic doctrines are quite Anglican and that Herbert's poetry illustrates much of Reformation theology]

Wall, John N. *Transformations of the Word: Spenser, Herbert, Vaughan*. Athens: University of Georgia Press, 1988. [Discusses Herbert in Chapter 3, with emphasis on *The Temple* and *The Country Parson*]

Wengen-Shute, Rosemary Margaret van. *George Herbert and the Liturgy of the Church of England*. Oegstgeest: Drukkerij de Kampenaer, 1981. [Discusses necessary Anglican and liturgical background for reading Herbert]

Wickenheiser, Robert J. "George Herbert and the Epigrammatic Tradition." *George Herbert Journal* 1, no. 1 (1977): 39–56.

C. Poetry

1. *Latin and Greek Poetry*

Coulter, Cornelia C. "A Possible Classical Source for The Blackamoor Maid." *Philological Quarterly* 18 (1939): 409–10. [Argues that two passages from Vergil's *Eclogues* may have influenced Herbert's "Aethiopissa ambit Cestum Diuersi Coloris Virum"]

Doelman, James. "The Contexts of George Herbert's *Musae Responsoriae*." *George Herbert Journal* 15, no. 2 (1992): 42–54. [Provides background and history for understanding Herbert's response to Andrew Melville as a defense of a uniform British Church, but also as a relevant work published by Duport in 1662 for defending Restoration Uniformity]

Dowling, Paul M. "*Memoriae Matris Sacrum*: The Muse Displaced: The Architecture of *Memoriae Matris Sacrum*." In *Like Season'd Timber: New Essays on George Herbert*, edited by Edmund Miller and Robert DiYanni, 181–90. New York: Peter Lang, 1987. [Notes various structural and linking techniques in the work, such as themes, antitheses, echoes, and images of the River Thames]

Dust, Philip. "The Sorrow of a Black Woman in a Seventeenth-Century Neo-Latin Poem." *College Language Association Journal* 18 (1975): 516–20. [Analyzes "Aethiopissa ambit Cestum Diuersi Coloris Virum" and contends that the poem was sent to Sir Francis Bacon as an objection to slavery]

Fruchter, Barry. "Andrewes and Herbert: Empty Music: Andrewes in the Elegiac Verse of Herbert and Milton." In *Like Season'd Timber: New Essays on George Herbert*, edited by Edmund Miller and Robert DiYanni, 219–30. New York: Peter Lang, 1987. [Discusses Herbert's tribute to Lancelot Andrewes, Bishop of Winchester, in his dedicatory epigram in *Musae Responsoriae*, noting that Herbert sees him as a shepherd, scholar, and heroic figure for the English Church]

Hovey, Kenneth Alan. "'Inventa Bellica'/'Triumphus Mortis': Herbert's Parody of Human Progress and Dialogue with Divine Grace." *Studies in Philology* 78 (1981): 275–304. [Argues that "Inventa Bellica" is an early poem parodying a poem by Thomas Reid that glorifies human progress. Notes that Herbert's later version of this poem is titled "Triumphus Mortis" and is a serious poem concerning the Christian response to death]

Kelliher, W. Hilton. "The Latin Poetry of George Herbert." In *The Latin Poetry of English Poets*, edited by J.W. Binns, 26–57. London and Boston: Routledge and Kegan Paul, 1974. [Criticism of the Latin poems, emphasizing *Memoriae Matris Sacrum* as "the masterpiece of Herbert's Latin poetry"]

Meyer, Gerard Previn. "The Blackamoor and Her Love." *Philological Quarterly* 17 (1938): 371–76. [Argues that Herbert's "Aethiopissa ambit Cestum Diuersi Coloris Virum" inspired poems by Henry Rainolds, Henry King, and John Cleveland]

Pearlman, E. "George Herbert's God." *English Literary Renaissance* 13 (1983): 88–112. [Argues that the poems of *Memoriae Matris Sacrum* reveal that Herbert felt he fulfilled his mother's expectations in writing poetry, that he describes his mother and

God in similar terms, and that he expresses maternal security in
his images of enclosure and spaces]

2. *Sonnets 1 and 2* (from Walton's *Lives*)

Christensen, Philip Harlan. "The Sonnets from Walton's *Life*: Sonnets
of the Sonne." In *Like Season'd Timber: New Essays on George
Herbert*, edited by Edmund Miller and Robert DiYanni, 169–80.
New York: Peter Lang, 1987.

3. *The Temple*

a. *The Temple* in General and Its Unity

Asals, Heather A.R. *Equivocal Predication: George Herbert's Way to
God*. Toronto: University of Toronto Press, 1981. [Emphasizes
Herbert's Anglicanism, the church of the middle way, and
outward form. Sees punning (equivocation) as opening the body
of Christ (the Word) for eucharistic partaking by Herbert's
reader]

Austin, Frances. *The Language of the Metaphysical Poets*. New York:
St. Martin's Press, 1992. [Chapter 3 is on Herbert.]

Bell, Ilona. "Circular Strategies and Structures in Jonson and Herbert."
In *Classic and Cavalier: Essays on Jonson and the Sons of Ben*,
edited by Claude J. Summers and Ted-Larry Pebworth, 157–70.
Pittsburgh: University of Pittsburgh Press, 1982.

Bell, Ilona. "'Setting Foot into Divinity': George Herbert and the
English Reformation." *Modern Language Quarterly* 38 (1977):
219–41. [With concentration especially on "The Thanksgiving,"
the essay argues that in *The Temple* Herbert emphasizes a
reformed, Calvinistic insistence upon Christ's past sacrifice,
rather than a medieval, Roman Catholic devotional reenactment.]

Benet, Diana. *Secretary of Praise: The Poetic Vocation of George
Herbert*. Columbia: University of Missouri Press, 1984.
[Examines the poetry both from the perspective of the "typical
Christian" speaking and from an autobiographical view toward
Herbert's choices of "poetic" and "priestly" vocations]

Bienz, John. "Images and Ceremonial in *The Temple*: Herbert's Solution
to a Reformation Controversy." *Studies in English Literature,
1500–1900* 26 (1986): 73–95. [Contends that, despite Reformation
doctrines in Herbert, the poet was receptive to techniques and
styles of worship drawing on ceremonies and images not
associated with the Reformers]

Bloch, Chana. *Spelling the Word: George Herbert and the Bible.*
    Berkeley and Los Angeles: University of California Press, 1985.
    [Studies Herbert's biblical sources and references, with close
    readings of many poems of *The Temple*]
Booty, John E. "Contrition in Anglican Spirituality: Hooker, Donne and
    Herbert." In *Anglican Spirituality*, edited by William J. Wolf, 25–
    48. Wilton, Connecticut: Morehouse-Barlow Co., 1982. [Argues
    that *The Temple* "moves from contrition to praise and is imbued
    with contrition in all its parts"]
Booty, John E. "George Herbert: *The Temple* and *The Book of
    Common Prayer.*" *Mosaic* 12, no. 2 (1979): 75–90. [Notes the
    influence of the Prayer Book on *The Temple*, in such matters as a
    contrition and praise structure and poems on matins and
    evensong]
Carnes, Valerie. "The Unity of George Herbert's *The Temple*: A
    Reconsideration." *ELH* 35 (1968): 505–26. [Argues that the
    three-part structure of *The Temple* embodies (1) the preacher
    expressing the sacred Word as it descends in visual form with
    simple image and didactic intent, (2) the poet re-expressing
    through the secular word with symbol, and (3) the redeemed soul
    experiencing reunion of secular word and sacred Word with
    mystic expression]
Charles, Amy. "The Williams Manuscript and *The Temple.*"
    Renaissance Papers (1972 [for 1971]): 59–77. [Argues that
    Herbert's early manuscript of his work is quite important in
    assessing its eventual title, divisions, and order of poems]
Clements, Arthur L. *Poetry of Contemplation: John Donne, George
    Herbert, Henry Vaughan, and the Modern Period.* Albany: State
    University of New York Press, 1990. [Chapter 3 covers Herbert.]
Clifton, Michael. "Staking his Heart: Herbert's Use of Gambling
    Imagery in *The Temple.*" *George Herbert Journal* 8, no. 1
    (1984): 43–55. [Notes imagery of wins and losses that apply
    spiritually]
Colie, R[osalie] L. "*Logos* in *The Temple*: George Herbert and the
    Shape of Content." *Journal of the Warburg and Courtauld
    Institutes* 26 (1963): 327–42. [Proposes that Herbert is most
    concerned with reflecting that the "idea of God, God-the-Word, is
    the ultimately self-sufficient idea, the idea of ideas which, if
    understood, satisfies, suffices, fills and makes content"]
Colie, Rosalie. *The Resources of Kind: Genre-Theory in the
    Renaissance.* Berkeley and Los Angeles: University of California
    Press, 1973. [The second essay ("Small Forms: *Multo in Parvo*")
    relates some of Herbert's poems and *The Temple* itself to the
    emblem tradition.]

Cook, Elizabeth. *Seeing Through Words: The Scope of Late Renaissance Poetry*. New Haven and London: Yale University Press, 1986. [Chapter 3 concerns Herbert.]

Davidson, Clifford. "Herbert's 'The Temple': Conflicts, Submission and Freedom." *English Miscellany* 25 (1975–76): 163–81. [Argues that *The Church-porch* and *The Church* are parts of a single design, but that *The Church Militant* probably is an early poem merely placed at the end without being closely integrated with the rest of *The Temple*. Sees *The Church* as embodying the creation and thus presents man's spatial and temporal journey (from West and death to East and life) through creation and experience, even into the "chancel" of heaven itself]

Dickson, Donald R. "Between Transubstantiation and Memorialism: Herbert's Eucharistic Celebration." *George Herbert Journal* 11, no. 1 (1987): 1–14.

Dickson, Donald R. *The Fountain of Living Waters: The Typology of the Waters of Life in Herbert, Vaughan, and Traherne*. Columbia: University of Missouri Press, 1987. [Chapter 4 is "Herbert and the Waters from the Heart."]

Dickson, Donald R. "Grace and the 'Spirits' of the Heart in *The Temple*." *John Donne Journal* 6 (1987): 55–66.

Edgecombe, Rodney. *"Sweetnesse readie penn'd": Imagery, Syntax and Metrics in the Poetry of George Herbert*. Salzburg: Institut für Anglistik und Amerikanistik, Universität Salzburg, 1980.

El-Gabalawy, Saad. "George Herbert and the Emblem Books." *English Miscellany* 26–27 (1977–78): 173–84.

Elsky, Martin. "Polyphonic Psalm Settings and the Voice of George Herbert's *The Temple*." *Modern Language Quarterly* 42 (1981): 227–46. [Contends that Herbert employs equivalents of musical polyphony (used for psalm settings) to represent divine and human voices in *The Temple*]

Endicott, Annabel M. "The Structure of George Herbert's *Temple*: A Reconsideration." *University of Toronto Quarterly* 34 (1964–65): 226–37. [Disagrees with any attempt to impose the structure of the Hebrew temple upon Herbert's work and contends that the satirical *The Church Militant* concerning the earthly church does not complete the pattern of ascending to God's heaven with the Church Triumphant]

Ferry, Anne. "Titles in George Herbert's 'little Book.'" *English Literary Renaissance* 23 (1993): 314–44. [Discusses the uniqueness of Herbert's titles for a book of poetry at the time. Relates his titles to those commonly used for topics in commonplace books and suggests that his book also might be modeled on the psalter]

Fischlin, Daniel T. "'And tuned by thee': Music and Divinity in George Herbert's Poetry." *Explorations in Renaissance Culture* 16 (1990): 87–99. [Argues that Herbert uses the associative power of musical imagery to lead the reader into the presence of God]

Fish, Stanley. *The Living Temple: George Herbert and Catechizing.* Berkeley: University of California Press, 1978. [Argues that Herbert the poet catechizes the reader in *The Temple*, as Herbert the priest would catechize a pupil in the church]

Freer, Coburn. *Music for a King: George Herbert's Style and the Metrical Psalms.* Baltimore and London: Johns Hopkins University Press, 1972.

Glaser, Joseph A. "George Herbert's *The Temple*: Learning to Read the Book of Nature." *College Language Association Journal* 25 (1982): 322–30. [Emphasizes nature imagery as central and evolving in the design of *The Temple*]

Goldberg, Jonathan. *Voice Terminal Echo: Postmodernism and English Renaissance Texts.* New York and London: Methuen, 1986. [Chapter 5 is "The Dead Letter: Herbert's Other Voices."]

Grant, Patrick. *The Transformation of Sin: Studies in Donne, Herbert, Vaughan, and Traherne.* Montreal and London: McGill-Queen's University Press; Amherst: University of Massachusetts Press, 1974. [Chapters 3 and 4 focus on Herbert in Augustinian and Franciscan contexts. Chapter 5 focuses on Vaughan but includes a comparison of Herbert and Vaughan.]

Hanley, Sara William. "Temples in *The Temple*: George Herbert's Study of the Church." *Studies in English Literature, 1500–1900* 8 (1968): 121–35. [Proposes that the title of Herbert's work provides the major principle of unity for the entire work, for sequences within it, and for individual poems. One should, however, remember the contention by Amy Charles and others that Nicholas Ferrar, not Herbert, provided the title for the work as published after Herbert's death.]

Hermann, John P. "Herbert's 'Superliminare' and the Tradition of Warning in Mystical Literature." *George Herbert Journal* 4, no. 1 (1980): 1–10.

Higbie, Robert. "Images of Enclosure in George Herbert's *The Temple*." *Texas Studies in Literature and Language* 15 (1973–74): 627–38. [Argues that the images of enclosure become a major principle of unity in *The Temple*]

Hughes, Richard E. "George Herbert and the Incarnation." *Cithara* 4, no. 1 (1964–65): 22–32. [Contends that the doctrine of the Incarnation provided Herbert with subject, form, technique, and meaning and that Herbert saw poetry itself as a miniature version of the Incarnation and each poem as a microcosm of the Incarnation]

Hunter, Jeanne Clayton. "*Mine-Thine* in Herbert's *The Temple* and St. John's Gospel." *Notes and Queries* 29 (1982): 492–93. [Sees Herbert's phrasing in some poems as a reflection of Christ's plain language]

Hunter, Jeanne Clayton. "Salvation Under Covenant: Herbert's Poetry and Puritan Sermons." In *Praise Disjoined: Changing Patterns of Salvation in 17th-Century English Literature*, edited by William P. Shaw, 201–19. New York: Peter Lang, 1991. [Argues for the importance of the Covenant of Grace as a motif of salvation in *The Temple*]

Huttar, Charles A. "Herbert and the Emblem: Herbert and Emblematic Tradition." In *Like Season'd Timber: New Essays on George Herbert*, edited by Edmund Miller and Robert DiYanni, 59–100. New York: Peter Lang, 1987. [Thorough examination of emblems and emblematic elements in *The Temple*, with detailed references to scholarship and criticism on the subject]

Johnson, Bruce A. "Theological Inconsistency and Its Uses in George Herbert's Poetry." *George Herbert Journal* 15, no. 2 (1992): 1–18. [Sees many inconsistencies in theological doctrines, especially in the mixed Arminianism and Calvinism in Herbert's poetry, but contends that this is deliberate by Herbert to appeal to a broad, common Christianity]

Johnson, Lee Ann. "The Relationship of 'The Church Militant' to *The Temple*." *Studies in Philology* 68 (1971): 200–206. [Argues that *The Church Militant* is a separate composition that is structurally unrelated to the other two sections of *The Temple*]

Judge, J. Sargent. "Beyond the Branches: The Nature of George Herbert's Protestantism." *Cithara* 29, no. 2 (1989–90): 3–19.

Lewalski, Barbara Kiefer. *Protestant Poetics and the Seventeenth-Century Religious Lyric*. Princeton, New Jersey: Princeton University Press, 1979. [Chapter 9 is "George Herbert: Artful Psalms from the Temple in the Heart."]

Lewalski, Barbara K. "Typology and Poetry: A Consideration of Herbert, Vaughan, and Marvell." In *Illustrious Evidence: Approaches to English Literature of the Early Seventeenth Century*, edited by Earl Miner, 41–69. Berkeley: University of California Press, 1975. [Argues that typological formulations from a Protestant perspective unify *The Temple* both structurally and thematically]

Linkin, Harriet Kramer. "Herbert's Reciprocal Writing: Poetry as Sacred Pun." In *Traditions and Innovations: Essays on British Literature of the Middle Ages and the Renaissance*, edited by

David G. Allen and Robert A. White, 214–22. Cranbury, New
    Jersey: Associated University Presses, 1990. [Argues that "as the
    Eucharist manifests a kind of sacred pun in presenting Christ's
    body and blood as bread and wine, Herbert approximates the
    duality of the Eucharist in a poetry composed of sacred puns and
    hieroglyphic verse"]
Lynch, Kathleen. "*The Temple*: 'Three Parts Vied and Multiplied.'"
    Studies in English Literature, 1500–1900 29 (1989): 139–55.
    [Argues that the three sections of *The Temple* are "three different
    views of human experience, each reiterating the same vision of
    redemption and containing the same promise of release from
    temporality"]
Maleski, Mary A., ed. *A Fine Tuning: Studies of the Religious Poetry of
    Herbert and Milton*. Binghamton, New York: Center for
    Medieval and Early Renaissance Studies, State University of New
    York at Binghamton, 1989. [Contains six essays on Herbert]
Manley, Frank. "Toward a Definition of Plain Style in the Poetry of
    George Herbert." In *Poetic Traditions of the English Renaissance*,
    edited by Maynard Mack and George deForest Lord, 203–17.
    New Haven and London: Yale University Press, 1982.
Marcus, Leah Sinanoglou. *Childhood and Cultural Despair: A Theme
    and Variations in Seventeenth-Century Literature*. Pittsburgh:
    University of Pittsburgh Press, 1978. [Chapter 3 is "The Poet as
    Child: Herbert, Herrick, and Crashaw."]
Marcus, Leah Sinanoglou. "George Herbert and the Anglican Plain
    Style." In *"Too Rich to Clothe the Sunne": Essays on George
    Herbert*, edited by Claude J. Summers and Ted-Larry Pebworth,
    179–93. Pittsburgh: University of Pittsburgh Press, 1980.
    [Argues that Herbert stylistically is between the "Anglican high
    style" and the "Puritan plain style," since Herbert felt that
    language should be used in humble submission to God but with
    the embodiment of an ideal of beauty and order]
Martin, Louis. "The Trinitarian Unity of *The Temple*: Herbert's
    Augustinian Aesthetic." *George Herbert Journal* 13 (1989–90):
    63–77. [Emphasizes Herbert's creation of various three-part
    structures and Trinitarian themes, among other significant
    numerological aspects, in *The Temple*]
Martz, Louis L. *The Poetry of Meditation: A Study in English Religious
    Literature of the Seventeenth Century*. New Haven: Yale
    University Press, 1954. [Two chapters and portions of several
    others are devoted to Herbert]
McCanles, Michael. *Dialectical Criticism and Renaissance Literature*.
    Berkeley: University of California Press, 1975. [Pp. 74–95
    discuss some of Herbert's poems.]

McLaughlin, Elizabeth, and Gail Thomas. "Communion in *The Temple.*" *Studies in English Literature, 1500–1900* 15 (1975): 111–24. [Sees the tripartite structure of *The Temple* corresponding to Anglican preparation for communion, communion itself, and consequences of communion for believers]

Meilaender, Marion. "Speakers and Hearers in *The Temple.*" *George Herbert Journal* 5 (1981–82): 31–44. [Argues that, through using various speakers and hearers, Herbert dramatizes God's pursuit of the soul as the soul resists]

Miner, Earl. *The Metaphysical Mode from Donne to Cowley.* Princeton, New Jersey: Princeton University Press, 1969.

Nestrick, William V. "'Mine and Thine' in *The Temple.*" In *"Too Rich to Clothe the Sunne": Essays on George Herbert,* edited by Claude J. Summers and Ted-Larry Pebworth, 115–27. Pittsburgh: University of Pittsburgh Press, 1980. [Notes recurrence of the words in Herbert's work to express the paradox of human separation from, but union with, God]

Nuttall, A.D. *Overheard by God: Fiction and Prayer in Herbert, Milton, Dante and St. John.* London and New York: Methuen & Co., 1980. [Over one half of the book is devoted to Herbert, and it is concerned especially with a Calvinistic context for *The Temple.*]

Ostriker, Alicia. "Song and Speech in the Metrics of George Herbert." *PMLA* 80 (1965): 62–68.

Paynter, Mary. "'Sinne and Love': Thematic Patterns in George Herbert's Lyrics." *Yearbook of English Studies* 3 (1973): 85–93. [Sees God's love set against sin through *The Temple*, with love portrayed in images of eucharistic feast and sin in images of the stony heart and the box]

Pennel, Charles A., and William P. Williams. "The Unity of *The Temple.*" *Xavier University Studies* 5 (1966): 37–45. [Argues that the central part of *The Temple* is patterned after a pilgrimage, depicting the "progress of the pilgrim soul, under the care of Christ's church"]

Pollard, David L. "The Organs of the Eye and Ear: Complementary Modes of Perception in George Herbert's *The Temple.*" *Cithara* 22, no. 2 (1982–83): 62–72. [Discusses the centrality of the imagery of sight and hearing in *The Temple*, with emphasis on the unifying theme of hearing and being heard by God]

Rickey, Mary Ellen. *Utmost Art: Complexity in the Verse of George Herbert.* Lexington: University of Kentucky Press, 1966.

Rollin, Roger B. "Self-Created Artifact: The Speaker and the Reader in *The Temple.*" In *"Too Rich to Clothe the Sunne": Essays on George Herbert*, edited by Claude J. Summers and Ted-Larry Pebworth, 147–61. Pittsburgh: University of Pittsburgh Press,

1980. [Categorizes poems of *The Temple* in three groups (Sacred Poems, Private Ejaculations, and Mixed Poems), according to the type of human speakers]

Sandler, Florence. "'Solomon vbique regnet': Herbert's Use of the Images of the New Covenant." *Papers on Language and Literature* 8 (1972): 147–58.

Schoenfeldt, Michael C. "'Respective Boldnesse': Herbert and the Art of Submission." In *A Fine Tuning: Studies of the Religious Poetry of Herbert and Milton*, edited by Mary A. Maleski, 77–94. Binghamton, New York: Center for Medieval and Early Renaissance Studies, State University of New York, 1989. [Sees Herbert's "Dedication" exploiting "tensions inherent in the literature of clientage to create a succinct but complex account of the goals and obstacles of his own poetic project"]

Schoenfeldt, Michael C. "Submission and Assertion: The 'Double Motion' of Herbert's 'Dedication.'" *John Donne Journal* 2, no. 2 (1983): 39–49.

Seelig, Sharon Cadman. *The Shadow of Eternity: Belief and Structure in Herbert, Vaughan and Traherne*. Lexington: University Press of Kentucky, 1981. [Chapter 1 is "Between Two Worlds: Herbert."]

Severance, Sibyl Lutz. "Numerological Structures in *The Temple*." In *"Too Rich to Clothe the Sunne": Essays on George Herbert*, edited by Claude J. Summers and Ted-Larry Pebworth, 229–49. Pittsburgh: University of Pittsburgh Press, 1980.

Shaw, Robert B. *The Call of God: The Theme of Vocation in the Poetry of Donne and Herbert*. Cambridge, Massachusetts: Cowley Publications, 1981.

Shawcross, John T. "Herbert's Double Poems: A Problem in the Text of *The Temple*." In *"Too Rich to Clothe the Sunne": Essays on George Herbert*, edited by Claude J. Summers and Ted-Larry Pebworth, 211–28. Pittsburgh: University of Pittsburgh Press, 1980. [Argues that six poems as ordinarily printed actually should be divided into twelve separate poems]

Sherwood, Terry G. *Herbert's Prayerful Art*. Toronto: University of Toronto Press, 1989.

Singleton, Marion White. *God's Courtier: Configuring a Different Grace in George Herbert's "Temple."* Cambridge: Cambridge University Press, 1987. [Emphasizes the role of the speaker as "God's Courtier," drawing upon the importance of Renaissance courtesy books and the courtly ideal as applied by Herbert to spiritual relationships]

Slights, Camille Wells. *The Casuistical Tradition in Shakespeare, Donne, Herbert, and Milton*. Princeton, New Jersey: Princeton

University Press, 1981. [Chapter 5 is "Casuistry in *The Temple*," in which the speaker is seen as a casuist, one who applies moral theology to practical, daily actions.]

Stambler, Elizabeth. "The Unity of Herbert's 'Temple.'" *Cross Currents* 10 (1960): 251–66. [Perceives a unifying element present in *The Temple* in its resemblance to courtly love lyrics, especially in the speaker-lover, themes of loss and discipline, and shifting emotional states]

Stanwood, P.G. "Time and Liturgy in Herbert's Poetry." *George Herbert Journal* 5 (1981–82): 19–30. [Argues for the importance of Anglican liturgy and the *Book of Common Prayer* to Herbert's composition of *The Temple*, contending that liturgy describes the structure, the outward form, of *The Temple* itself]

Summers, Joseph H. "Sir Calidore and the Country Parson." In *Like Season'd Timber: New Essays on George Herbert*, edited by Edmund Miller and Robert DiYanni, 207–17. New York: Peter Lang, 1987. [Treats Sir Philip Sidney's influence on Herbert]

Taylor, Mark. *The Soul in Paraphrase: George Herbert's Poetics*. The Hague and Paris: Mouton, 1974.

Thekla, Sister Maria. *George Herbert, Idea and Image: A Study of "The Temple."* North Yorkshire, England: The Greek Orthodox Monastery of the Assumption, Normanby, Whitby, 1974.

Thorpe, Douglas. "'Delight into Sacrifice': Resting in Herbert's *Temple*." *Studies in English Literature, 1500–1900* 26 (1986): 59–72. [Sees individual poems in *The Temple* as visible signs, metaphors of "the man remade"]

Todd, Richard. *The Opacity of Signs: Acts of Interpretation in George Herbert's "The Temple"*. Columbia: University of Missouri Press, 1986. [Argues that *The Temple* is Herbert's interpretation of his relationship with God and that the reader must interpret the opacity in the poems as an analogy to Herbert's interpretation of God's signs]

Toliver, Harold. "Herbert's Interim and Final Places." *Studies in English Literature, 1500–1900* 24 (1984): 105–20. [Notes Herbert's recurrent concerns with placing, situating God and with emphasizing God's "in-dwelling presence," as opposed to a "transcendent law giver"]

Toliver, Harold. *Pastoral Forms and Attitudes*. Berkeley and Los Angeles: University of California Press, 1971. [Chapter 6 ("Poetry as Sacred Conveyance in Herbert and Marvell") argues that the "temple" is "a house of sacraments and sacred objects, the poet's book of verse, and the inner self of the sinner" and emphasizes Herbert's changing of secular means into sacred means of praise]

Van Nuis, Hermine. "Sincerity of Being and Simplicity of Expression: George Herbert's Ethics and Aesthetics." *Christianity and Literature* 27, no. 1 (1977): 11–21.

Vendler, Helen. *The Poetry of George Herbert.* Cambridge, Massachusetts: Harvard University Press, 1975.

Walker, John David. "The Architectonics of George Herbert's *The Temple.*" *ELH* 29 (1962): 289–305. [Proposes that the three-part structure of *The Temple* is analogous (1) to the division of the Hebraic temple into porch or courtyard, holy place, and holy of holies; (2) to a spatial perspective of lower, middle, and upper regions; and (3) to a temporal perspective of youth, maturity, and old age-death]

Watson, George. "The Fabric of Herbert's *Temple.*" *Journal of the Warburg and Courtauld Institutes* 26 (1963): 354–58. [Contends that the most important "temple" is Herbert the priest]

Watson, Thomas Ramey. "God's Geometry: Motion in the English Poetry of George Herbert." *George Herbert Journal* 9, no. 1 (1985): 17–25.

White, Helen C. *The Metaphysical Poets: A Study in Religious Experience.* New York: The Macmillan Company, 1936. [Chapters 6 and 7 concern Herbert.]

Whitney, Charles. "Bacon and Herbert: Bacon and Herbert as Moderns." In *Like Season'd Timber: New Essays on George Herbert,* edited by Edmund Miller and Robert DiYanni, 231–39. New York: Peter Lang, 1987.

Wilcox, Helen. "Herbert's Musical Contexts: Countrey-Aires to Angels Musick." In *Like Season'd Timber: New Essays on George Herbert,* edited by Edmund Miller and Robert DiYanni, 37–58. New York: Peter Lang, 1987.

Yearwood, Stephenie. "The Rhetoric of Form in *The Temple.*" *Studies in English Literature, 1500–1900* 23 (1983): 131–44. [Asserts that Herbert's purpose is to change lives and that his poems call forth an emotional and spiritual response from the reader]

Ziegelmaier, Gregory. "Liturgical Symbol and Reality in the Poetry of George Herbert." *American Benedictine Review* 18 (1967): 344–53.

b. *The Church-Porch*

Blau, Sheridan D. "The Poet as Casuist: Herbert's 'Church-Porch.'" *Genre* 4 (1971): 142–52. [Sees *The Church-Porch* as "a sort of sermon based on practical divinity or casuistry" and its purpose "to prepare its auditors for the prayers of *The Church*"]

Hinman, Robert B. "The 'Verser' at *The Temple* Door: Herbert's *The Church-porch*." In *"Too Rich to Clothe the Sunne: Essays on George Herbert*, edited by Claude J. Summers and Ted-Larry Pebworth, 55–75. Pittsburgh: University of Pittsburgh Press, 1980. [Contends that Herbert plays on "Verser" in the first stanza to imply, in one sense, a huckster or trickster who dupes the reader into surrendering to God's game, to God's pleasures]

Kessner, Carole. "Entering 'The Church-porch': Herbert and Wisdom Poetry." *George Herbert Journal* 1, no. 1 (1977): 10–25. [Argues that the apocryphal *Wisdom of Joshua Ben Sira* (or *Ecclesiasticus*) is the "spiritual and poetic ancestor" of Herbert's *The Church-Porch*]

c. *The Church* and Its Individual Poems

Adler, Jacob H. "Form and Meaning in Herbert's 'Discipline.'" *Notes and Queries* 5 (1958): 240–43. [Analysis of the poem, especially in terms of paradox, tone, and man-God relationship]

Allen, Don Cameron. "George Herbert's 'Sycomore.'" *Modern Language Notes* 59 (1944): 493–95. [Notes that "sycomore" in "The World" refers to the fig-tree of Genesis and traces through various versions of the Bible to show why Herbert would choose this word]

Allen, Don Cameron. *Image and Meaning: Metaphoric Traditions in Renaissance Poetry.* New Enlarged Edition. Baltimore, Maryland: Johns Hopkins Press, 1968. [Chapter 6 is "George Herbert: 'The Rose.'" Examines the classical and Christian symbols and associations upon which the doctrine of the rose in Herbert's poem rests]

Anderson, Jan. "Further Biblical Allusions in Herbert's 'Love' Poems." *George Herbert Journal* 12, no. 1 (1988): 41–44.

Anselment, Raymond A. "George Herbert's 'The Collar.'" *Neuphilologische Mitteilungen* 3 (1983): 372–75. [Supports several ironies and implications in the poem by citing relevant biblical and emblematic echoes and parallels]

Asals, Heather. "The Voice of George Herbert's 'The Church.'" *ELH* 36 (1969): 511–28. [Notes the importance to Herbert's poetry of the psalms and commentaries on them by St. Augustine and others and argues that the several speakers of Herbert's poems ultimately are voices of the one "voice of the Church"]

Bache, William B. "A Note on Herbert's 'Coloss. 3. 3.'" *George Herbert Journal* 6, no. 1 (1982): 27–30. [Argues that one should read and reread the italicized diagonal line in its accumulating parts completed successively by the remainder of the horizontal lines in order to perceive the full meanings embedded in the poem]

Bell, Ilona. "The Double Pleasures of Herbert's 'Collar.'" In *"Too Rich to Clothe the Sunne": Essays on George Herbert*, edited by Claude J. Summers and Ted-Larry Pebworth, 77–88. Pittsburgh: University of Pittsburgh Press, 1980. [Contends that, in addition to the internal debate of the speaker that is seen by most critics of the poem, there also is a second reading in which Christ's voice is echoing and reinterpreting the speaker's words]

Bell, Ilona. "Revision and Revelation in Herbert's 'Affliction (I).'" *John Donne Journal* 3 (1984): 73–96. [Reads the poem as embodying a change in Herbert's sympathies "from Hooker and the high Anglicans toward Calvin and the reformers"]

Benjamin, Edwin B. "Herbert's 'Vertue.'" *The Explicator* 9 (1950–51): Item 12. [Emphasizes the structure of the poem, in which the first three stanzas are contrasted to the last by thought, repetition and variation, and shifting accents and stops within individual lines]

Bevan, Jonquil, and Alastair Fowler. "Herbert's Vitruvian 'Man': Symmetry in the Stanza Structure." *Notes and Queries* 32 (1985): 156–59. [Analyzes stanza structure and rhyme in terms of complex number symbolism]

Bickham, Jack M. "Herbert's 'The Collar.'" *The Explicator* 10 (1951–52): Item 17. [Adds a third meaning by means of another pun in the title (added to those noted by Dan S. Norton in 1944–45): suggests that there is a "caller," God, in the poem]

Bienz, John. "George Herbert and the Man of Sorrows." *University of Hartford Studies in Literature* 11 (1979): 173–84. [Argues that the opening poems of *The Temple* should be read in the context of the pictorial tradition of the Man of Sorrows]

Bienz, John. "Herbert's 'Daily Labour': An Eschatological Pattern in 'The Church.'" *George Herbert Journal* 12, no. 1 (1988): 1–15. [Argues for a subdued eschatological theme that pervades *The Church*, through which Herbert expresses his concern with preparation for the end of time]

Boenig, Robert. "George Herbert and John Climicus: A Note on 'Prayer (I).'" *Notes and Queries* 37 (1990): 209–11. [Notes striking parallels and similarities in some phrases of "Prayer (1)" and a passage in Climicus's *Heavenly Ladder*, suggesting Climicus as a possible source]

Boenig, Robert. "Herbert's Poor Reed: Musical Irony in 'Employment (I).'" *Notes and Queries* 35 (1988): 64–66. [Argues that Herbert's revision of the poem's last two lines to a musical metaphor creates deliberate irony in that the musician is using an outmoded, inappropriate instrument and one at which he is not adept]

Boenig, Robert. "Listening to Herbert's Lute." *Renaissance and Reformation* 8 (1984): 298–311. [Notes some of Herbert's poems possibly written for lute accompaniment—specifically, "Denial," "The Thanksgiving," "Sunday," and "Virtue"]

Boenig, Robert. "The Raising of Herbert's Broken Consort: A Note on 'Doomsday,' 29–30." *Notes and Queries* 31 (1984): 239–41. [Suggests that the musical elements in the last two lines of the poem serve metaphorically as the "Christian's change in life leading to salvation"]

Bonnell, William. "*Anamnesis*: The Power of Memory in Herbert's Sacramental Vision." *George Herbert Journal* 15, no. 1 (1991): 33–48. [Argues that, for Herbert, one participates in God's grace through *anamnesis* (i.e., active, lively remembrance of our salvation as wrought by Christ on the cross and of our consequent relationship to God)]

Bonnell, William. "The Eucharistic Substance of George Herbert's 'Prayer' (I)." *George Herbert Journal* 9, no. 2 (1986): 35–47.

Bowers, Fredson. "Herbert's Sequential Imagery: 'The Temper.'" *Modern Philology* 59 (1961–62): 202–13. [Uses "The Temper" to illustrate how Herbert employs strains of images in one poem and in others of its sequential grouping to make larger thematic comments]

Braden, Gordon. "Unspeakable Love: Petrarch to Herbert." In *Soliciting Interpretation: Literary Theory and Seventeenth-Century English Poetry*, edited by Elizabeth D. Harvey and Katharine Eisaman Maus, 253–72. Chicago: University of Chicago Press, 1990. [Concerns Herbert's adaptation of the Petrarchan lover who cannot speak]

Breiner, Laurence A. "Herbert's Cockatrice." *Modern Philology* 77 (1979–80): 10–17. [Argues that Herbert's use of the cockatrice in "Sin's Round" is most likely referring to the alchemical *cockatrice*, "the final stage in the procedure by which the philosopher's stone was achieved"]

Brower, Reuben Arthur. *The Fields of Light: An Experiment in Critical Reading*. 1951. Reprint. New York: Oxford University Press, 1968. [Comments on "Love (3)" (pp. 28–30) and "The Windows" (pp. 45–48 and 59–61)]

Brown, C.C., and W.P. Ingoldsby. "George Herbert's 'Easter-Wings.'" *Huntington Library Quarterly* 35 (1971–72): 131–142. [In a full reading of the poem, the authors consider Greek, Hebrew, and Christian sources and analogues; pattern poems; biblical echoes; symbolism of the wings; and the context of other poems of *The Church*]

Brown, Cedric C., and Maureen Boyd. "The Homely Sense of Herbert's 'Jordan.'" *Studies in Philology* 79 (1982): 147–61. [Surveys the various meanings and allusions that have been proposed for the title of Herbert's two poems, insisting on the primacy of the story of Naaman and analyzes both of the poems so titled]

Brunner, Larry. "Herbert's 'Affliction' (I) and 'The Flower': Studies in the Theme of Christian Refinement." *Christianity and Literature* 26, no. 3 (1977): 18–28. [Sees the two poems moving one "from rebellion to acceptance, from pride to humility, from pain to that peace which perceives the love behind the severity of Christian suffering"]

Burden, Dennis H. "George Herbert's 'Redemption.'" *Review of English Studies* 34 (1983): 446–51. [Emphasizes the legal imagery and its Old Testament associations as well as the liturgical nature of the poem]

Carney, Frank. "George Herbert the Musician: Integration of Music into Poetry." *Explorations in Renaissance Culture* 4 (1978): 17–31.

Carpenter, Margaret. "From Herbert to Marvell: Poetics in 'A Wreath' and 'The Coronet.'" *Journal of English and Germanic Philology* 69 (1970): 50–62. [Includes a reading of Herbert's "A Wreath" in order to compare and contrast it to Marvell's poem]

Clark, Ira. *Christ Revealed: The History of the Neotypological Lyric in the English Renaissance.* Gainesville: University Presses of Florida, 1982. [Chapter 4 is "'Lord, in thee The *beauty* lies in the *discovery*': 'Love Unknown' as George Herbert's Neotypological Lyric Paradigm."]

Clements, A.L. "Theme, Tone, and Tradition in George Herbert's Poetry." *English Literary Renaissance* 3 (1973): 264–83. [With primary focus on a reading of "Artillery," the essay notes a central theme of submission to God's will in *The Temple*.]

Collmer, Robert G. "Herbert's 'Businesse,' 15–30." *The Explicator* 16 (1957–58): Item 11. [Sees five different kinds of death in the poem]

Cramer, Carmen. "Herbert's 'Ungratefulness.'" *The Explicator* 41, no. 4 (1983): 17–19. [Argues for the centrality of enclosure imagery in interpreting the poem]

Cunnar, Eugene R. "Herbert and the Visual Arts: *Ut Picture Poesis*: An Opening in 'The Windows.'" In *Like Season'd Timber: New Essays on George Herbert*, edited by Edmund Miller and Robert DiYanni, 101–38. New York: Peter Lang, 1987. [Emphasizes the image of the Word as light, arguing that Herbert pictures the Word as light by its living embodiment in the preacher. Says that the poem is "both a silent sermon and a speaking picture with light as the new common ground between word and image"]

Daniels, Earl. *The Art of Reading Poetry*. New York: Rinehart & Co., 1941. [Brief comments on "Prayer (1)" and "The Pulley"]

Daniels, Edgar F. "Herbert's 'The Quip,' Line 23: 'Say, I am Thine.'" *English Language Notes* 2 (1964–65): 10–12. [Notes the ambiguity of "say, I am thine," in that it can mean either "say that I (man) am Thine (God's)" or "say, 'I (God) am thine (man's).'" Argues that the latter reading better fits the thematic unity of the poem]

Daniels, Edgar F. "Herbert's 'The Quip, 23.'" *The Explicator* 23 (1964–65): Item 7. [Argues that "at large" in "Speak not at large" means "at length, in full, fully," rather than "in a general way"]

Davies, H. Neville. "Sweet Music in Herbert's 'Easter.'" *Notes and Queries* 15 (1968): 95–96. [Comments on the associations of the image of the crucified Christ's stretched sinews with the idea that a fully stretched string on a musical instrument produces music valued for its sweetness and with the common reference to Christ's sweetness]

Dessner, Lawrence J. "A Reading of George Herbert's 'Man.'" *Concerning Poetry* 5, no. 1 (1972): 61–63. [Proposes that the poet is criticizing the speaker of the poem who is proud and uses false logic]

Di Cesare, Mario A. "God's Silence: On Herbert's 'Deniall.'" *George Herbert Journal* 10 (1986–87): 85–102. [Focuses on prosody and on the theme of "spiritual dryness"]

Di Cesare, Mario A. "Image and Allusion in Herbert's 'Prayer (I).'" *English Literary Renaissance* 11 (1981): 304–28.

Doerksen, Daniel W. "Recharting the *Via Media* of Spenser and Herbert." *Renaissance and Reformation* 20 (1984): 215–25. [Argues that Herbert endorses the middle way between Rome and Geneva in order and ritual, in externals, rather than in doctrine. Cites "The British Church" as primary support]

Douds, J.B. "George Herbert's Use of the Transferred Verb: A Study in the Structure of Poetic Imagery." *Modern Language Quarterly* 5 (1944): 163–74. [Defines and illustrates the power of the "transferred verb" in various poems by Herbert]

Dyson, A.E., and Julian Lovelock. *Masterful Images: English Poetry from Metaphysicals to Romantics*. London: Macmillan; New York: Barnes and Noble, 1976. [Chapter 2 is "Herbert's 'Redemption'" and explicates the poem with an emphasis on its metaphysical characteristics, the quest of the simple *persona*, homely images, and use of St. Paul's theology]

Edgecombe, Rodney Stenning. "A Probable Source for Herbert's 'Whitsunday.'" *Notes and Queries* 39 (1992): 29–30. [Sees influence from a passage in St. Augustine's *Confessions*]

Eldredge, Frances. "Herbert's 'Jordan.'" *The Explicator* 11 (1952–53):
    Item 3. [Argues that the primary meaning in the title of the two
    poems is in reference to baptism and cites the Order of Baptism
    in the *Book of Common Prayer* to support the reference to
    Christ's baptism. Herbert, then, is baptizing his earlier verses.]
Elsky, Martin. *Authorizing Words: Speech, Writing, and Print in the
    English Renaissance.* Ithaca and London: Cornell University
    Press, 1989. [Chapter 5 is "The Space of the Hieroglyph: George
    Herbert and Francis Bacon."]
Elsky, Martin. "George Herbert's Pattern Poems and the Materiality of
    Language: A New Approach to Renaissance Hieroglyphics." *ELH*
    50 (1983): 245–60. [Comments on ways in which the designs of
    Herbert's pattern poems "spell God's Word by building up letters
    into pictures in which language, nature, and history merge with
    the poet's spoken utterances, recorded in his written words"]
Elsky, Martin. "The Sacramental Frame of George Herbert's 'The
    Church' and the Shape of Spiritual Autobiography." *Journal of
    English and Germanic Philology* 83 (1984): 313–29. [Using the
    perspective of Protestant typology, the essay views *The Church*
    as "a chronicle of the spiritual and emotional life lived in that
    ambiguous time between the Passion events ('The Sacrifice') and
    the end time ('Dooms-day'), between the partial fulfillment of the
    prophecy of redemption and its final fulfillment."]
Empson, William. *Seven Types of Ambiguity.* 2nd ed. London: Chatto
    & Windus, 1947. [Comments on "Affliction (1)," "Hope," "The
    Pilgrimage," and "The Sacrifice"]
Emslie, Macdonald. "Herbert's 'Jordan I.'" *The Explicator* 12 (1953–
    54): Item 35. [Explicates the poem and alternate meanings of
    various phrases, with emphasis on Herbert's attack on those who
    write religious verse in excessively elaborate and allegorical
    ways]
Ende, Frederick von. "George Herbert's 'The Sonne': In Defense of the
    English Language." *Studies in English Literature, 1500–1900* 12
    (1972): 173–82. [Analyzes the sonnet as a compact classical
    oration that defends the adequacy of English, evidenced primarily
    through the *sun-son* homonym]
Engel, Wilson F., III. "Christ in the Winepress: Backgrounds of a
    Sacred Image." *George Herbert Journal* 3 (1979–80): 45–63.
    [Examines the backgrounds of the winepress image and its
    associations in the Bible, theological writers, and English liturgy
    and its use by poets of the 16th and 17th centuries, emphasizing
    Herbert's in "The Agony"]
Entzminger, Robert L. "Doctrine and Life: George Herbert and the
    Augustinian Rhetoric of Example." *George Herbert Journal* 13

(1989–90): 37–47. [Argues that Herbert's poems present evidence of failure to attain the ideal of becoming like Christ, thus achieving the poetic purpose of picturing his own spiritual conflicts to comfort others]

Ericson, Edward E., Jr. "A Structural Approach to Imagery." *Style* 3 (1969): 227–47. [Examines external structuring of imagery in Herbert's poetry, seeing some poems that are unified throughout by imagery and others consisting of separate blocks of images connected "end to end"]

Evans, G. Blakemore. "George Herbert's 'Jordan.'" *Notes and Queries* 5 (1958): 215. [Supports (with seventeenth-century citations) Grosart's contention in his 1874 edition of Herbert that the two poems so titled suggest a contrast to Helicon and that God, not the Muses, is Herbert's inspiration]

Fallon, Robert Thomas. "'Artillerie': Herbert's Strange Warfare." In *Praise Disjoined: Changing Patterns of Salvation in 17th-Century English Literature*, edited by William P. Shaw, 221–36. New York: Peter Lang, 1991. [Argues that the star falling into the speaker's lap is God's gift of divine grace and that the speaker resists the offer until he successfully subdues his own sinful nature and surrenders his will]

Fish, Stanley E. *Self-Consuming Artifacts: The Experience of Seventeenth-Century Literature*. Berkeley, Los Angeles, London: University of California Press, 1972. [Chapter 3 is "Letting Go: The Dialectic of the Self in Herbert's Poetry."]

Flesch, William. *Generosity and the Limits of Authority*. Ithaca and London: Cornell University Press, 1992. [Chapter 1 is "'When Griefs Make Thee Tame': Public and Private in Herbert."]

Fowler, Anne C. "'With Care and Courage': Herbert's *'Affliction'* Poems." In *Too Rich to Clothe the Sunne": Essays on George Herbert*, edited by Claude J. Summers and Ted-Larry Pebworth, 129–45. Pittsburgh: University of Pittsburgh Press, 1980. [Regards "Affliction (1)" and "Affliction (4)" as the best of the five poems, especially because of the immature speakers' expression of emotional realities not available to the wiser voices of the other three poems]

French, Roberts W. "'My Stuffe is Flesh': An Allusion to Job in George Herbert's 'The Pearl.'" *Notes and Queries* 27 (1980): 329–31. [Notes that Herbert alludes to Job 6:12 in the third stanza of the poem, with the echo of Job's ". . . is my flesh of brass?" Argues that the reference serves to highlight the ego of the speaker]

Gaskell, Ronald. "Herbert's 'Vanitie.'" *Critical Quarterly* 3 (1961): 313–15. [Explicates "Vanity (1)" in terms of its critical attitude toward violators of nature and its uses of imagery, alliteration, and parallelism]

Getz, Thomas H. "Herbert's 'Confession.'" *The Explicator* 41, no. 1 (1982): 21–22.

Gilman, Ernest B. *The Curious Perspective: Literary and Pictorial Wit in the Seventeenth Century.* New Haven and London: Yale University Press, 1978. [Comments on "The Sacrifice" on pp. 191–94]

Gottlieb, Sidney, ed. *Approaches to Teaching the Metaphysical Poets.* New York: The Modern Language Association of America, 1990. [Herbert is a major focus in many of the essays and sections in this volume.]

Gottlieb, Sidney. "From 'Content' to 'Affliction' (III): Herbert's Anti-Court Sequence." *English Literary Renaissance* 23 (1993): 472–89. [Argues for seeing *The Temple* as not only a work of private devotion but also as "a cunning and curious as well as faithful examination of the inextricably linked realms of politics and prayer"]

Gottlieb, Sidney. "Herbert's Case of 'Conscience': Public or Private Poem?" *Studies in English Literature, 1500–1900* 25 (1985): 109–26. [Argues for the "public" side of Herbert's poetic concerns by perceiving conscience personified as a "nonconforming radical Protestant, a danger not only to one's peace of mind but also to one's church and society"]

Gottlieb, Sidney. "Herbert's 'Coloss. 3.3' and Thomas Jenner's *The Soules Solace*." *English Language Notes* 18 (1980–81): 175–79. [Notes a possible source from Jenner for the "one eye" image in Herbert's poem]

Gottlieb, Sidney. "Herbert's Political Allegory of 'Humilitie.'" *Huntington Library Quarterly* 52 (1989): 469–80. [Interprets the poem as a "witty political poem, an allegorical satire" on Jacobean patronage]

Gottlieb, Sidney. "How Shall We Read Herbert? A Look at 'Prayer' (I)." *George Herbert Journal* 1, no. 1 (1977): 26–38. [Argues for reading this poem and Herbert's others in the context of the surrounding verses]

Gottlieb, Sidney. "Linking Techniques in Herbert and Vaughan." *George Herbert Journal* 2, no. 1 (1978): 38–53. [Examines such techniques in Herbert as repetition and association of titles; repetition of words, images, and actions; question and answer; and thematic groupings. Reflects on ways in which Vaughan employs similar techniques under Herbert's influence]

Gottlieb, Sidney. "The Social and Political Backgrounds of George Herbert's Poetry." In *"The Muses Common-Weale": Poetry and*

Politics in the Seventeenth Century, edited by Claude J. Summers and Ted-Larry Pebworth, 107–18. Columbia: University of Missouri Press, 1988. [Argues that many topical references and controversial political, social, and ecclesiastical subjects in Herbert's poetry have been ignored and should be examined more fully, with examples of such topics related by Gottlieb to some of the poems]

Gottlieb, Sidney. "The Two Endings of George Herbert's 'The Church.'" In *A Fine Tuning: Studies of the Religious Poetry of Herbert and Milton*, edited by Mary A. Maleski, 57–76. Binghamton, New York: Center for Medieval and Early Renaissance Studies, State University of New York, 1989. [Argues that changes from Herbert's early version to his final one develop confirmation of Herbert's broad and inclusive Anglicanism]

Greenwood, E.B. "George Herbert's Sonnet 'Prayer': A Stylistic Study." *Essays in Criticism* 15 (1965): 27–45. [Emphasizes the movements of "Prayer (1)" from earth to heaven and heaven to earth, while also noting ambiguities and multiple possibilities in many of the words and phrases]

Halli, Robert W., Jr. "The Double Hieroglyph in George Herbert's 'Easter-Wings.'" *Philological Quarterly* 63 (1984): 265–72. [Argues that the patterns of the stanzas reflect hourglasses, as well as wings, and that the symbolism of mortality and immortality combined is important in the poem]

Hammond, Gerald. "Herbert's 'Prayer I.'" *The Explicator* 39 (Fall 1980): 41–43.

Harman, Barbara Leah. *Costly Monuments: Representations of the Self in George Herbert's Poetry*. Cambridge, Massachusetts: Harvard University Press, 1982.

Harnack, Andrew. "Both Protestant and Catholic: George Herbert and 'To all Angels and Saints.'" *George Herbert Journal* 11, no. 1 (1987): 23–39. [Argues for Herbert as both a "catholic" (i.e., universal) Christian and a Protestant, rather than as at the ecclesiastical extremes of embracing facets of older Roman Catholicism or of radical Puritanism]

Harnack, H. Andrew. "George Herbert's 'Aaron': The Aesthetics of Shaped Typology." *English Language Notes* 14 (1976–77): 25–32. [Analyzes "Aaron" as a shaped lyric perfectly fusing theme, verse form, expression, typography, sound, numerology, and tone]

Hart, Jeffrey. "Herbert's 'The Collar' Re-Read." *Boston University Studies in English* 5 (1961): 65–73. [Reads the poem in terms of

the Fall, Atonement, and Redemption, emphasizing the
importance of the Eucharistic imagery]

Häublein, Ernst. *The Stanza*. London: Methuen & Co., 1978. [Several
comments on Herbert, but especially on "Aaron" (pp. 104–105)
and "Virtue" (pp. 82–85)]

Hester, M. Thomas. "Altering the Text of the Self: The Shapes of 'The
Altar.'" In *A Fine Tuning: Studies of the Religious Poetry of
Herbert and Milton*, edited by Mary A. Maleski, 95–116.
Binghamton, New York: Center for Medieval and Early
Renaissance Studies, State University of New York, 1989.
[Argues that "The Altar" is "an unfolding series of verbal and
visual 'parts' of speech that serve as images of the speaker's self"]

Hilberry, Conrad. "Herbert's 'Dooms-day.'" *The Explicator* 16 (1957–
58): Item 24. [Explicates the poem, noting especially the bizarre
comic tone of the first four stanzas that shifts to a serious one in
the final stanza]

Hill, D.M. "Allusion and Meaning in Herbert's 'Jordan I.'"
Neophilologus 56 (1972): 344–52. [Sees a simple surface
argument representing a "wished-for clarity" existing together
with "unfolding intricacies and ambiguities"]

Hollander, John. *The Untuning of the Sky: Ideas of Music in English
Poetry, 1500–1700*. Princeton, New Jersey: Princeton University
Press, 1961. [Chapter 5 contains the section titled "Herbert's
Musical Temper."]

Hovey, Kenneth Alan. "Church History in 'The Church.'" *George
Herbert Journal* 6, no. 1 (1982): 1–14. [Discusses some scattered
poems that reflect the Church and its history in a chronological
sequence that parallels the life of the individual Christian depicted
in *The Church*]

Hovey, Kenneth Alan. "'Diuinitie, and Poesie, Met': The Baconian
Context of George Herbert's Divinity." *English Language Notes*
22, no. 3 (1985): 30–39. [Argues that Herbert, like Bacon, felt
that science should be separated from divinity (as well as reason
from faith) and that the clearest expression of this feeling is in
Herbert's "Divinity"]

Hughes, R.E. "George Herbert's Rhetorical World." *Criticism* 3 (1961):
86–94. [Illustrates the importance of Herbert's rhetorical way of
looking at experience and ideas with comments on "Prayer (1),"
"The Agony," "Redemption," "Christmas," "Easter," and "The
Pilgrimage"]

Hunter, C. Stuart. "Herbert's 'The Pulley.'" *The Explicator* 34 (1975–
76): Item 43. [Comments on the pulley conceit and the various
meanings of "rest," including uses of the word in the Bible to
imply spiritual rest]

Hunter, Jeanne Clayton. "George Herbert and 'Friend.'" *Notes and Queries* 32 (1985): 160–61. [Argues that the source of Herbert's use of "friend" in his poems to mean God or Christ is John 15:13–16]

Hunter, Jeanne Clayton. "Herbert's 'The Water-Course': Notorious and Neglected." *Notes and Queries* 34 (1987): 310–12. [Relates the flowing waters imagery to several biblical passages and to Calvinistic doctrines of grace and election]

Hunter, Jeanne Clayton. "'Silk Twist': Line of Grace in Herbert's *The Pearl. Matth. XIII.45.*" *Notes and Queries* 29 (1982): 19–20. [Argues that the "silk twist" is the Covenant of Grace, a reading supported by passages from John Calvin and John Preston]

Hunter, Jim. *The Metaphysical Poets.* 1965. Reprint. London: Evans Brothers Limited, 1968. [Chapter 7 concerns Herbert.]

Huntley, Frank L. "George Herbert and the Image of Violent Containment." *George Herbert Journal* 8, no. 1 (1984): 17–27. [Examines the importance of Herbert's images of containers of all sorts, climaxed by the containment within Christ of all human experience of sacrifice, love, tears, drama, cruelty, and forgiveness]

Jacobs, Edward C. "Herbert's 'The World': A Study of Grace." *Concerning Poetry* 8, no. 2 (1975): 71–74. [Explicates the poem in terms of an allegory of the "stately house" that leads to the necessity of God's grace for humanity to have an eternal dwelling]

Johnson, Bruce A. "Penitential Voices in Herbert's Poetry." *George Herbert Journal* 8, no. 2 (1985): 1–17. [Categorizes speakers in Herbert's penitential poems as of the following types: (1) one who "raises a voice of extreme self-abasement," (2) one who "examines himself calmly and deliberately" and exposes "his sinful attitudes to himself and God," and (3) one who "rails at God in ever increasing confusion until God intervenes, overwhelming the now penitent speaker"]

Johnson, Jeffrey S. "Recreating the Word: Typology in Herbert's 'The Altar.'" *Christianity and Literature* 37, no. 1 (1987): 55–65. [Argues that every aspect of "The Altar" reveals it to be a typological hieroglyph for spiritual conversion, especially emphasizing the relevance of St. Paul's idea of the circumcision of the heart]

Johnson, Parker. "'Worthy to be here': Protestant Sacramental Devotion and Herbert's 'Love' (III)." *George Herbert Journal* 13 (1989–90): 49–62. [Drawing upon Calvin, *The Book of Common Prayer*, and other commentators, this essay argues that the worth of the speaker "is the critical issue in the poem" and that the

"Protestant devotional tradition of sacramental preparation and self-examination" provides an important context for interpreting Herbert's poem.]

Johnson, Parker H. "The Economy of Praise in George Herbert's 'The Church.'" *George Herbert Journal* 5 (1981–82): 45–62. [Centers on Herbert's economic, legal, and mercantile imagery that explores "the difficulty of response to God and the problem of praise"]

Jones, Nicholas R. "Texts and Contexts: Two Languages in George Herbert's Poetry." *Studies in Philology* 79 (1982): 162–76. [Sees in many poems an interaction between a quasi-poem (a "text") that is pure, divine, and demanding interpretation in a way analogous to a scriptural passage and a "context" that is impure, willful, witty, human, and necessary for explanation]

Keizer, Garret. "Fragrance, 'Marie Magdalene,' and Herbert's *The Temple*." *George Herbert Journal* 4, no. 1 (1980): 29–50. [Examines "mutuality in the divine-human relationship" (i.e., "fragrance") in Herbert and as a reflection of biblical imagery]

Keizer, Garret. " A Possible Source for Herbert's 'Anagram.'" *English Language Notes* 16 (1978–79): 281–83. [Argues for a sermon by Lancelot Andrewes (preached in 1611 and published in 1629) as a possible source for the conceit of the tent in the poem]

Kinnamon, Noel J. "A Note on Herbert's 'Easter' and the Sidneian Psalms." *George Herbert Journal* 1, no. 2 (1978): 44–48. [Concerns possible influence on Herbert of the Countess of Pembroke's metrical version of Psalm 108]

Kinnamon, Noel. "Notes on the Psalms in Herbert's *The Temple*." *George Herbert Journal* 4, no. 2 (1981): 10–29. [Examines how Herbert employed Psalm structures, allusions to individual Psalm verses, and adaptation of some Psalms in many poems of *The Church*]

Klawitter, George. "The Problem of Circularity in Herbert's Wreath." *George Herbert Journal* 6, No. 1 (1982): 15–20. [Contends that "A Wreath" actually is a "double wreath" that "doubles back upon itself" midway through the poem, a feat achieved by Herbert's use of repetition, convoluted lines, and rhetorical devices]

Klopfenstein, Glenn. "Herbert's 'Heaven.'" *The Explicator* 51 (1992–93): 10–12. [Analyzes this penultimate poem of "The Church" primarily as the "soul's final catechism in preparation for the soul's glorification that is dramatized in 'Love III'"]

Knieger, Bernard. "Herbert's 'Redemption.'" *The Explicator* 11 (1952–53): Item 24. [Notes the poem's dual chronology, the fact that Christ grants the suit before it is stated, and associations of "dearly bought"]

Knieger, Bernard. "The Purchase-Sale: Patterns of Business Imagery in the Poetry of George Herbert." *Studies in English Literature, 1500–1900* 6 (1966): 111–24. [Examines Herbert's uses of commercial imagery, emphasizing particularly the idea of Christ's purchase and sale for mankind through the crucifixion]

Knieger, Bernard. "The Religious Verse of George Herbert." *College Language Association Journal* 4 (1960–61): 138–47. [Notes Herbert's universal themes and emphasizes his uses of business imagery]

Knights, L.C. *Explorations: Essays in Criticism Mainly on the Literature of the Seventeenth Century.* New York: George W. Stewart, Publisher, Inc., 1947. [Chapter 6 is "George Herbert," originally published in 1944 in *Scrutiny.* Knights concentrates on Herbert's "human value" and "craftsmanship," distinct from his Christian value, and he illustrates with excerpts from several poems of "The Church."]

Koretz, Gene H. "The Rhyme Scheme in Herbert's 'Man.'" *Notes and Queries* 3 (1956): 144–46. [Argues that the "rhyme scheme is consistently varied in stanzas of equal length" in such a way as to embody "the concepts of unity enveloping diversity, order governing abundance and variety"]

Kronenfeld, Judy Z. "Herbert's 'A Wreath' and Devotional Aesthetics: Imperfect Efforts Redeemed by Grace." *ELH* 48 (1981): 290–309. [Comments on "A Wreath" in light of its progression from an imperfect human maker trying to praise God into what God and his grace must do for the human]

Kronenfeld, Judy Z. "Probing the Relation between Poetry and Ideology: Herbert's 'The Windows.'" *John Donne Journal* 2, no. 1 (1983): 55–80. [Argues for concentrating on the poem as being about inner faith, rather than being about an Anglo-Catholic/Puritan conflict concerning "sacramentals" of the church]

Labriola, Albert C. "Herbert, Crashaw, and the *Schola Cordis* Tradition." *George Herbert Journal* 2, No. 1 (1978): 13–23. [Uses "The Bunch of Grapes" to show Herbert's relating of biblical passages and typological interpretations of them, especially in regard to the human heart]

Labriola, Albert C. "The Rock and the Hard Place: Biblical Typology and Herbert's 'The Altar.'" *George Herbert Journal* 10 (1986–87): 61–69. [Relates four biblical episodes (the transfiguration, the buffeting of Christ, the entombment of Christ, and Pentecost) to "The Altar"]

Leimberg, Inge. "Annotating Baroque Poetry: George Herbert's 'A
     Dialogue-Antheme.'" *George Herbert Journal* 15, no. 1 (1991):
     49–67.
Leishman, J.B. *The Metaphysical Poets: Donne, Herbert, Vaughan,
     Traherne.* 1934. Reprint. New York: Russell & Russell, 1963.
     [Second major section is "George Herbert."]
Lerner, Laurence. *An Introduction to English Poetry.* London: Edward
     Arnold Publishers, 1975. [Chapter 5 gives a reading of "The
     Bunch of Grapes," emphasizing the poem as an "intellectual
     exploration" and commenting on its typological and moral
     meanings.]
Linden, Stanton J. "Herbert and the Unveiling of Diana: Stanza Three of
     'Vanitie' (I)." *George Herbert Journal* 1, no. 2 (1978): 30–37.
     [Relates the image of the "Chymick" intruding into nature to
     common references of the time to intruding upon the privacy of
     the bathing Diana]
Lord, John B. "Herbert's Poetic Voice." *George Herbert Journal* 2, no.
     2 (1979): 25–43. [Phonological examinations of Herbert's poems,
     with primary illustrations from "The Windows," "Church
     Monuments," "The Quip," and "The Forerunners"]
Low, Anthony. "Herbert's 'Jordan (I)' and the Court Masque."
     Criticism 14 (1972): 109–18. [Sees the poem as critical of court
     masques and as itself a parody in the form of a miniature divine
     masque]
Low, Anthony. *Love's Architecture: Devotional Modes in Seventeenth-
     Century English Poetry.* New York: New York University Press,
     1978. [Chapter 4 is "George Herbert: Varieties of Devotion," and
     Herbert is also discussed briefly in Chapter 2 ("Divine Song").]
Lull, Janis. *The Poem in Time: Reading George Herbert's Revisions of
     "The Church".* Cranbury, New Jersey: Associated University
     Presses, 1990. [Examines Herbert's revised lyrics from the early
     Williams manuscript to the late Bodleian manuscript]
Luxton, Andrea. "The Rest That Remaineth: A Study of Five Poems by
     George Herbert." *George Herbert Journal* 11, no. 2,(1988): 49–
     62. [Discusses the relevance of Hebrews 3–4 and its concept of
     "rest" to "The Pulley," "Aaron," "Peace," "Sunday," and "Even-
     song"]
Lynch, Denise E. "Herbert's 'The H. Scriptures I and II.'" *The
     Explicator* 50 (1991–92): 139–42. [Examines the parallels in the
     two sonnets that reinforce their "thematic links"]
Lynch, Denise. "Herbert's 'Love (III)' and Augustine on Wisdom."
     English Language Notes 27, no. 1 (1989): 40–41. [Proposes as a
     possible source for Herbert the reading of Proverbs 9:1–5 in St.
     Augustine's *The City of God*]

Lyons, Bridget Gellert. "Poetic Affinities: Metaphysical and Modern
Poets." In *Approaches to Teaching the Metaphysical Poets*, edited
by Sidney Gottlieb, 114–19. New York: Modern Language
Association of America, 1990. [Relates several characteristics of
Herbert's poetry (such as forms, diction, and dramatic voices) to
Robert Frost's]

Mahood, M.M. "Something Understood: The Nature of Herbert's Wit."
In *Metaphysical Poetry*, edited by Malcolm Bradbury and David
Palmer, 123–47. London: Edward Arnold, 1970. [Comments on
form, craftsmanship, and wordplay in such poems as "Faith,"
"Repentance," "Prayer (1)," "The Pearl," "Mortification,"
"Church Monuments," "Death," "Constancy," "Love Unknown,"
"Virtue," and "Love (3)"]

Malpezzi, Frances M. "Herbert's 'The Thanksgiving' in Context."
Renascence 34 (1981–82): 185–95. [Sees the poem as dramatizing
"a man who has much to learn about giving thanks" and as a part
of a cluster of poems showing a speaker that "painfully makes his
way toward humility and enlightenment"]

Malpezzi, Frances M. "The Withered Garden in Herbert's 'Grace.'"
John Donne Journal 4 (1985): 35–47. [Examines the poem in the
context of others that concern spiritual barrenness (or its
opposite) in *The Temple* and sees this poem as a "nadir for the
persona"]

Malpezzi, Frances M. "Thy Cross, My Bower: The Greening of the
Heart." In *"Too Rich to Clothe the Sunne": Essays on George
Herbert*, edited by Claude J. Summers and Ted-Larry Pebworth,
89–100. Pittsburgh: University of Pittsburgh Press, 1980. [A
Reading of "The Flower" in its context following "The Cross"
and in relation to associations of paradise and gardens]

Manning, Stephen. "Herbert's 'The Pearl,' 38." *The Explicator* 14
(1955–56): Item 25. [Argues that the "silk twist" is faith]

Matar, Nabil I. "George Herbert, Henry Vaughan, and the Conversion
of the Jews." *Studies in English Literature, 1500–1900* 30 (1990):
79–92. [Comments on Herbert's "The Jews," observing that the
sympathetic note in it is not the dominant one in his other poems
and prose, which primarily reflect the hostility and dogmatism of
King James and the Church of England at the time]

McColley, Diane. "The Poem as Hierophon: Musical Configurations in
George Herbert's 'The Church.'" In *A Fine Tuning: Studies of the
Religious Poetry of Herbert and Milton*, edited by Mary A.
Maleski, 117–43. Binghamton, New York: Center for Medieval
and Early Renaissance Studies, State University of New York,
1989. [Examines some of Herbert's poems as "hierophons"—i.e.,
sacred "composures." Argues that they "display configurations of

'concent' comparable to kinds of music Herbert heard, played,
and sang"]

McGrath, F.C. "Herbert's 'The Bunch of Grapes.'" *The Explicator* 29
(1970–71): Item 15. [Notes the poem's final insistence on the
"fundamental difference between the pre-Christian promise of
everlasting joy and the Christian promise of salvation in the
crucified and resurrected Christ"]

McGuire, Philip C. "Private Prayer and English Poetry in the Early
Seventeenth Century." *Studies in English Literature, 1500–1900*
14 (1974): 63–77. [Explores the influence of private prayer upon
some poems by Jonson, Donne, and Herbert. Comments on "The
Altar" as a prayer of praise and petition and sees the phrase "this
frame" as referring both to the altar of the speaker's heart and to
the poem itself]

McMahon, Robert. "Herbert's 'Coloss. 3.3' as Microcosm." *George
Herbert Journal* 15, no. 2 (1992): 55–69. [Places "Coloss. 3.3" in
the tradition of Christian uses of Plato's *Timaeus*, specifically
asserting that Christ the "sun of righteousness" is implied in the
poem and that the poem "mimes the movements of the sun in
nature and the movement of Redemption in history"]

Merrill, Thomas F. *Christian Criticism: A Study of Literary God-Talk.*
Amsterdam: Rodopi N.V., 1976. [Chapter 2 is "Devotion and
'The Flower,'" and Chapter 4 is "Herbert's Poetic God-Talk."]

Merrill, Thomas F. "George Herbert's 'Significant Stuttering.'" *George
Herbert Journal* 11, no. 2 (1988): 1–18. [Concerns the difficulty
of Herbert's devotional language for modern readers because this
language is "God-talk"—i.e., "language 'stretched' beyond its
functional limits to address supernatural 'facts'"]

Miller, William R. "Herbert's Approach to God in 'The Bag.'" *English
Language Notes* 29, no. 1 (1991): 38–44. [A reading of the poem
that centers on the conceit of Christ's wound as a mail bag, with
the final stanza paradoxically turning to the needless nature of
words when Christ has returned to glory]

Mollenkott, Virginia R. "George Herbert's 'Redemption.'" *English
Language Notes* 10 (1972–73): 262–67. [Argues that the speaker
is the "spiritual nature of Everyman, not thriving under the Old
Testament covenant" who seeks a New Testament one and that
grace is the smaller rent that replaces the "old lease of the law."
Feels that God "had 'dearly bought' the world long ago, by the act
of creation, and because of the Fall must now 'take possession' by
buying the world back—redeeming it—on the cross"]

Mollenkott, Virginia Ramey. "The Many and the One in George
Herbert's 'Providence.'" *College Language Association Journal* 10
(1966–67): 34–41.

Moloney, Michael F. "A Note on Herbert's 'Season'd Timber.'" *Notes and Queries* 4 (1957): 434–35. [Argues that in this phrase from "Virtue" Herbert primarily stresses the fact that, just as seasoned timber resists structural strains without warping, so does the virtuous soul resist with integrity the burden of temptation and that, because of its spiritual steadfastness, the soul will "chiefly live" when the world has been consumed]

Montgomery, Robert L., Jr. "The Province of Allegory in George Herbert's Verse." *Texas Studies in Literature and Language* 1 (1959–60): 457–72. [Sees the fable as "the core of Herbert's allegorical method"]

Moreland, Kim. "The Rooted Flower and the Flower that Glides: An Interpretation of Herbert's 'The Flower.'" *George Herbert Journal* 6, no. 2 (1983): 37–45. [Argues for the poem as "the spiritual climax of the smaller pattern that exists within the larger pattern of *The Temple*," the pattern being movement from "spiritual aridity" to "spiritual joy"]

Morillo, Marvin. "Herbert's Chairs: Notes to *The Temple*." *English Language Notes* 11 (1973–74): 271–75. [Notes various kinds of "chairs" referred to in Herbert's poems]

Mulder, John R. *The Temple of the Mind: Education and Literary Taste in Seventeenth-Century England*. New York: Pegasus, 1969. [Herbert is referred to many times throughout, and a section of Chapter 6 is "The Spiritual Temple of George Herbert."]

Mustazza, Leonard. "Herbert's 'The Forerunners.'" *The Explicator* 44, no. 3 (1986): 21–23. [Regards the poem as embodying the poet's ambivalence toward his craft of poetry as "a vehicle of divine praise"]

Nelson, T.G.A. "Death, Dung, the Devil, and Worldly Delights: A Metaphysical Conceit in Harington, Donne, and Herbert." *Studies in Philology* 76 (1979): 272–87. [Notes Herbert's use of "dung" as worldly delights in "The Forerunners," as well as a similar idea in "The Rose"]

Norton, Dan S. "Herbert's 'The Collar.'" *The Explicator* 2 (1943–44): Item 41. [Notes the contrast between images of fertility and freedom and sterility and constriction in the poem, as well as irony at the end which causes the reader to review the images in specifically Christian terms]

Norton, Dan S. "Herbert's 'The Collar.'" *The Explicator* 3 (1944–45): Item 46. [Notes the play on "collar" and "choler" and cites seventeenth-century uses of "rope of sand" as a symbol of "futile or impossible industry"]

Olson, John. "Biblical Narratives and Herbert's Dialogue Poems." *George Herbert Journal* 12, no. 1 (1988): 17–28. [Examines "The

Collar" and "Love (3)" in light of influences upon them from various Old Testament and New Testament dialogues]

Ormerod, David. "Number Theory in George Herbert's 'Trinity Sunday' and 'Trinitie Sunday.'" *George Herbert Journal* 12, no. 2 (1989): 27–36. [Examines "Trinity Sunday" from the Williams manuscript and "Trinitie Sunday" from *The Temple* in light of Herbert's interest in Christian numerology, "divine mathematics"]

Otten, Charlotte F. "'The Thankfull Glass, / That Mends the Lookers Eyes' in Herbert's 'The Holy Scriptures I.'" *Notes and Queries* 38 (1991): 83. [With support from a book by the 16th-century Dutch physician Levinus Lemnius, argues that these lines suggest that "as by looking into a mirror the brain of the looker is activated and new spirits are created which renew eyesight, so by looking into the Scriptures the soul of the reader is activated by the Holy Spirit, who restores the soul in the very act of reading"]

Ottenhoff, John H. "Herbert's Sonnets." *George Herbert Journal* 2, no. 2 (1979): 1–14. [Divides Herbert's sonnets into "narrative" and "meditative or contemplative" and discusses some of the experimental elements of form]

Pahlka, William H. *Saint Augustine's Meter and George Herbert's Will.* Kent, Ohio: Kent State University Press, 1987. [Argues that Herbert's meter functions in the dramatic conflict of his will with God's]

Passarella, Lee. "The Meaning of the Tent in George Herbert's 'Anagram.'" *English Language Notes* 21, no. 2 (1983): 10–13. [Relates the image of the "tent" to (1) the first repository of the Ark of the Covenant, the Tabernacle of Witness; (2) the Virgin Mary's womb; (3) the body of Christ; (4) the human body; and (5) the temporary residence of the Church on earth]

Powers-Beck, Jeffrey. "'Whence com'st thou . . . so fresh and fine?': The King's Stamp and the Origins of Value in Herbert's 'Avarice.'" *English Language Notes* 30, no. 3 (1993): 14–23. [Analyzes "Avarice" as a bitter sonnet in which the speaker is troubled by "the human parody of redemption that coining enacts," through which humanity becomes dross itself and loses its true kingdom]

Pruss, Ingrid. "George Herbert's 'Prayer' (I): From Metaphor to Mystery." *George Herbert Journal* 12, no. 2 (1989): 17–26.

Randall, Dale B.J. "The Ironing of George Herbert's 'Collar.'" *Studies in Philology* 81 (1984): 473–95. [Concentrates on the several meanings proposed in the past for "collar" and suggests that also relevant are puns on *color* and *colour*, as well as reference to an iron collar used on sinners, mad people, slaves, and animals]

Ray, Joan Klingel. "Herbert's 'Easter-Wings.'" *The Explicator* 49 (1990–91): 140–42. [Comments on the appropriateness of larks, given their natural habits, symbolically in the poem and argues that Herbert is making an implied pun on "*exaltation* of larks"]

Ray, Joan Klingel. "Myth, Microcosm, and Method in George Herbert's 'Prayer'(I)." *George Herbert Journal* 12, no. 2 (1989): 37–42.

Ray, Robert H. "Ben Jonson and the Metaphysical Poets: Continuity in a Survey Course." In *Approaches to Teaching the Metaphysical Poets*, edited by Sidney Gottlieb, 89–95. New York: Modern Language Association of America, 1990. [Argues for the importance of Ben Jonson's classical style in shaping Herbert's poems, beyond the influence of Donne and the "metaphysical" characteristics, with primary examples seen in "Virtue" and "The Windows"]

Ray, Robert H. "Herbert's 'Prayer I.'" *The Explicator* 51 (1992–93): 215–16.

Ray, Robert H. "Spatial and Aural Patterns in 'The Windows.'" *George Herbert Journal* 1, no. 2 (1978): 38–43. [Argues that each stanza spatially proceeds from God to preacher to congregation (beyond windows to chancel to nave) and that nasal sounds increase in the poem to the climactic "ring" as the last word of the poem]

Reeves, Troy D. "Herbert's 'The Agonie.'" *The Explicator* 39, no. 1 (1980): 2–3. [Emphasizes that the second stanza concerns blood in the Garden of Gethsemane and the third stanza concerns blood on Calvary and that Christ is "tested by torture," with the reader "invited to test for himself the fruit of that act of love"]

Renaux, Sigrid. "George Herbert's 'The Windows' Illuminated: A Critical Approach." *George Herbert Journal* 9, no. 1 (1985): 26–32. [Concentrates on closely analyzing the "man-window" metaphor as the key to understanding the poem, while noting some elements that earlier critics seem to have overlooked or misread]

Richey, Esther Gilman. "Words Within the Word: The Melodic Mediation of 'To all Angels and Saints.'" *George Herbert Journal* 15, no. 2 (1992): 33–41. [Sees the poem as being "far from Puritan" and, in fact, one that honors the angels and saints because they carry the words of God himself]

Richey, Esther Gilman. "'Wrapt in Nights Mantle': George Herbert's Parabolic Art." *John Donne Journal* 9 (1990): 157–71. [Argues that Herbert's narrative poems scattered through his work reveal his affinity with the Christian humanists and with the patristic theories of Origen, Gregory of Nyssa, Chrysostom, and Augustine]

Rickey, Mary Ellen. "Herbert's Fool for Christ's Sake: A Note on
    'Joseph's Coat.'" *George Herbert Journal* 1, no. 1 (1977): 57–60.
    [Argues for echoes of the fool in folk festivals and of one of the
    fool's songs in *King Lear*, adapted for Christian purposes]
Roche, Thomas P., Jr., ed. *Essays by Rosemond Tuve: Spenser,
    Herbert, Milton*. Princeton, New Jersey: Princeton University
    Press, 1970. [Contains Tuve's "George Herbert and *Caritas*" and
    "Sacred 'Parody' of Love Poetry, and Herbert"]
Roche, Thomas P., Jr. "Typology, Allegory, and Protestant Poetics."
    George Herbert Journal 13 (1989–90): 1–17. [Uses a reading of
    Herbert's "Aaron" to show the "intimate and intricate relationship
    between allegory and typology"]
Rosenthal, M.L., and A.J.M. Smith. *Exploring Poetry*. New York:
    Macmillan Co., 1955. [Brief comments on "Virtue" (pp. 416–17)
    and "The Pulley" (pp. 544–45)]
Rubey, Daniel. "The Poet and the Christian Community: Herbert's
    Affliction Poems and the Structure of *The Temple*." *Studies in
    English Literature, 1500–1900* 20 (1980): 105–23. [Sees the five
    "Affliction" poems moving from "the individual and
    autobiographical" to the "communal and typological" and
    contends that this movement "parallels the larger organizational
    structure of *The Temple* as a whole"]
Ruud, Jay. "Herbert's 'Sinnes Round.'" *The Explicator* 34 (1975–76):
    Item 35. [Contends that in "vent the wares" Herbert is using an
    older meaning of *ware* as "pus" or "matter" and that the image is
    of the mouth spitting forth words as "pus-like infection"]
Scheurle, William H. "A Reading of George Herbert's 'Content.'" *The
    University of South Florida Language Quarterly* 4, nos. 1–2
    (1965): 37–39.
Schleiner, Louise. "Jacobean Song and Herbert's Metrics." *Studies in
    English Literature, 1500–1900* 19 (1979): 109–26. [Discusses the
    possible influence of music composed by others or by himself on
    some of Herbert's stanzas]
Schleiner, Louise. *The Living Lyre in English Verse from Elizabeth
    through the Restoration*. Columbia: University of Missouri Press,
    1984. [Chapter 3 examines some of Herbert's poems in light of
    song, metrics, and prosody.]
Schoenfeldt, Michael C. "'That Ancient Heat': Sexuality and Spirituality
    in *The Temple*." In *Soliciting Interpretation: Literary Theory and
    Seventeenth-Century English Poetry*, edited by Elizabeth D.
    Harvey and Katharine Eisaman Maus, 273–306. Chicago:
    University of Chicago Press, 1990. [Argues that there are some
    occurrences of sexual puns and sexual connotations in Herbert's
    words and phrases that some critics have hitherto not perceived

or have resisted because of being uncomfortable with the bawdy implications]

Schwartz, Helen J. "Herbert's 'Grief.'" *The Explicator* 31 (1972–73): Item 43. [Argues that the speaker's "overflowing, immeasurable" grief is conveyed by images of overflowing, but also by the facts that the essentially sonnet form overflows by an extra quatrain and part-line and that redundant phrases also are an overflowing]

Severance, Sibyl Lutz. "Self-Persistence in *The Temple*: George Herbert's 'Artillerie.'" *University of Hartford Studies in Literature* 15–16 (1983–84): 108–19. [Regards "Artillery" as "one of Herbert's most intricate lyrics" and one that "vividly illustrates thought and devotion united—and the fragility of such a union, the plight of the mind that refuses to slight its mission as God's instrument"]

Sharp, Nicholas. "Herbert's 'Love (III).'" *The Explicator* 33 (1974–75): Item 26. [Argues that the situation in the poem with Love as a host at a banquet also suggests the "host" of communion, the communion wafer, in which Christ is present]

Shullenberger, William. "*Ars Praedicandi* in George Herbert's Poetry." In *"Bright Shootes of Everlastingnesse": The Seventeenth-Century Religious Lyric*, edited by Claude J. Summers and Ted-Larry Pebworth, 96–115. Columbia: University of Missouri Press, 1987. [Argues that "Herbert's lyrics appeal to, and force a crisis in, his reader's penchant for clear predication," with emphasis on readings of "Prayer (1)" and "The Windows"]

Simpson, David L. "Herbert's 'Vertue.'" *The Explicator* 37, no. 1 (1978): 46–47. [Argues that "seasoned timber" suggests that it is not only sweet and powerful, but also tempered, ripened, and hardened. Also notes that the phrase may echo the connotations of the biblical cedars of Lebanon, since they were strong, durable, and fragrant]

Slights, Camille. "Herbert's 'Trinitie Sunday.'" *The Explicator* 38, no. 1 (1979): 13. [Sees the poem as emphasizing "the reciprocity of divine and human action"]

Smith, A.J. *Metaphysical Wit*. Cambridge: Cambridge University Press, 1991. [Pp. 151–72 comment on several poems that illustrate Herbert's wit.]

Smith, Barbara Herrnstein. *Poetic Closure: A Study of How Poems End*. Chicago and London: University of Chicago Press, 1968. [Discusses closure in "Virtue," "Mortification," and "Redemption"]

Smith, Thomas R. "The Mystical Vineyard in George Herbert's 'Redemption.'" *Studia Mystica* 13, no. 1 (1990): 46–54. [Argues that parables of unproductive vineyards in Isaiah and the New

Testament parallel Herbert's poem in both "narrative events" and in allegorical references to "the old covenant of God with the Jews and the new covenant of God with the Christians"]

Smithson, Bill. "Herbert's 'Affliction' Poems." *Studies in English Literature, 1500–1900* 15 (1975): 125–40. [Proposes a new order for the five "Affliction" poems of *The Temple* and discusses each one]

Spence, Martin. "Herbert's 'Employment II.'" *The Explicator* 44, no. 3 (1986): 18–21. [Argues that the poem centers on "the paradox of 'busy' to 'still'" and focuses on multiple meanings and suggestions in many words of the poem]

Steele, Oliver. "Crucifixion and the Imitation of Christ in Herbert's 'The Temper' (I)." *George Herbert Journal* 5 (1981–82): 71–74. [Emphasizes that the speaker identifies with Christ on the cross, as seen in the typology of the harp as the crucifixion, the spanning of arms, and the images of stretching]

Stewart, Stanley. *The Enclosed Garden: The Tradition and the Image in Seventeenth-Century Poetry.* Madison, Milwaukee, and London: University of Wisconsin Press, 1966.

Strier, Richard. "Herbert and Tears." *ELH* 46 (1979): 221–47. [Argues that Herbert's theology is always strongly Protestant, emphasizing the mercy of God over the sinner's contrition or tears. Analyzes particularly "Marie Magdalene," "Grief," and "Praise (3)" in this light]

Strier, Richard. "History, Criticism, and Herbert: A Polemical Note." *Papers on Language and Literature* 17 (1981): 347–52. [Argues that Herbert is Calvinistic in theology and that he maintains the middle way between Rome and Geneva only in worship and church government, not in doctrine]

Strier, Richard. *Love Known: Theology and Experience in George Herbert's Poetry.* 1983. Reprint. Chicago and London: University of Chicago Press, 1986. [Views Herbert's poems as embodying the doctrine of grace ("justification by faith") and the view of knowing love through knowing both sin and the inadequacy of reason]

Strier, Richard. "Songs and Sonnets Go to Church: Teaching George Herbert." In *Approaches to Teaching the Metaphysical Poets,* edited by Sidney Gottlieb, 127–31. New York: Modern Language Association of America, 1990. [Argues for using Donne's *Songs and Sonnets* as a way to make a transition into Herbert's poetry and to compare and contrast Herbert and Donne. Suggests specific pairings of poems and lines in the two poets]

Strier, Richard. "'To all Angels and Saints': Herbert's Puritan Poem." *Modern Philology* 77 (1979–80): 132–45. [In contrast to previous criticism, proposes that the poem does not show Herbert's conservative Anglican attraction to old devotions, but rather it shows in this particular instance in Herbert's work a Puritan stance taken with "evident discomfort"]

Stull, William L. "Sacred Sonnets in Three Styles." *Studies in Philology* 79 (1982): 78–99. [Brief comments on "Joseph's Coat," "Love (1)," "Love (2)," "The H. Scriptures (1)," and "The H. Scriptures (2)" in light of Herbert's use of "Petrarchan conceits and hyperboles" for "praise of divine love and Holy Scripture"]

Summers, Claude J. "The Bride of the Apocalypse and the Quest for True Religion: Donne, Herbert, and Spenser." In *"Bright Shootes of Everlastingnesse": The Seventeenth-Century Religious Lyric*, edited by Claude J. Summers and Ted-Larry Pebworth, 72–95. Columbia: University of Missouri Press, 1987. [Argues that "The British Church" condemns the Roman Catholic and Genevan Churches in its endorsement of the English Church of the middle way]

Summers, Claude J., and Ted-Larry Pebworth. "The Politics of *The Temple*: 'The British Church' and 'The Familie.'" *George Herbert Journal* 8, no. 1 (1984): 1–15. [Uses "The British Church" and "The Family" to illustrate how Herbert does engage "in sectarian controversy, consistently rebuking Puritan attacks on the Established Church," defending the Church's authority and deploring its fragmentation by Puritans]

Summers, Joseph. "From 'Josephs coat' to 'A true Hymne.'" *George Herbert Journal* 2, no. 1 (1978): 1–12.

Summers, Joseph H. "Herbert's 'Trinitie Sunday.'" *The Explicator* 10 (1951–52): Item 23. [Feels that the poem is a prayer for Trinity Sunday, comments on its tripartite divisions and sets of three, and sees the poem as an application of Trinitarian doctrine to personal life]

Swaim, Kathleen M. "Herbert's 'Paradise.'" *George Herbert Journal* 8, no. 2 (1985): 19–31. [Analyzes the importance in the poem of verbal pruning as "progressive purifying of self" and of circularity as a return "to the perfection of God's grace-full, fruit-full garden"]

Swaim, Kathleen M. "The 'Season'd Timber' of Herbert's 'Vertue.'" *George Herbert Journal* 6, no. 1 (1982): 21–25. [Focuses on two meanings of "coal" in the last stanza, arguing that *cinders* applies to the destruction of the world by fire and that *charcoal* applies to the soul that will continue to "live," just as charcoal burns with intense fire]

Thorpe, James. "Herbert's 'Love (III).'" *The Explicator* 24 (1965–66): Item 16. [Argues that this poem, like several of Herbert's, is conducive to the fourfold interpretation usual in medieval scriptural exegesis: literal, anagogical, allegorical, and tropological. Illustrates the allegorical interpretation centering on the Eucharistic feast, with parallels to the service of Holy Communion in *The Book of Common Prayer*]

Tuve, Rosemond. "George Herbert and *Caritas*." In *Essays by Rosemond Tuve: Spenser, Herbert, Milton*, edited by Thomas P. Roche, Jr., 167–206. Princeton, New Jersey: Princeton University Press, 1970.

Tuve, Rosemond. *A Reading of George Herbert*. Chicago: University of Chicago Press, 1952. [Argues for reading Herbert in liturgical and typological contexts to understand him]

Tuve, Rosemond. "Sacred 'Parody' of Love Poetry, and Herbert." In *Essays by Rosemond Tuve: Spenser, Herbert, Milton*, edited by Thomas P. Roche, Jr., 207–51. Princeton, New Jersey: Princeton University Press, 1970.

Van Nuis, Hermine J. "Herbert's 'Affliction' Poems: A Pilgrim's Progress." *Concerning Poetry* 8, no. 2 (1975): 7–16. [Argues that the five "Affliction" poems reduce Herbert's and Everyman's "stubborn will to God's just will and ways" and that this reflects an overall movement in *The Temple* as a whole]

Vickers, Brian. *Classical Rhetoric in English Poetry*. 1970. Reprint. Carbondale and Edwardsville: Southern Illinois University Press, 1989. [Comments on Herbert throughout, but more extensively on "The Wreath" (pp. 163–66)]

Waddington, Raymond B. "The Title Image of Herbert's 'The Pulley.'" *George Herbert Journal* 9, no. 2 (1986): 49–53. [Argues that the connotation of the "pulley" (also known as the "squassation") in the sense of an instrument of torture used in the Inquisition is relevant in this poem and relates to the afflictions and vacillations of the human condition throughout Herbert's poems]

Wanamaker, Melissa C. *Discordia Concors: The Wit of Metaphysical Poetry*. Port Washington, New York: Kennikat Press, 1975. [Chapter 3 is "George Herbert: Discovery of Occult Resemblances."]

Wardropper, Bruce W. "The Religious Conversion of Profane Poetry." In *Studies in the Continental Background of Renaissance English Literature: Essays Presented to John L. Lievsay*, edited by Dale B.J. Randall and George Walton Williams, 203–21. Durham, North Carolina: Duke University Press, 1977. [Discusses the long tradition of adapting secular songs and poems to Christian purposes, a tradition reflected by Herbert in some poems]

Weatherford, Kathleen J. "Sacred Measures: Herbert's Divine Wordplay." *George Herbert Journal* 15, no. 1 (1991): 22–32.

[Discusses the importance of "measure," both as word and concept, throughout Herbert's poetry]

Weibly, P.S. "George Herbert's 'Heaven': The Eloquence of Silence." *George Herbert Journal* 4, no. 2 (1981): 1–9. [Examines the use of the echo device to imply the speaker's silence before God as his questions have been answered with God's Word]

Werner-King, Janeen. "Herbert's 'Charms and Knots.'" *The Explicator* 48 (1989–90): 244–45. [Notes that the third couplet echoes a familiar analogy to distinguish logic and rhetoric and contends that in this poem Herbert is using rhetoric to tell complex truths with simplicity in a way that people will remember them and repeat them to others]

West, David. "Easter-Wings." *Notes and Queries* 39 (1992): 448–52. [Considers early manuscript and printed versions, emphasizing as primary the image of larks' wings and the prevalence of the letter 'e' ending the lines, suggesting that Herbert deliberately wanted the leading edge of each wing to be the first letter of "Easter"]

West, David. "Easter-Wings: Addendum." *Notes and Queries* 39 (1992): 489–90. [Furthers the argument that the earliest manuscript version (usually referred to as "W") should be taken as authoritative in its *uncorrected* version and that someone other than Herbert corrected this manuscript, a view that contradicts that of most Herbert scholars and editors]

West, Michael. "Ecclesiastical Controversy in George Herbert's 'Peace.'" *Review of English Studies* 22 (1971): 445–51. [Argues that the poem primarily criticizes sects and factions of the church and defends solid traditionalism of the Church of England]

Westerweel, Bart. *Patterns and Patterning: A Study of Four Poems by George Herbert.* Amsterdam: Rodopi, 1984. [Although many of Herbert's poems are mentioned, this study emphasizes "The Altar," "Easter-wings," "Love (3)," and "The Pilgrimage" in the context of the tradition of pattern poems.]

Westgate, Sam. "George Herbert: 'Wit's an Unruly Engine.'" *Journal of the History of Ideas* 38 (1977): 281–96. [Examines Herbert's concept of wit and cites examples from his poems]

Whitlock, Baird W. "The Sacramental Poetry of George Herbert." *South Central Review* 3, no. 1 (1986): 37–49. [Emphasizes Herbert's expression of traditional Anglican sacramental concepts as embodied in the forms of his poems]

Williams, Anne. "Gracious Accommodations: Herbert's 'Love III.'" *Modern Philology* 82 (1984–85): 13–22. [Argues that Herbert uses as a center for the poem the theological concept of accommodation, a term that "denotes the variety of ways in which

God has manifested himself to man since the Fall." Suggests that
the poem is more a parable than it is an allegory]

Williams, Donald T. "Thou Art Still My God: George Herbert and the
Poetics of Edification." *Christian Scholar's Review* 19 (1989–90):
271–85. [Holds up Herbert as a model for any would-be Christian
poet, noting his combination of sense of vocation, awareness of an
audience of both God and humans, devotion to craftsmanship, and
use of images drawn from biblical story and common experience]

Williamson, George. *Six Metaphysical Poets: A Reader's Guide.* New
York: Farrar, Straus & Giroux, 1967. [Chapter 5 concerns
Herbert and presents general paraphrases of some poems.]

Wilson, F.P. "A Note on George Herbert's 'The Quidditie.'" *Review of
English Studies* 19 (1943): 398–99. [Argues that "most take all" is
a proverb meaning "the most powerful take all," and in this case
it refers to God taking complete possession of the speaker]

Winters, Yvor. *Forms of Discovery: Critical and Historical Essays on
the Forms of the Short Poem in English.* Chicago: Alan Swallow,
1967. [Discusses "Church Monuments" on pp. 83–88, noting the
sophistication of its style and the effectiveness of its syntax,
diction, and tone]

Wolfe, Jane E. "George Herbert's 'Assurance.'" *College Language
Association Journal* 5 (1961–62): 213–22. [Sees the poem as
"spiritual biography" and analyzes its ideas, biblical echoes,
images, and tone]

Wood, Chauncey. "An Augustinian Reading of George Herbert's 'The
Pulley.'" In *A Fine Tuning: Studies of the Religious Poetry of
Herbert and Milton,* edited by Mary A. Maleski, 145–59.
Binghamton, New York: Center for Medieval and Early
Renaissance Studies, State University of New York, 1989.
[Detailed examination of the probable influence of St. Augustine's
work on Herbert's poem, especially in the ideas of "rest" and
God's goodness]

Wood, Chauncey. "A Reading of Herbert's 'Coloss. 3.3'" *George
Herbert Journal* 2, no. 2 (1979): 15–24.

Wood, Chauncey. "Sin and the Sonnet: Sidney, St. Augustine, and
Herbert's 'The Sinner.'" *George Herbert Journal* 15, no. 2
(1992): 19–32. [Argues primarily that Herbert in "The Sinner"
parodies the first sonnet of Sidney's *Astrophil and Stella*]

Woods, Susanne. "The 'Unhewn Stones' of Herbert's Verse." *George
Herbert Journal* 4, no. 2 (1981): 30–46. [Argues for seeing each
of Herbert's poems as an "altar, centered by the poet's God-hewn
hard heart, on which the sacrifice of his priestly poetic is
performed or through which it is made manifest"]

Yunis, Susan S. "George Herbert's 'Jordan (I)': Catching the Sense at Two Removes." *English Language Notes* 27, no. 3 (1990): 20–26. [Contends that the poem "discovers the difficulty" of actually praising plainly and that this leads to the "conciliatory tone of the final stanza." Also argues that "Prime" may refer to the elaborate choral service virtually eliminated from the *Book of Common Prayer* and thus suggests poetry sacrificed for the plain speaking insisted upon by Puritans]

d. *The Church Militant*

Anselment, Raymond A. "'The Church Militant': George Herbert and the Metamorphoses of Christian History." *Huntington Library Quarterly* 41 (1977–78): 299–316. [Sees Herbert as a poet-prophet in this poem in which past and present are defined in terms of a future to which history points]
Hovey, Kenneth Alan. "'Wheel'd about . . . into *Amen*': 'The Church Militant' on Its Own Terms." *George Herbert Journal* 10 (1986–87): 71–84. [A reading of the poem, section by section, for its own meaning and value, as opposed to the question of its structural unity with other divisions of *The Temple*. Emphasizes that Herbert uses "Sin" in the poem specifically to denote "false religion, the worship of anything but the true God"]
Levang, Dwight. "George Herbert's 'The Church Militant' and the Chances of History." *Philological Quarterly* 36 (1957): 265–68. [Notes that a Puritan preacher (Samuel Ward) was imprisoned in 1635 for making the statement that "Religion and the Gospel stood on tiptoes ready to be gone," a direct allusion to Herbert's "Religion stands on tip-toe in our land, / Readie to passe to the American strand" from *The Church Militant*]
Weinberger, G.J. "George Herbert's 'The Church Militant.'" *Connecticut Review* 4, no. 2 (1971): 49–57. [Argues that *The Church Militant* is a historical parallel to individual experience in *The Church*: for example, sin acts on religion in *The Church Militant* as it acts on the individual Christian in *The Church*]

4. *To the Queen of Bohemia*

Hovey, Kenneth Alan. "George Herbert's Authorship of 'To the Queene of Bohemia.'" *Renaissance Quarterly* 30 (1977): 43–50. [Argues that the poem should be verified as Herbert's, rather than classified as a "doubtful poem," as it is in Hutchinson's edition of Herbert]

5. *To the Right Hon. the L. Chancellor* (Bacon)

Dinshaw, Fram. "A Lost MS. of George Herbert's Occasional Verse and the Authorship of 'To the L. Chancellor.'" *Notes and Queries* 30 (1983): 423–25. [Argues that "To the L. Chancellor" should be verified as Herbert's, rather than considered to be one of his "doubtful poems"]

6. Miscellaneous and More Than One Type of Poem

Bennett, Joan. *Four Metaphysical Poets: Donne, Herbert, Vaughan, Crashaw*. Cambridge: Cambridge University Press, 1934. [Chapter 4 is "George Herbert, 1593–1633."]

Blair, Rhonda L. "George Herbert's Greek Poetry." *ELH* 64 (1985): 573–84. [Notes that the form and language of the Greek poems of *Memoriae Matris Sacrum* show Herbert echoing great classical and post-classical poets that aid him in praising his mother]

Daalder, Joost. "Herbert's 'Poetic Theory.'" *George Herbert Journal* 9, no. 2 (1986): 17–34. [Citing several poems from *The Church*, as well as the sonnets to Herbert's mother, the essay argues that there is no one "poetic theory" that Herbert "consistently adhered to" and that Herbert's "attitude to poetic craftsmanship varies and evolves"]

Gallagher, Michael P. "Rhetoric, Style, and George Herbert." *ELH* 37 (1970): 495–516. [Concerns Herbert's use of the classical "plain style" and "rhetoric of plainness" as promoted for Christian work by St. Augustine]

Gaston, Paul L. "The Excluded Poems: Steps to the Temple." In *Like Season'd Timber: New Essays on George Herbert*, edited by Edmund Miller and Robert DiYanni, 151–68. New York: Peter Lang, 1987. [Discusses the six poems in Herbert's early manuscript (Williams manuscript) that he excluded from his final work, finding them of interest in revealing Herbert's demanding standards, his poetic development, his range, and some foreshadowings of the mature genius of Herbert]

Hayes, Albert McHarg. "Counterpoint in Herbert." *Studies in Philology* 35 (1938): 43–60. [Uses "counterpoint" to mean Herbert's technique of constructing "the pattern of his line lengths independently of the pattern of his rimes" and thus to defeat the "excessive expectation of rime by making its position unpredictable"]

Mazzaro, Jerome. "Donne and Herbert: Striking through the Mask: Donne and Herbert at Sonnets." In *Like Season'd Timber: New Essays on George Herbert*, edited by Edmund Miller and Robert

DiYanni, 241–53. New York: Peter Lang, 1987. [Discusses some of the sonnets of *The Church*, as well as one of those written to Herbert's mother. Emphasizes Herbert's "challenges to the traditional style and themes of his day in order to assert sincerity"]

Roberts, John R., ed. *Essential Articles for the Study of George Herbert's Poetry*. Hamden, Connecticut: Archon Books, 1979. [Categorizes and prints 34 previously published essays]

Stein, Arnold. *George Herbert's Lyrics*. Baltimore, Maryland: Johns Hopkins Press, 1968. [Detailed study of Herbert's style, language, prosody, and form]

Young, Diane. "The Orator's Church and the Poet's Temple." *George Herbert Journal* 12, no. 2 (1989): 1–15. [Notes Herbert's continued concern with the problems of the English church from *Musae Responsoriae* through *Passio Discerpta* and *Lucus* to several poems of *The Temple*]

D. Prose

1. *The Country Parson* (*A Priest to the Temple*)

Blau, Sheridan D. "George Herbert's Homiletic Theory." *George Herbert Journal* 1, no. 2 (1978): 17–29. [Primarily examines Chapter 7 ("The Parson Preaching") of *The Country Parson* and concludes that Herbert advocates a plain and practical way of preaching, the three major principles of which are indicated in this chapter]

Cooley, Ronald W. "'Untill the Book Grow to a Compleat Pastorall': Re-Reading *The Country Parson*." *English Studies in Canada* 18 (1992): 247–60. [Examines the functions of first-person and third-person voices, as well as the "interaction between doubt and assurance, restlessness and security" in the work. Also argues for reading this work in light of the poems (whereas critics usually do the reverse) in order to see some features that have escaped notice]

Doerksen, Daniel W. "'Too Good for Those Times': Politics and the Publication of George Herbert's *The Country Parson*." *Seventeenth-Century News* 49 (1991): 10–13. [Argues that there were attempts to have *The Country Parson* published before 1641 but that Laudian censors did not approve the manuscript, indicating that Arminian politics kept it from the press]

Kollmeier, Harold H. "*The Country Parson*: The Country Parson in Its Time." In *Like Season'd Timber: New Essays on George Herbert*, edited by Edmund Miller and Robert DiYanni, 191–206. New

York: Peter Lang, 1987. [Primarily discusses Barnabas Oley's use
of Herbert's work to give a vision of "the good, of what should
be" and "a vision by contrast of evil, of what is but should not
be," in the condition of the clergy and the Church of England
during its embattled state in 1652]

Wolberg, Kristine. "All Possible Art: *The Country Parson* and
Courtesy." *John Donne Journal* 8 (1989): 167–89. [Argues that
Herbert's main concern in the work is with the pastor's correct
public image and appearances, rather than with private and
inner spiritual matters and that the work is modeled upon
courtesy books]

2. *Outlandish Proverbs* (*Jacula Prudentum*)

Benet, Diana. "Herbert's Proverbs: The Magic Shoe." In *Like Season'd
Timber: New Essays on George Herbert*, edited by Edmund
Miller and Robert DiYanni, 139–50. New York: Peter Lang,
1987. [Notes that many of Herbert's proverbs are adapted,
echoed, or paralleled in his poems and in *The Country Parson*]

Piret, Michael. "Canon Hutchinson and the *Outlandish Proverbs*." *Notes
and Queries* 34 (1987): 312–13. [Corrects a statement by
Hutchinson in his edition of Herbert: the erasure of the attribution
to Herbert appears on the title page of a copy of *Witts Recreations*
(1640), not on the title page of the 1651 printing of *Jacula
Prudentum*]

Thorpe, James. "Reflections and Self-Reflections: *Outlandish Proverbs*
as a Context for George Herbert's Other Writings." In *Illustrious
Evidence: Approaches to English Literature of the Early
Seventeenth Century*, edited by Earl Miner, 23–37. Berkeley, Los
Angeles, London: University of California Press, 1975. [Notes
how the proverbs in Herbert's collection are used also in various
forms in his letters, in *The Country Parson*, and in some poems
of *The Temple*. Argues that Herbert was interested in ordinary
human behavior and in useful aims for himself and others]

Wilson, F.P. "English Proverbs and Dictionaries of Proverbs," *The
Library* 4th ser. 26 (1946): 51–71. [Discusses Herbert's
Outlandish Proverbs in the context of other collections in English]

3. Miscellaneous and More Than One Type of Prose Work

Bell, Ilona. "Herbert's Valdésian Vision." *English Literary Renaissance*
17 (1987): 303–28. [Argues that Herbert's notes on Nicholas
Ferrar's translation of the *Considerations* of John Valdessso (i.e.,
Juan Valdés) and Herbert's letter to Ferrar about the work reveal

the following as part of a core of religious assumptions that
Herbert shared with Valdés: (1) Protestantism, especially belief in
predestination, covenant theology, and justification by faith;
(2) emphasis on Christ's divinity and an inward vision of Christ;
and (3) a progressive, spiritual vision of piety]

VI. GENERAL BACKGROUND

Alexander, H.G. *Religion in England, 1558–1662.* London: University
of London Press, 1968.
Cirlot, J.E. *A Dictionary of Symbols.* New York: Philosophical
Library, 1962.
Heninger, S.K., Jr. *A Handbook of Renaissance Meteorology, With
Particular Reference to Elizabethan and Jacobean Literature.*
1960. Reprint. New York: Greenwood Press, 1968.
Jones, Richard Foster. *Ancients and Moderns: A Study of the Rise of the
Scientific Movement in Seventeenth-Century England.* 1936.
Reprint. Berkeley and Los Angeles: University of California
Press, 1965.
Meadows, A.J. *The High Firmament: A Survey of Astronomy in
English Literature.* Leicester: University of Leicester Press,
1969.
New, John F.H. *Anglican and Puritan: The Basis of Their Opposition,
1558–1640.* Stanford, California: Stanford University Press,
1964.
Ruthven, K.K. *The Conceit.* London: Methuen, 1969.
Shullenberger, William. "The Word of Reform and the Poetics of the
Eucharist." *George Herbert Journal* 13 (1989–90): 19–36.
Tillyard, E.M.W. *The Elizabethan World Picture.* London: Chatto &
Windus, 1943.